POLITICAL COMMUNICATION

THE PUBLIC LANGUAGE
OF POLITICAL ELITES
IN INDIA AND THE UNITED STATES

POLITICAL COMMUNICATION

THE PUBLIC LANGUAGE
OF POLITICAL ELITES
IN INDIA AND THE UNITED STATES

SATISH K. ARORA
National Institute of Community Development
Hyderabad, India

HAROLD D. LASSWELL
Yale University Law School

HOLT, RINEHART AND WINSTON, INC.
New York   Chicago   San Francisco   Atlanta   Dallas
Montreal   Toronto   London   Sydney

PREFACE

The first years of independence are uniquely significant for the political evolution of any nation. They set the frame of reference in which the course of public life develops. Ensuing years usually bring great changes, yet the impact lingers on. It is in the early years that heroic figures form national traditions by historic acts of successful affirmation of the collective self. Their words and deeds provide an interpretative gloss on constitutional charters and international agreements. The norms of the time are subsequently available for capture by all who would initiate movements for the regeneration of belief, faith, and loyalty.

Our interest in this book is in the interplay between India and the United States. We are in search of a means of making accessible to concerned citizens of both countries an understanding of their likenesses and differences. The study of political rhetoric provides a suitable beginning for reciprocal insight and understanding—as the authors have discovered in their own experience. The language of politics is part of the exposure of all who follow public affairs. We have sought to present the public utterances of the top figures of India and the United States at the same cross-section in time, and to do so in an analytic framework designed to bring out the points at which they diverge or converge in relation to one another.

The modern study of public communication has begun to utilize highly sophisticated techniques. We have decided against presenting computerized results until they could be summarized in a wider comparative context, and until various technical problems have been more satisfactorily met than they can be at present. We trust that we have chosen enough excerpts to give a sense of reality to the flow of discourse, and to enable the reader to achieve a degree of empathy with the political life of India and the United States.

This book, we hope, can provide an impetus for the emergence of a series of investigations which can mitigate some of the psychological distress which accompanies intercultural encounters. It is conventional to regard countries such as India as transitional, but in the sense that both the United States and India are dynamic, they are both transitional societies. We hope that this book will contribute to a conscious control over the transitional processes in both societies.

One cannot fail to note the global impact that change within these two polities can effect, nor can one overlook the creative future that their elites can usher in. The focus and the shifts in the flow of political symbols which we observe in the public political communication of American and Indian elites testify to the enduring importance of such comparative inquiries on a world scale. Insofar as these studies permit realistic and nonparochial definitions of self, they assist man in the process of making history instead of remaining largely a passive victim of unfolding events.

Among those to whom we owe acknowledgement for indispensable assistance, we single out for special mention the officers of the Ralph E. Ogden Foundation of Cornwall, New York. More specifically, we are grateful to the judgment and patience of H. Peter Stern, vice president.

S.K.A.
H.D.L.

November 1968

CONTENTS

CHAPTER 1 · THE ROLE OF ARTICULATE GENERALIZATION IN POLITICS

The future course of world politics will be deeply affected by the relationships between India and the United States. The formidable challenge to accelerate India's development must be met in part with outside assistance; and one of the largest reservoirs of potential support, tendered under conditions of minimum subserviency, is the United States. The long-range security of the United States depends in no small degree upon the growth of an Indian state that is fully able to minister to the rising expectations of the Indian people within the framework of popular government.

Although on reflection such fundamental interdependencies are clear to any candid observer, they will not necessarily determine the future course of Indian, American, or world politics. Indian leaders who desire a flourishing and powerful nation-state may agree that the statements made above are true. Nevertheless, Indian policy may veer away from the United States as a by-product of tactical manipulations carried out by politicians who assume that the United States will make more concessions if India seems to be gravitating toward sovietism. Decision makers of the United States, finding these tactics provocative, may postpone—perhaps too long—measures fundamentally acceptable to both sides.

In addition to tactical sources of friction, full weight must be given to more fundamental differences. It is often said that two more contrasting societies than India and the United States cannot be found. The Indian tradition, we are told, is introspective, withdrawn, other

worldly; the United States is supposed to be a cradle of activists. However true or false, these images are among the significant facts of political
life, and must be taken into account in any assessment of the future.

Whatever throws light on the government, law, and politics of either
country contributes to the discovery of common objectives and the invention of realistic strategies. The present study explores the relatively
stable perspectives of responsible leaders on both sides.

Public communications provide a multitude of direct clues to the perspectives involved. Acts of public communication are not isolated from
other features of the political process. They affect, and in turn are
affected by, private communication, public and private deeds, and
events in the physical environment. Hence the language of public
communication, if examined with care and caution, can disclose many
fundamental demands, expectations, and perceptions of identity. This
is particularly true of public communications made by members of the
political leadership, the elite. It may be that an element of conscious
deception is present in many public statements. Language, however,
deceives the deceiver; it cannot be stripped bare of its complex relation
to a total flow of subjectivity. Within limits, it remains an unwilling
"mirror of the soul."

The public language of politics, in common with all modes of communication, is a complicated blend of general and particular statements. Conceptual terms are indispensable in referring to particular
individuals, deeds, and physical happenings: a "man" is also a Nehru, a
prime minister, and an eminent figure. From the conceptual requirements of thought and language come the relative stabilities of perspectives and communication that comprise an ideology. The stabilities they
achieve enter into the experience of all who speak or listen, and aid
in sustaining dependable patterns of conduct.

Contemporary India and the United States afford remarkable opportunities for the study of articulate generalizations in the political
process. Both nations are passing through momentous though contrasting
phases of development. The experience of secession from a larger political unit and the discovery of an enduring identity is ancient history in
the United States. But Indian independence is a new and formidable
fact; and if it is to remain a fact, independence must be buttressed at
every point. The United States is struggling to fulfill the world role
that recent changes enable it to play. For a century after separating
from the British Empire the people of America expanded westward
across a thinly held continent. Toward the end of the nineteenth
century, when this process was concluded, the United States began to
play a more positive part in world politics. One major step was to
intervene in and encourage Cuba to throw off the imperial authority

of a European power. Another step was to tip the balance of power in two world wars against the aggressive bid of Germany to dominate Europe. Since the end of World War II abundant resources have enabled the United States to face the Soviet coalition in a relatively bipolar division of the globe.

The lack of synchronization between the political challenges that confront the United States and India is evident. In the years before 1947 the principal problem of India's rising leadership was to obtain independence. Since 1947 the problem has been to keep it. With a huge population possessing few centers of modern science and technology, the overwhelming task has seemed to be internal integration, interpreted to imply minimal foreign commitments. In the meantime the United States, intent on safeguarding itself and all non-Communist states from Soviet domination, was bound to treat any declaration of non-involvement with suspicion.

As it happens several factors simplify some features of the task of studying the language of politics in the two countries. Both the apex elite of India and the whole leadership of the United States rely on the English language as the principal means of communicating with one another. Hence it is feasible to compare at least part of the elite press of India and the United States without the need of translation. For this purpose the New York *Times* and the *Times of India* (Bombay and New Delhi) are obvious choices. In every modern country there is a single newspaper, or a very small number of papers, which it is taken for granted the national political elite will read or know about. The New York *Times* undoubtedly belongs to this select list; although the *Times of India* is one among perhaps four pre-eminent newspapers, it, too, is a clear choice. Other possibilities in India are the *Hindu* (Madras), the *Statesman* (Calcutta and Delhi), and the *Hindustan Times* (Delhi). It is of interest that the *Times of India* started publication much earlier than the New York *Times,* the respective dates being 1838 and 1851. Both newspapers identify themselves, and are so identified by readers, as "independent." (*N. W. Ayer & Son's Directory: Newspapers and Periodicals, 1961,* identifies the New York *Times* as "independent"; the *Indian Press Year Book, 1956,* states that the policy of the *Times of India* is "Independent, Liberal, supporter of Democratic Govt.") Both newspapers reach a national audience and neither one of them has extraordinary circulation figures.

The prestige of the *Times of India* depends not only upon the fact that it is an old and established newspaper. It is also the central link of a chain of newspapers and periodicals that belong to it. The *Times of India* chain includes among others the *Illustrated Weekly of India,* the Indian counterpart of *Life* magazine in America. It is also the only

major daily newspaper that for many years has received the services of
The Associated Press (of the United States) and maintains a press
service of its own, having special correspondents in India and abroad
(a practice not too common in India). We noted that at the time of our
survey the standard sources showed that taken together all the English-
language newspapers enjoyed 23.4 percent of the total circulation in India.
The Hindi-language newspapers are second with 18.8 percent of the total
circulation. Since Hindi is the official national language it is of interest
that the number of English language newspapers has increased absolutely
and in terms of circulation. According to *Times of India Directory and
Yearbook, 1958–59,* as of December 31, 1956, the language-wise distribution figures of newspapers showed: English-language newspapers, total
number 1133; percentage of distribution 17.2; Hindi-language newspapers, total number 1254; percentage of distribution 19.1.

In explaining the influence of English-language newspapers account
must be taken of the fact that English has been, and remains, an
official language; and that in practice it is the preferred language of the
administrator and the intellectual. Since foreign news is carried largely
in the English-language press, rather than in Hindi or other vernacular
organs, the chief interpreters of foreign news are writers in the *Times
of India* and its counterparts. The journalists and editors who are all-
India figures are those who are active in the English-language press.

The role of the elite press is underlined when we note that radio
is government controlled. Moreover, the journalists and editors are not
subjected to the competition of private experts on foreign politics. The
relevance of this point is clarified when we find that organizations
interested in foreign affairs in India are few in number compared to
the United States where nearly 5000 unofficial institutions interest themselves in foreign affairs.

It would be too much to assume that every politician who thinks
about national or international issues reads all the pages of either
newspaper. No one is far wrong, however, who asserts that top elite
members follow these publications with enough care to absorb the front
pages and some inner pages as well. Whatever appears in news and
editorial columns instantly enters the public domain, and elite individuals are presumed to be as aware of what is published as though a
town crier has shouted every item in his hearing.

The phenomenon of an elite press is to be found in every nation-
state, totalitarian or pluralistic. In Moscow, for instance, there is *Pravda;*
in Peking, *Jen-Min Jin-Pao.* In a scientific and technological era intra-
elite communication is particularly important as a means of accelerating
the tempo of policy agreement and interpretation. The press is a convenient instrument of elite contact since the boundaries of the elite are
somewhat ambiguous, and speed is important. When societies enter the

world of modern technology they soon acquire a more acute awareness of time. The scheduling of transportation, as of all collective activities, calls for chronometers that register narrow intervals. The synchronizing of operations must be worked out by the expanding corps of elite and mid-elite persons who exercise effective control over the inception and execution of most collective activities. They plan and guide production; they direct and administer military, police, and other public services; they edit and disseminate news and comment; they are in charge of schools and other institutions of learning; and so on through the network of social institutions. If elite and mid-elite elements are to adapt their choices and decisions to one another, they must be regularly and rapidly informed of changing military, fiscal, and other circumstances.

The dependence of elite members on a common stream of information goes considerably beyond the need for technical detail. They are in need of a stable map of the context; likewise, they require access to information that nourishes fundamental perspectives of faith, belief, and loyalty. The major proposition is that unless the focus of attention of elite members is reached and perspectives are patterned by media of communication, common experiences fade, common goal values are in confusion, and common identities dissolve. As the ideological structures that confer a measure of continuity on the problem-solving process lose coherence, behavioral maladaptations are more frequent and more threatening to public order.

Even large-scale industrial societies might conceivably depend on the exclusive use of closed rather than open systems of intra-elite communication. To some extent, of course, closed systems of communication are to be found among the elite of every society. It is taken for granted that closed circuits will connect top military and political figures on security matters. Nevertheless, no modern society relies entirely on closed systems of intra-elite contact. As suggested above, this is partly to be explained by the need of reaching an audience whose boundaries, even in a totalitarian state, are somewhat vague and variable. When traditional societies are modernized, eliteship ceases to be a closed rank and in varying degrees becomes an open class. In totalitarian powers, it is noteworthy that the elite includes more than members of the monopoly party. It embraces nonparty professionals who have many skills at their command, and operate at many levels of responsibility. Effective eliteship reflects the facts of control; and control is a fluctuating magnitude.

Although the New York *Times* and the *Times of India* perform functions which are broadly equivalent to *Pravda* or *Izvestia* in Moscow, it is obvious that in a relatively open and a relatively closed system the nuances of the role of the elite press differ enormously from one another. The front pages of the New York *Times* and the *Times of India* ac-

curately mirror the decision process of pluralistic bodies politic. In
pluralistic states the differences which remain covert, delayed, and
ultimately explosive in totalitarian states are permitted to emerge
overtly, immediately, and persuasively.

If we were to construct a detailed theoretical model to guide enquiry
into the political process of relatively pluralistic bodies politic, such as
India and the United States, it would be necessary to deal exhaustively
with the elite press. Obviously the front pages are available to both
official and unofficial spokesmen in such pluralistic systems. Publication
gives exposure to speeches by top figures in the cabinet and the political
parties, including weighty oppositional elements. Leaders of economic
life—bankers, industrialists, merchants, trade-unionists, agrarians, for
example—appear side by side with eminent figures in religion, science,
medicine, or indeed in any sector of society. The exploratory model
should be built to investigate the hypothesis that the elite press enables
the members of the top leadership to become aware of one another;
hence they are able to discern the potential limits of cooperation on
policy issues. The model must be designed to account for changes that
occur in the language of politics as new occurrences and policy orienta-
tions are introduced. Ultimately it will be possible to demonstrate how,
in the bound and rebound of everyday discourse, clauses are trimmed to
phrases, and phrases are polished to key symbols which influence the
concentration or dispersion of sentiment, and guide reflection.

Our expectation is that when all relevant data are ultimately available concerning the period under review in the present report the
relative perpetuity of the printed page will be understood to have played
a unifying and stabilizing role in both India and the United States.
Since it is possible to store and retrieve print with comparative ease,
a published newspaper has an impact on politics that goes beyond the
immediate audience. It is in the area of translocal politics that printed
pages come into their own, pending the day when a documentary
function is integrated with television. Newspapers count for little at
the level of local affairs when printed documentation is relatively
meager, and when the disciplined memories of a preliterate age continue to play a part.

One of the principal hypotheses about the role of the elite press is
that it is a major factor in mediating between the political ideology
of a nation-state and the daily stream of contemporary events.[1] More
explicitly:

The ideological framework affects the recognition of an event as news-

[1] Conceptions of "ideology" and "elite" vary among political and social scientists
in degree of inclusiveness or exclusiveness. For orientation: D. E. Apter (ed.), *Ideology
and Discontent* (New York: The Free Press, 1964 [International Yearbook of Political

worthy The findings of the present investigation will show how world events in New York and New Delhi are refracted through the ideologies of the two countries. Many sources of information which are treated as credible in one city are unacceptable in the other.

An ideology provides a set of fundamental expectations about future developments The morale of a body politic, it is often observed, depends in part on confidence in a benevolent even though difficult future. Confidence is a means of avoiding the panic that results from surprise. To the scientific observer of elite communication it is often evident that a quoted leader is attempting to prepare the community to take in stride some approaching military or economic reverse. When setbacks have come, the interpreter's task is to use them to strengthen the ideology rather than to allow disappointments to militate against faith, belief, and loyalty. After all, says the interpreter, were difficulties not foreseen and discounted in advance by all who understood the basic myth of the body politic?

Ideology provides a vision of the past that helps to make the present and the future relatively intelligible to elite and non-elite elements alike We shall see that the New York *Times* and the *Times of India* often give prominence to statements that make shrewd use of yesterday as a storehouse of precedent for today and tomorrow.

Ideology provides explanatory categories which add analytic depth to the task of comprehending past, present, or prospective events If politics are seen in highly personal terms, or, on the contrary, as an interplay of vast material and ideological forces, such categories are available to guide understanding.

An ideology is a frame of reference in which the goals and objectives of public policy can be clarified This is accomplished by distinguishing the collective identity from other such identities, and by grounding and specifying the values sought. If at a given moment prominent leaders propose different policies, the elite press is often able to quote an elite member who shows how if the basic ideology is correctly understood these seemingly contradictory alternatives can be reconciled with one another. The clarifying function is also performed when the challenge of a counterideological system must be met. We suggest, in fact, that an established ideology is likely to be made more rather than less

Behavior Research]); H. D. Lasswell and Daniel Lerner (eds.), *World Revolutionary Elites; Studies in Coercive Ideological Movements* (Cambridge, Mass.: M.I.T. Press, 1966; Lucian W. Pye (ed.), *Communications and Political Development*, Princeton: Princeton University Press, 1963; and the other volumes entitled *Studies in Political Development*, sponsored by the Committee on Comparative Politics of the Socia Science Research Council (Gabriel A. Almond, Joseph LaPalombara, Myron Wiener, and others).

effective by the experience of coping with counter systems. American and Indian elites have some experience of this kind.

Although it is correct to speak of an elite press it is worth emphasizing that members of the mid-elite and of the rank and file are not necessarily excluded from access to what is published. When illiteracy is high, it is often an established practice for literate persons to read aloud to audiences. In literate and industrially developed countries the level of political participation is high, and the content of the elite press is widely relayed through the nation. The same message may be disseminated by several transmission belts. For instance, it is not unusual for the same person to receive messages that originated in a single source—such as the New York *Times*—and are filtered to him by a local editor, pastor, radio-TV commentator, luncheon club speaker, and neighbor who reads the *Times*.

We have been discussing the elite press of India and the United States as though they were read only by the national elite of both nations. Because of the role they are assumed to play in their respective countries the foreign office of each nation reads and summarizes the content of messages to which they attach significance. Many of the quoted speeches by Prime Minister Nehru or President Eisenhower were undoubtedly directed, in part, to each other, and beyond them to the interested elements in each nation. The present study is not concerned with this aspect of the matter, although the data also contribute to an understanding of Indian–United States diplomacy. Our enquiry is principally concerned with the dynamics of ideology inside national bodies politic.

To say that an ideological system is by definition somewhat stable is not to assert that it is rigid. On the contrary, a degree of flexibility is required if key symbols, slogans, and doctrines are to be kept in touch with ever-changing realities. The problem-solving role of an ideology implies that it must contain principles of procedure for thinking about particular events in the light of general principles of content. Reference was made above to goals, trend, condition, projection, and alternative. These terms refer to intellectual tasks that must be performed by individuals and groups in seeking to think about any problem. Since the various tasks cannot be performed all at once, an agenda is implied. An agenda exemplifies the procedural principles that are latent—or explicit—in all ideological systems.

When it is suggested that political ideologies provide problem-solving guidance, the implication is that every phase of the community process of decision is affected. The press—and especially the elite press—of India and the United States is part of the total process of decision. It might be analyzed to throw light on every phase. For comparative purposes we distinguish seven decision phases: *intelligence* and planning, or the gathering, analysis, and dissemination of information: *promotion,* or the use of persuasion (or other means) of affecting results; *prescription,* or lawmaking; *invocation,* or the preliminary characterization of a concrete situation in terms of prescriptions; *application,* or the putting of prescriptions into effect in concrete circumstances; *appraisal,* or the characterizing of the trend of events according to the policy objectives achieved or frustrated; and *termination,* or the ending of a prescription and the adjustment of claims based on expectations created during the period when the prescription was in effect.[2]

The politically specialized means of communication in a body politic are involved in all seven functions. The most obvious participation, no doubt, is in the intelligence process. But promotion is plainly involved, since many reported speeches or statements are propaganda for or against a controversial public policy. The act of giving dissemination to propaganda is part of the promotional phase of community action. Clearly enough a newspaper is not an authorized legislature. Nonetheless it participates directly in the process of crystallizing authoritative expectations in the body politic. This act of formulating authoritative general prescriptions is what is meant by lawmaking. Legislation is not to be confused with such specific operations as passing a statute. (Some statutes do not sufficiently affect community expectations to be called "law.")

Communication media are also implicated in the invoking and applying functions, since space is given to specific complaints and to actions in particular cases. The appraisal phase of decision likewise figures extensively in public media, since assertions are continually being quoted about the success or failure of policies to date. The termination function may be affected—perhaps unintentionally—in several ways, such as by failing to mention past prescriptions, hence contributing to their obsolescence.

In the present inquiry the *Times of India* and the New York *Times* are examined chiefly in reference to their intelligence role. What national leaders are brought to the reader's focus of attention? What parts of the world are referred to by elite members? What problems are dealt with? What articulate generalizations employ what criteria of evaluation?

The speeches and other public pronouncements in the press are themselves news; what is said is news within the news. We describe

[2] For more detail see Chapters 3 and 4 of H. D. Lasswell, *The Future of Political Science* (New York: Atherton Press, 1963).

what is referred to because the status of the communicator gives it importance.

What parts of the environment are important enough to elite members to be the subject matter of pronouncements that are also disseminated to other elite members? A reply to this question calls for a more refined set of hypotheses about elite communication than those formulated above. An explicit theory of elite attention is required. What events are sufficiently salient to be disseminated in elite media?

The maximization postulate holds that what people feel, think, and do is determined by their expectations of net value advantage. If we use this postulate to guide enquiry into elite communication, various hypotheses are suggested. Presumably the members of an elite evaluate their value position in terms of power. It is not necessary to assume that power is the dominant value in order to suppose that it is at least among the values of importance to the politically active class in nations such as India and the United States. The implication is that elite attention will probably be directed to present or prospective events that are perceived as affecting the elite's actual position. The effect may be indulgent: power is gained or maintained against loss. The effect may be deprivational: power is lost or gains are blocked. Attention will presumably go to (a) elite members (the self-included), (b) counter-elite members (the disloyal opposition), and (c) the elite of other bodies politic. The most general hypothesis is that attention is given to elite rather than non-elite participants in the arena of politics. Elites are presumably more directly significant for value change, whether indulgent or deprivational.

The competitive relationship of elites and elite members to one another furnishes a clue to a fundamental role performed by a regularly appearing elite press. To "possess" enough power to belong to a ruling class implies that one is vulnerable to deprivations of power by those who strive more actively and effectively to obtain it. When the press continues to appear, the reassuring implication usually is that the public order—including one's position—is intact. Intact, that is, from fellow cabinet members, bureau chiefs, department factions, and party factions, as well as from revolutionists or foreign powers.

Clearly a channel of communication builds up expectations that politically salient features of the world will be reported and interpreted in a relatively stable format. Newspapers such as the New York *Times,* and the *Times of India* do much more than furnish selected information to their readers. By appearing regularly they prevent the upsurge of anxieties that might arise if readers were deprived of reassurance that things remain basically the same. Even threatening events are treated as topics of stabilized expectation; great changes typically arrive in slow motion.

When we recognize that an elite press performs a stabilizing function for the elite—and hence for the whole body politic—by the simple act of appearing on schedule, a latent threat is also implied. The practice of expecting and demanding reassurance indicates a dependent status that can be exploited by revolutionary or counterrevolutionary elements to obtain the advantages of shock and surprise. Calculated nonappearance is a means of sowing anxiety, panic, and disorganization. During the period of our investigation of India and the United States no subversive organizations attempted to seize power, and no officeholders used the "blackout" to engineer a seizure of unauthorized power at any level. There were, however, incidents that provided at least a faint foretaste of what large-scale stoppages might accomplish. Newspaper strikes in a modern metropolis occasionally impose suspensions of publication, whose impact, though dampened by the presence of radio and television, creates the sense of malaise, of something wrong, that adds a touch of anxiety (and of emptiness) to life, especially among the educated classes.

The dependence of the elite audience on the press (and related media) has a further consequence. Once in operation a newspaper survives only by continuous activity. It is impracticable to suspend publication for a day because nothing "important" has happened. Hence marginal news and comment—items that would be left to one side on interesting days—are used to fill space. The readership is less upset by triviality than by the publication of nothing whatever.

The news initially regarded as marginal does not always remain so. Judgment changes. "Trivial" items often arouse a modicum of interest; and the mere fact of publication begins to modify current perspectives about what is properly disseminated by an elite organ. Hence trend description may show that the coverage of sources is changing. Various government activities, once disregarded, become eligible for mention in elite media. The number of quoted political party or pressure group figures may increase; other social institutions, too, may command attention. In consequence the scope of understanding—of empathy—is extended to include social groups who were previously overlooked. Such a development contributes to a fundamental goal of popular government by helping to achieve a decision process in which diverging viewpoints obtain effective and empathic consideration. Effective power is indicated by taking a significant part in decision. The giving and receiving of empathic consideration is a more refined level of political life. At such a level there is awareness of the thoughts and feelings of others in the community; hence even the perspectives of the human beings who occupy different value positions are part of the self system of all. The conception of the national self becomes a richly refined image, suffused with warm appreciation of the meaning of human experience in many localities, functional activities, and class levels. Differences of outlook and expression are not ignored; rather, they are viewed with the connoisseurship of enlightened respect and affection.

The expectations built up by an elite press include the assumption that attention will be given to counter-elites. While statements made by a revolutionary leader may be quoted, it is more likely that assertions will be circulated *about* the movement.

An elite press is also expected to guide attention to the outside world, and especially to opponents, allies, or noncommitted powers. The assumption is that the press acts as an agent of the power elite in observing who interprets the global context in ways that are intelligible to the specialists among the elite who perform the interpretative role for their more parochial colleagues.

The elite press adapts itself to such expectations. The New York *Times* is wealthy enough to maintain an independent corps of correspondents who girdle the globe. The *Times of India* is more dependent on news services, other media of communication, and interviews with official or private sources at home. Both papers are notably stable in the attention they give to the world arena. Thus they *maintain their credibility* by publishing about the same amount of foreign material even when the happenings may be of little interest to many readers. A cumulative reputation for knowledge depends in part on displaying knowledge even when an audience is little interested in the items themselves.

The present investigation chose 1950 as the starting point with several considerations in mind. The early years of a nation exercise a deep and persisting influence on its subsequent development. Although India achieved independence in August 1947, the partition of the subcontinent with Pakistan and the consequent transfer of population (estimated as high as 10 million) almost exclusively occupied the energies of the new state. The present study uses the year 1950 as a base because the early turmoil of partition and transfer had died down, and more problems were coming to attention. Nineteen-fifty is a usable base line for future surveys of changing emphasis upon the ideology of India.

Since the chief focus is on emergent India, the year 1950 was chosen with no particular regard for the significance of the year in the perspective of United States history. As it happens, the period immediately after 1950 was of no small consequence to the United States, and provided ample opportunity for the ideological orientation of the nation to come to the surface. The Korean conflict did obtain somewhat disproportionate prominence; however, it is to be recalled that since the end of World War II the United States has usually been involved in "little wars" or threats of war in some part of the globe. By extending the termination date of the main study to 1958 the presidential campaign of 1956 receded to the background, and a wider range of questions came to public notice.

If the flow of news is to be analyzed to bring out its ideological significance, methods must be employed that indicate the degree of intensity with which values are stressed in the rhetoric of public discourse. In examining the value criteria employed by members of a political elite we do not assume that even in the realm of national policy the only goal, or even the principal aim, is power. We think at once of wealth outcomes, recognizing that independent India will presumably put a premium on higher standards of consumption by encouraging modernized production. Among other valued outcomes we shall find that respect plays an important part, since modern conceptions of human dignity, which include equality of opportunity, render caste or racial restrictions obsolete. Closely intertwined with political, economic, and respect perspectives, although separable from them, are demands for shared enlightenment, skill, well-being, and affection. Of particular interest, in view of the religious tradition of India, is the amount of emphasis on considerations of rectitude, sacred or secular.

If we are to put the pursuit of power in proper relation to other values in the social process of India or the United States, it is necessary to employ a comprehensive method. The categories employed to designate the values must be inclusive. And the list should be short; otherwise, comparisons become unwieldy. The list needs to be related to the specialized fields of knowledge about politics and society, since the data obtained by various bodies of scholars can be conveniently incorporated and compared in this way. As it happens, most of the obvious value shaping and sharing processes in any society have been the object of specialized professional study in the universities. For instance, power is the principal field of research among political scientists, jurists, and students of international relations. The mass media are the principal research field at schools of communication. Economists focus on wealth; public-health specialists on health; educationists on skill; sociologists on the family; sociologists and social psychologists on caste and class; students of comparative religion and ethics on rectitude.

When we refer to evaluative criteria, then, we have eight categories

of culminating events in mind: the giving and receiving of power, enlightenment, wealth, well-being, skill, affection, respect, rectitude. Moreover, we make explicit our preference for widespread rather than narrow participation in the sharing of each category of valued outcome.
The specifications in the Universal Declaration of Human Rights are
compatible with value-sharing norms; for example, democracy in government, widespread enjoyment of the fruits of modern production,
general access to the knowledge necessary for enlightened civic judgment, opportunities to benefit from modern medicine, freedom to found
a family and to choose friends, freedom from social discrimination,
freedom of worship and of ethical choice.

In the everyday rush of public affairs not many reported speeches
devote themselves exclusively to ideological questions. Hence if the
changing significance of ideology is to be uncovered, a search must be
made for largely implicit or incidental value statements. The method is
to analyze all quotations or summarized statements which are reported on
the front pages of the New York *Times* and the *Times of India*. In order
to communicate a full sense of ideology in action, many representative
excerpts are reproduced here, and some indication is given of the quantitative picture.

Each statement is classified according to categories designed to disclose
the significance of the statement for comparative and systematic political
analysis. Since a major question in political analysis refers to the sense
of identity, we take note of statements that deal expressly with the
national "self" or with the self of an "other." A communicator may
refer to his primary ego ("I," "me") or to collective terms ("we," "they").
The assertion may boldly declare one's identity ("I am Indian"); or
depict an image of the national self (or other) by imputing traits (the
"rich Americans").

The references made in a statement may assert a matter of fact. From
an analytic point of view the criterion employed in this case is enlightenment ("our northern neighbor"; that is, a neighbor is to the north).
The words comprising a statement may express a positive or negative
preference or volition ("our sinister neighbor"; that is, the neighbor is
threatening to our power position). The expression "rich Americans" is,
on the face, an evaluation of Americans in economic terms. "Dishonest"
could be understood to be an evaluation according to rectitude. "Disease
ridden" refers to the state of well-being. Some expressions convey contempt (disrespect) or admiration (positive respect). "Friendly" characterizes affection.

Matter-of-fact statements allude to present, past, or future events; or
to conditioning factors. Historical references, predictions of the future,

or assertions of the role of science or technology come within "expectations."

The fundamental categories of statement analysis, then, are these: identity (self, other), value demand (power, enlightenment, wealth, well-being, skill, affection, respect, rectitude), and expectations (past, present, future; conditioning factors).

Political analysts must be concerned with both ideologies and counter-ideologies. Ideologies, of course, are the affirmations put forward by the elite of an established order; counter-ideologies are rejections of the prevailing order. To the extent that the Congress party of India agitated actively in support of national independence it was counter-ideological in orientation toward the established order of the British period of supremacy. After 1947 the party became the principal stabilizer and defender of the newly established system.

Detailed statement analysis is a tool that aids in the task of exhibiting ideology in daily action. By comparing the elite press of India and the United States during the years selected it is possible to throw light on the depth of penetration achieved by the ideologies of the two countries. Do ideological criteria figure explicitly in the statements that are regarded as worthy of dissemination? In particular, do the popular images of India and the United States gain confirmation, or do they distort reality? For instance, is rectitude an omnipresent criterion of public policy in India? Is the United States entirely secularized, so that references to theology, for example, drop completely out of sight?

Questions of this kind—and they could be multiplied a hundredfold—can be answered within rather clear limits. In addition to the problems suggested by popular imagery, many issues have been formulated in the course of systematic studies of political ideology. One question can be taken as representative of many others: Does political theory play a particularly prominent role among the elite of newly independent states? In the past, political research has not been carried far enough to provide empirical knowledge of how much attention has been given to ideological matters among new or long-established states. The present report provides some bench marks for this line of enquiry.

The context of the present investigation can be most readily understood by examining the magnitude of the problems confronting the active elements in the leadership of India and the United States in recent years. It is helpful to narrow the question somewhat by focusing on the relationship of the top elite to the communication situation. Every elite adopts strategies of communication management. These strategies are deeply affected by the objectives sought: to consolidate independence, to maintain high levels of military preparation as a guarantor of national security, and so on. Strategies also depend on the characteristics of the specialized network of communication, and of the potential audience. The communication situation, in turn, is intimately bound up with the entire context of value shaping and sharing, and of institutional development.

On most matters the study of India and the United States is a study in extreme contrasts. The estimated population of India is upward of 438 million (1961). In 1960 the census figure for the United States was less than 180 million. India, with one third the land available in the United States, has more than twice as many people. The per-capita income of Indians is $60 a year; for Americans the level is more than $2000 per year. This figure alone is sufficient to indicate why economic development has become a principal goal of Indian policy, and why the United States is partially taken as a model and viewed as a source of assistance.

Both countries possess democratic institutions of government. Yet many factors combine to require the government of India to supply the initiative that in the United States is forthcoming throughout an industrialized society that has evolved a vast network of pluralistic associations to connect localities with regional, national, and transnational activities. The great body of the Indian people is not yet in effective control of enough knowledge and skill of the kinds suitable to continuing and impactful participation in the national process of decision. According to the 1951 census, literacy in India was 16.61 percent; the American figure was more than 95 percent. The network of communication in India, when compared with the United States, provides a relatively rudimentary means of contact between leaders and led. The figure for daily newspapers per 1000 of population in the United States was 337; in India, it was 9. In 1958 the number of radio receiving sets in India was 1,560,000; the comparable number in the United States was 161,-000,000. More than 50 million television sets were operating in the United States; none were in India.

The barriers of communication in India are far more numerous and significant than these figures suggest. In terms of diversity, India and the United States could, for most purposes, be placed at opposite ends. In the matter of language alone, the 1951 census of India reported 845 languages or dialects spoken, and the Indian Constitution recognizes no less than 14 official languages (in addition to English). More than 80 percent of Indians reside and work in the villages; they lack exposure to urban life, which is the dominant style of industrial societies. As a result of the arrangement of conditioning factors in history, the socio-economic climate in India is authoritarian, status-bound, and basically rigid, while the American society is basically egalitarian, with great fluidity in the status structure.

Communication and politics proceed in India on two relatively distinct planes: the local village plane, and the national or metropolitan level. The tentacles of the mass media reach into even the remotest corner of America in a multiplicity of forms; in India, for the vast majority of the people communication is oral communication. Lacking integration with the national arena, the communication and politics of the majority of the Indian population are parochial, oblivious to national issues. While the name of an Eisenhower would be familiar to most Americans, even a personality such as Nehru will not have been heard of in many of India's villages. (An Indian newspaper records that some villages in South India had never heard of Mahatma Gandhi a decade after he died; there have been cases in Bengal where villagers did not know that the British had ruled India for more than two centuries.)

It is impossible to review these facts about the role of leaders and led in India without obtaining a renewed impression of the formidable tasks with which they were confronted after independence. The official and unofficial leaders of the United States were functioning in the most modern and potent national unit of power in the globe. By contrast, India's technology was archaic and its power, though formidable, remained latent and potential.

The present analysis of public communication is a short though essential step toward understanding the complex role of communication in the political process of bodies politic in general, and of India and the United States in particular. Classical studies of political life emphasize the "philosophy" of law, government, and politics; and philosophy presumably refers to the stable generalizations that provide a problem-solving frame of reference to all who participate in the decision process at every level or phase. The interplay of one set of generalizations with another, and of generalizations with particular statements, is a process of enormous subtlety that must eventually be traced through all the media of public and private communication. A central channel in all this flow is the elite press; and of critical interest is the role of articulate generalization in the political act.

The plan of the following chapters is to move from the quotations that refer to the internal arenas of India and the United States to the presentation of quotations that have to do with the external arenas of each nation. Within this broad framework successive chapters give prominence to themes that emphasize the identifying symbols of the "self" and "others" (the nation, external allies or antagonists, internal components), or exemplify the general and specific value demands and expectations that figure in the stream of political communication. The concluding chapter considers the significance of the material for the theoretical issues to which some allusion has been made in the preceding pages.[3]

[3] See Appendix B for details concerning the sources and procedures utilized in this investigation.

PART I · THE INNER ARENA

INDIA

CHAPTER 2 · THE
INDIAN CONCEPTION
OF THE SELF

Each nation conceives of itself in a manner that suggests certain qualities of human character are its special province. The shaping of the national image is largely dictated by experiences of the past. But from the multitude of characteristics that the past furnishes, an elite can select, within varying limits, particular aspects for special attention. Through the process of selection and emphasis, identity can be shaped to effect national behavior and the future course of events.

When the nation is as diverse and as rich in its historical past as India, the opportunity for forging national identity and lending coherence to self imagery becomes a political task of a high order. Upon emerging from the colonial past, elites have a unique opportunity to stress the distinctive, though often dormant, components of the self. But in order for a degree of versatility to enter into the creation of a national identity, it is essential that the elite demonstrate a grasp of the complex and rich heritage of its people. In the case of the Indian elite there are few indications that much energy has been invested in the formulation of a recognizable and meaningful identity.

Innovation in the creation of a national self has been minimal. The battery of unifying national symbols that a new nation demonstrably requires has been slow in manifesting itself. Members of the Indian elite have been prone to evoke those aspects of the Indian tradition and past that are related to the passive-resistance phase of the independence movement. The rhetoric of that phase, dominated largely by Gandhian values and the language of morality, appears congenial to the present elite, and it has clearly become a major component of its political style. By perpetuating this rhetoric, the elite has been able to rely on an established mode of communication with the masses. Excessive linkages with the agitational phase of the independence struggle may evince little effort on the part of the elite, but it may also be true that this does not assist in confronting contemporary dilemmas emerging from a newly acquired sense of nationhood.

Typifying this type of rhetoric is the statement of Finance Minister Morarji Desai, who, in addressing industrialists, declared that the most basic characteristic of Indians was their capacity to derive happiness from sacrificing for the happiness of others. It was this, he said, which "had preserved Indian civilization through several vicissitudes," and it was this same sacrificial tradition which present and future generations had the responsibility to enrich.[1] Whether or not empirically supported, this element of self-sacrifice has been repeatedly articulated within the Indian tradition, and Desai but echoed ideological sentiments which a typical Indian has undoubtedly been assimilating since childhood. According to the karma theory of reincarnation, an individual must do good and sacrifice for the happiness of others if he aspires to a more benign future in his next birth. This does not mean Indians are dissuaded from pursuing economic gain. Note, for instance, that Desai is addressing large-scale industrialists. But even pronouncements in ancient Indian literature exhort the individual to hold his wealth "in trust" for society; and he is told that to gain religious merit, he must utilize this wealth for the happiness and enrichment of the less fortunate. In this same vein, Rajendra Prasad, the late president of India, called upon Indians to "be prepared to make sacrifices," to "stick to what is right despite overwhelming difficulties," and to attempt to "enter into the skin of others and make their suffering and sorrows one's own."[2]

The Indian elite appear constantly preaching to its people to search within, reflect, and then act in what is conceived to be the truly moral way. "Let each of us examine his or her own life to see how far he or she conforms in daily dealings to the ordinary standard that is generally accepted in society," declared the president.[3] Even Prime Minister Nehru, secular and modern in bent of mind, would proclaim to Parliament that "only a return to moral and spiritual values could control nuclear energy and save mankind."[4] This is the language of morality and the rhetoric is one that demands introspective analysis. We identify this as a dominant mode of reflection and communication. There is little evidence from our study to indicate that the self-scrutiny preferred by the

[1] *Times of India*, March 15, 1958. (The following notes, unless otherwise indicated, are from the same source.)

[2] August 15, 1952.

[3] August 15, 1952.

[4] April 1, 1955.

Indian elite is formulated along definite and measurable lines. Where the American counterpart finds it often congenial to describe the national self in quantitative terms, the Indian elite rarely displays any knowledge of the complex and variegated social fabric of Indian society. The Indian elite appears to make few demands upon itself to support communications with data even when they are readily accessible. Where the American elite is likely to be descriptive in political rhetoric, the Indian top leadership is more often than not prescriptive; where the American elite seeks to enlighten or indulge the audience, the Indian elite's target for indulgence appears to be the self.

The Indian belief system instructs one to approach the affairs of society and politics with the same moral dedication that should characterize the pursuit of personal salvation. The emphasis upon moral action approaches religious fervor. As President Prasad expounded: "Our hands may shake, our feet may falter, but let not our vision be dimmed nor our determination to follow the true path be weakened."[5] This moral consciousness is articulated in nearly every sphere of activity, public and private, domestic affairs and foreign relations. Although the traditional Indian concept of the self embodies this moral emphasis, we draw attention to the fact that in modern India such an emphasis is especially symptomatic of periods of stress. Moral exhortations are universally resorted to at times of crisis in order to marshal inner resources. From 1950 to 1958 the Indian elite was acutely conscious of such a crisis. It expressed a sense of urgency and a recognition that disaster might lurk around the corner: it felt justified in demanding a great deal of the people. The President indicated this in an Independence Day address to the nation in 1951.[6] Six years later, reinforcing the impression that the climate of crisis had not appreciably receded, he reiterated his belief that the Indian people would not be "cowed down by any difficulties and that, to a man, the whole nation will rise to the occasion and make sacrifices, so that a better, brighter, and more prosperous India may be built."[7]

Although the Indian people are encouraged to make sacrifices of the self and they are described as being resilient in the face of crisis, the inherited political pattern has been one of dependency. The government has been conceived as a source of nurturance, and the people have tended to regard the government as their *maa-baap* (mother and father). The paternalism of the British civil services in India served to reinforce these tendencies. The President felt the necessity of admonishing the people against their excessive dependence upon the government. He

5 August 15, 1952.
6 August 15, 1951.
7 August 15, 1957.

declared that such dependence "must give place to a robust consciousness and steady confidence that it is for us and up to us as a people to conquer all our difficulties."[8] The Indian people have demonstrated excessive dependency upon government, and partly because of this attitude there has been a relative absence of organized groups which could function as mediators between people and the government. Governmentally induced changes in India have activated groups that were previously latent in public affairs; and new groups arise continuously which make competing demands upon resources.

In an economically underdeveloped country such as India, possessing inadequate channels of communication, the elite occupies an especially crucial position. Furthermore, in view of the multifarious regional language and religious differences among the people, a foremost task of the leadership is to establish the rules of the game of politics: they, in fact, become teachers of the rudiments of appropriate political behavior upon which depends the nation's survival. The legacy of the struggle against alien rulers has not entirely benefited this end: largely characterized by negative protest, and led by a monolithic nationalist movement, the struggle provided little experience in group-to-group intercourse and negotiation. In addition, traditional political patterns scarcely serve the purposes of a government engaged in modernizing the society. It is true that homage may still be paid to some of these traditional patterns, and that some ideological survivals are useful to the elite, who reinforce them through exhortation. Usually, however, the traditions lose their original meaning and purpose through the new interpretation.

An especially useful analytical device with which to differentiate political cultures is the identification of instrumentalities and strategies by which political innovation and social change are effected.

The institution of government can be all-embracing, or it can leave varying degrees of function to organized private associations and to individuals. In executing its role, governments can rely on coercion or persuasion in all proportions. Today the government of India is far from all-embracing, but it performs many enterprisory, regulative, and supervisory functions that express and consolidate national authority.

One implication of the present situation is that the government advocates the settling of differences and disputes on the basis of negotiation rather than through direct, violent means to which Indian sectional groups and interests are sometimes prone to resort. Prime Minister Nehru spoke of "one's duty to smoothen . . . out" differences of opinion

8 August 15, 1952.

rather than quarrel over "petty differences."[9] Such a position characterizes all democratic governments where the rules of the political game
are clear and widely understood.

In India, however, this appeal to settle disputes and to change the
status quo by peaceful means is not merely based upon the fact that
such means are essential to any democratic order. The accent is upon
the moral nature of such a course, with deliberate attention drawn to
indigenous modes of action. The Gandhian emphasis on the purity of
means in politics, for instance, is linked with Hindu–Buddhist traditional prescriptions for the behavior of individuals. The Prime Minister
vividly demonstrated this linkage during a speech at Sanchi, when he
noted that the teachings of Buddha, such as love and compassion,
could provide a useful path to progress and prosperity.[10]

Even members of opposition parties share the feeling that the moral
approach must be utilized to solve social problems. Asoka Mehta, then
leader of the Praja Socialist party, spoke of "moral courage" as the "last
arsenal on which human beings could depend."[11]

The emphasis upon the preferred modes of conflict resolution lead
us to examine pronouncements on the problem of disunity and harmony,
conceived to be historically the most enduring of the nation's problems.
Until recently, a major problem of Indian unity centered on Hindu–
Muslim relations. The partition of the country in 1947 did not by any
means wholly resolve this problem. The top elite of India has consistently and vigorously advocated a secular state. But in both sections
of the subcontinent strains between the two communities are scarcely
concealed.[12]

The post-independence period has brought to the fore even greater
problems of national integration. Never in Indian history has the
authority of the central government extended so widely. In the past
national unity was precarious and short-lived; and even today there is
reason to fear dissolution of the country into separate nationalities,

9 December 1, 1967. There is frequent use of the word "petty" in terms of disputes
and the exhortation is to rise above these "petty" disputes, to be above such matters.
A typical example of this is the remark of the Home Minister G. B. Pant in the lower
house of Parliament during the course of a debate on the States Reorganization Commission Report: "Let us not be involved in petty squabbles. Let us resolve our differences through the peaceful means of negotiations." (*Times of India*, December 15,
1957.)

10 December 1, 1952.

11 January 1, 1954.

12 In a separate section we consider this problem of "communalism." Here we note
that in India today the tensions between the majority (Hindu) and minority (Muslim)
communities are more frequently latent than manifest.

each exercising autonomous power. Cultural groups, such as Bengalis, Punjabis, Gujeratis, each comprising tens of millions and each having separate languages and customs, have existed for centuries. For the first time in Indian history, however, it has become something of a problem to move freely between the borders of the constituent states of the republic. The riots between the Assamese-speaking and the Bengali-speaking Indians in eastern India have highlighted the precarious nature of Indian unity. Movements for secession have, at various times, been active in various regions of the country, especially in South and East India.

Deputy Prime Minister Sardar Patel, in a speech delivered in Calcutta, condemned provincialism and urged the people to turn from lawlessness to production.[13] Nehru would often repeat that "fissiparous tendencies . . . benefit neither the region concerned nor the country."[14] In an Independence Day message to the nation the President gave the following version of the problem:

> We have people following different religions, speaking different languages, following many and varied customs, and complete understanding and toleration of each other and full freedom to each to live his own life and to rise to his fullest height without interfering with similar rights of others are essential. This, in one word, is what is meant by calling our state a secular state, and today it is obvious that the first condition not only of all progress, but also of our bare existence, is peace based on mutual respect.[15]

These interregional, interlinguistic rivalries are not merely because of cultural differences; they are based on serious economic considerations. Each group finds itself threatened by members of the other communities—the Gujeratis are feared because they dominate the business of Bombay; the Assamese rise up violently against the Bengalis because the latter occupy some of the most coveted posts in their state. The late G. V. Mavlankar, speaker of the Lok Sabha, may plead with the members of his own Maharashtrian community "to recognize the limits of their love of language and region" and to place national unity above all other problems.[16] But the speeches of the leadership divulge little serious thought on the ways and means of achieving national unity. As a rule lofty exhortations are devoid of concrete proposals. Illustrative of this style is the following statement of the President, who, in the name of Mahatma Gandhi and his creed, appealed to the people "to learn to live and let others live, none trying to dominate, none trying to

[13] January 16, 1950.
[14] November 1, 1955.
[15] August 15, 1952.
[16] November 1, 1953.

exploit, none trying to humiliate others. This can be secured only on the basis of nonviolence which the Father of the Nation taught us as of yore."[17]

Problems of social and political unity can not be considered outside the context of economic inequality and the existence of scarce wealth resources. The national self image of the Indian elite clearly demonstrates anxiety regarding the political survival of the nation. Economic deprivation is perceived to be a legacy of the past and an integral part of the present. The vague and allusive quality of the political communication of the Indian leadership mirrors itself in discourses on problems of wealth and welfare. On these problems, data for precision and specificity are certainly more accessible, but we do not discover any persuasive evidence which would indicate that the normal diffuseness of style has undergone the requisite transformation.

That the people of India live under severely deprivational economic conditions is well known; that within India exist extremes of economic well-being is also generally acknowledged. Soon after independence, the government launched a planned program of economic development, aimed not only at the rational exploitation of resources, but designed to bridge the gap between the few rich and the many poor. Thus, a variety of socialism, or at least of welfare economics, became the official ideology of the government.

The partition of the country caused tremendous social and economic upheavals, and intensified the problem of food shortages. In the 1940s India had undergone what was probably the worst famine in modern times; the tragedy was only further exaggerated by the fact that the famine was limited largely to the state of Bengal. In the post-independence period, elected officials stressed the fact that negligence in transferring resources from one region to another could not be tolerated. We get some idea of this felt urgency in Nehru's broadcast to the nation on the question of the food shortages of 1950–1951:

> We cannot tolerate that there should be any abundance in one part and starvation in another. . . . If we spread out this burden and all of us share it, then we may well pass this critical period of the next few months. Therefore, let us come to grips with this problem in all earnestness and determination. Let there be no waste. Let no man shift for himself at the cost of his neighbor. It is a common peril that faces us, and we can only meet it together as comrades, helping each other and thus lightening each other's distress. We have a hard time ahead. We will not escape it by running away from it or by blaming others or by futile argument.[18]

[17] August 15, 1952.
[18] January 1, 1951.

Vague and patriotic sentiments are reiterated. The tenor of such speeches seems to be that of a schoolteacher or an elder speaking to a child. Note, for instance, the President, on the occasion of India's Independence Day celebrations, calling upon the nation to rid itself of "sloth and laziness" so as to better utilize its energies in productive work.[19]

Occasionally, rather extraordinary and specific demands are made upon the people. For example, the Chief Minister of Mysore state K. Hanumantaiya, visiting the Kolar Gold Mines, asked the workers their opinion of prohibition. All workers opposed it. Noting that prohibition was introduced to ensure that all wages went into food and clothing, he then declared: "Surely, you workers in the Kolar gold fields are not overpaid. Your leaders tell me that you are underpaid, and the money you get is not sufficient for two meals a day."[20]

Victorian paternalism, although characteristic of leadership at the national level, goes to even greater lengths at the state level.

Clearly the Indian elite perceives the necessity for vast changes in the distribution of wealth and welfare. The preferred ideology is egalitarian, and its chief exponents have charted the future in terms that demand a narrowing of class divisions in the future. The national self toward which the elite strives is a commonwealth of shared wealth and welfare.

Prime Minister Nehru is the person most responsible for having articulated the objectives of Indian economic development. He enunciated them in broad terms before the All-India Manufacturers' Organization: "We must fight and remove social injustices which come in the way of human welfare, progress, and cooperation."[21] And in addressing a group such as the Associated Chambers of Commerce he did not hesitate to state that heavy taxation was a necessity and that it was the object of taxation to equalize income. For, Nehru said, in the conditions prevalent in India, "obviously a modern social outlook could not endure such a terrific difference."[22] With similar directness, the Finance Minister C. D. Deshmukh declared that measures were necessary to strike a balance between the public and the private sectors of the national economy, because "class jealousy" was already tending to paralyze the country.[23]

Economic development, rationally planned, may eventually serve as an integrative factor; it cannot be assumed, however, that economic development will automatically bring about political stability. Indeed,

[19] August 15, 1952.
[20] September 1, 1955.
[21] April 15, 1956.
[22] December 15, 1953.
[23] March 15, 1951.

some of the most stable groups politically are often the most backward economically. Perhaps a more accurate picture is one of competing local interests demanding what they deem to be their share of the available resources, irrespective of the effect on others. It appears necessary, there-fore, for the leaders to expound national development goals in such a way that the allocation of resources is seen to be rational in the in-clusive interest of the whole nation. The overriding necessity then, under prevailing Indian conditions, is to evolve symbols of national policy that have currency everywhere. Such symbols must gain definite-ness and win support by the advocacy of programs that marshal the resources of the nation without providing opportunity for the programs to be labeled as favoring particular groups or areas.

The leaders of contemporary India have sought to define the national image of the self in a framework of tradition modified by demands for the consolidation of independence, unity, and economic growth. The appeal to unity, it is often recognized, is an appeal to history. The statements and key symbols that refer to the past appeal to common knowledge and themselves provide an experience of unity. Historical references are part of the "collective memory"; their recall can serve the purposes of the living.

In a newly independent country such as India it is important to note what aspects of history are brought to the focus of public attention. The dominant and respected political leadership can and does influence the academic specialists who interpret the past. Political reinterpretations of history have particular impact in a developing nation which is by and large illiterate, and whose historical memories are chiefly religious in nature; if the general level of information is low, it is likely that the historical information selected and disseminated by the elite will become the basis for belief and action.

More than one competent historian has observed that if among the great world civilizations the Chinese have been the most historically minded, the Indians are the least so. Records from the past have been few indeed, and most early Indian history has had to be reconstructed from religious and literary tracts, coins, pillars, and artifacts. With the Islamic invasions, historical accounts begin to appear in some quantity. Individual scholars have gone so far as to suggest that the notion of historical records is itself part of the legacy bestowed upon India by the British raj, and that Indian history as we know it today rests largely on the work of European, especially British, scholars. If we accept these observations as substantially accurate, it becomes especially interesting and important to see how India's new elite has made public use of the past.

It is not only totalitarian elites who patronize the art of revising accounts of the past; nationalists of all subjugated countries have utilized history as a justification for national survival and autonomy. Since history can enhance the self-respect of nationalistic leaders and of those whom they seek to recruit, history is an aid to establishing both a personal and a national identity at a time when the self is threatened by rapid and erratic pressures from alien sources. Linkage to the past constitutes one of the most potent motivations for stepping into the future as a shaper of tomorrow's history.

In the period January 1950 to June 1958 Indian leaders refer to history primarily to stress the fact that national unity is imperative. Prime Minister Nehru indicated that in both the past as well as the present the greatest danger India has had to face has not come from outside, but from the disunity within the country.[24] Some months later, Nehru again warned an audience at a public meeting to remember its Indian history, when the Rajputs were vanquished and the country overrun by the British because of a divided Indian people.[25] And the Governor of Bombay Harekrushna Mahtab, in a broadcast on Independence Day, states:

> When India went down in the past, it was not as if there was no achievement to her credit then. In spite of the Buddha, Shankara, and a host of other saints, and in spite of the high civilization which India had built up in the course of hundreds of years, she went down in the past because of internal dissension and intolerance.[26]

By and large, we may note, the elite does *not* blame external forces for previous defeats in Indian history. Rather, it is generally accepted that internal weakness has accounted for reverses in the past. This attitude may be explained partially by the fact that the secular leadership of India cannot afford to interpret history in a way that would directly damage either the Muslims who conquered India or the British. Damaging the former would be unwise because Hindu–Muslim tensions are still a source of anxiety. Cordial relations with the Great Britain of today (including the fact of membership in the Commonwealth of Nations) preclude statements directly attacking the last and most successful of India's overlords. In the light of these two factors until now it has been difficult to utilize external enemies as historical scapegoats. Indeed, a rare item in our study is the report of a talk by the Prime Minister's sister, Mme. V. L. Pandit, before an American audience of relatively conservative businessmen and community leaders. She told them that it had been "centuries of foreign imperialist exploitation"

[24] November 1, 1955.
[25] June 15, 1956.
[26] August 15, 1956.

which had impoverished modern India, and which was now forcing her to catch up with lost time.[27] It is to be noted, however, that these remarks were made outside of India, and during the first year covered by our study. A far more typical reference to colonialism is found in the Prime Minister's speech of December 1, 1957. He drew attention to the fact that despite great cultural versatility and innovativeness, India lost her independence because of domestic "internecine quarrels" among her own people.[28]

Indirectly, a proud and sensitive elite, aware of its past, can almost arrogantly relegate the years of foreign domination to but an interlude of no great consequence. Note, for instance, how Prime Minister Nehru explained the introduction of the decimal coinage system:

> We are not adopting something alien to India. Indeed, we are going back to something which was originally the product of Indian genius. India gave to the world long ago the great discovery of the zero and numerals, and later the beginnings of what subsequently came to be known as the metric system saw light through Indian genius. So we go back to our own.[29]

The elite repeatedly links the past with events, discoveries, and occurrences of the present day. The Prime Minister, addressing the Indian Science Congress, remarked that India was "a bundle of ages and somehow we jog along. The cow and the tractor going along side by side seem terribly incongruous."[30] He noted how he seemed to associate in his mind the memory of a recent visit to Nalanda, the great ancient university, founded 2500 years ago, and Hirakud, the new dam built under the Five-year Plan. Both were to him illustrative of his nation's greatness.

Prime Minister Nehru, born a Hindu, a professed agnostic, identified deeply with Buddhism. The creed taught by Buddha and the execution of that creed by Emperor Ashoka left a deep imprint on his mind. Nehru consciously utilized symbols associated with Emperor Ashoka. He has recounted how both the Ashoka *chakra* (wheel) on the national flag and the Ashoka lions on the national emblem had been deliberately selected as symbolic of a sincere desire for peace.[31] Even the Panchshila—the "Five Principles" agreement between India and China—had been, according to Prime Minister Nehru, an inherent part of Indian tradition, implicit in Ashoka's philosophy.[32]

[27] May 1, 1950.
[28] December 1, 1957.
[29] April 1, 1957.
[30] January 15, 1957.
[31] December 1, 1952.
[32] December 1, 1955.

But while a Nehru can express pride in Indian history without appearing too immodest, this is by no means the case with those members of the elite whose roots are solely in traditional India, and who have been barely touched or influenced by Western modes of life and thought. The traditionalists feel there is very little which cannot be learned from India's past. This attitude is, in reverse, quite like the patronizing attitude which Indians are likely to encounter in the West. For example, the heir to Gandhi's spiritual leadership, Vinoba Bhave, told an American student that "He thought the element of aggressiveness in Western culture might be owing to its being very young, compared to Indian culture, which dated beyond the very dawn of history. This element would perhaps wane away with the culture attaining maturity, he added."[33]

This type of superiority concerning history and culture is likely to play an increasingly important role in the politics of the coming decades, especially as the cosmopolitan and Westernized leadership gives place to traditionalist leadership from the provinces. Such attitudes can have an appreciable effect not only at home in India but in the wider context of India's relationship with the Western world. During the years of his ascendancy, the influence of Prime Minister Nehru was a restraining force, at least within his political party.

But even Prime Minister Nehru had to operate and contend with the dominant feelings in his society. He, too, felt compelled to place traditional historical figures within politically appropriate contexts. The case of the Mahratta chieftain Shivaji, who challenged the might of the Muslim rulers of India, illustrates this. Shivaji has represented militant Hinduism and has been the acknowledged hero of the neo-fascist Hindu organizations as well as the Hindu traditionalists. Yet, called upon to unveil the statue of Shivaji, Nehru insisted "that while Shivaji fought his enemies bitterly, he was never against Muslims or Islam. He was a national leader fighting for the freedom of his people."[34] Nehru also laid great stress on the differences between Indian and foreign authors regarding Shivaji's relations with Muslims. "He said that from childhood he had regarded Shivaji as one of the great men of India and it pained him to read from history books written by foreigners that Shivaji had deceived Afzal Khan. But reading books written on this incident by Indian authors, the doubt in his mind had been cleared."[35]

He ended the unveiling ceremony by noting that India needed men and women as valorous as Shivaji and, appropriate to the occasion, he stated "but bravery without unity is futile."[36]

[33] August 15, 1957.
[34] December 1, 1957.
[35] December 1, 1957.
[36] December 1, 1957.

Historical reinterpretation becomes more feasible with the passage of time. Due homage may be paid to Gandhi, but policies can be followed which are quite contrary to his teachings. Justifications for such a course will often assume forms such as are indicated in a remark by Nehru, who noted that while Gandhian principles were still adhered to, history taught that policies must change in accordance with the times.[37]

Nations often claim to possess historical bonds even with nations with whom contact has been minimal. Our investigation discloses few references to historical ties with specific countries. One such reference concerned Tibet at the time of Chinese military operations there. Addressing the Parliament, Nehru stated: "Tibet is not only a neighbor of India, but has had close cultural and other ties with her for ages past. India must, therefore, necessarily concern herself with what happens in Tibet and hope that the autonomy of this peaceful country will be preserved."[38] Tibet was incorporated into China after the military invasion. Less than two years after this the Prime Minister's sister led the Indian Cultural Delegation to China. In Peking, Mme. Pandit recounted the significance of her visit:

> My colleagues and I, who form the first official delegation from free India to New China, feel happy and proud that we should have been called upon to walk in the footsteps of those early pilgrims and pioneers, crossing the mountains and deserts of Central Asia or the perilous seas of Southeast Asia, traveling from India to China and China to India.[39]

It is perhaps of some significance to note that the three areas about which references are made—Tibet, China, and Southeast Asia—are precisely those areas with which Indian contact was great more than a thousand years ago. There has been very little intercourse over the past few centuries. References to ancient contacts such as the Indian elite have made is known to serve the specific purpose of heightening self-respect at a historical moment when objective conditions provide little sustenance to national dignity.

The long span of India's existence is a feature of the national image always available for mention. Handled with creativity, this can assist in the formation of a viable national self.

It is clear from this discussion of the national self that the Indian elite has not demonstrated any great virtuosity in the manipulation of symbols to create a sense of collective identity demanded by a period of national reconstruction. Exhortations cannot provide a substitute for a

[37] January 15, 1958.
[38] November 15, 1950.
[39] May 1, 1952.

sensitive definition of the self. There is, it appears, a lack of *élan* and self-confidence on the part of the Indian elite in seeking to extend into a post-independence era the rhetoric of the agitational phase of the freedom struggle. The demands of national unity and reconstruction have produced a national image that largely fails to exploit the richness of the cultural diversity with all its attending complications. Insofar as the national elite has failed to provide an identity appropriate to prevailing conditions and the extension of these conditions into the future, the problems of mobilization have been inadequately tackled. Manifestly, this failure to articulate a sensitive new image of the collective self relegates to history a task which could have been constructively performed by the elite. For, lacking a clear self-identity, a new nation can only blindly grope through the future.

CHAPTER 3 · POLITICAL
PERSPECTIVES
AND MOVEMENTS

The generalized image of the self that has been projected during recent years in the new India gains depth and definiteness when it is linked with the chief political perspectives and movements that have found expression in the internal arena of the nation. The struggle for freedom was not over with the formal attainment of independence; its repercussions gave distinctiveness to many elite communications to one another and to the larger public. The Congress party—the self-chosen instrument of nationalism—had the formidable task before it of moving from a negative and largely agitational stance to a fully responsible and affirmative way of life. On the ideological front socialism played a far from simple role; and constitutionalism stood athwart many of the fondest hopes and aims of India's top elite. We shall give attention to these several manifestations of the Indian outlook in internal matters.

THE STRUGGLE FOR FREEDOM

The mobilization of hopes and their channeling into an action-oriented movement aimed at the capture of power from alien overlords —this might serve as a partial definition of the struggle for freedom. Movements of a mass nature involve the mobilization of large numbers around common perspectives and key symbols. Not only are future rewards offered, but also the opportunity to sacrifice in the name of the common good. All such movements are headed by an elite which articulates the goals, gives content to the aspirations, and forges strategy and tactics. Hence, not the aggregated mass as such, but the group of individuals acting on behalf of the mass give precise meaning and orientation to the struggle for freedom.

By observing how Indian leaders interpret the freedom movement *after* the culmination of the struggle, we may be able to arrive at a concise record of the national past as presently redefined by the active leadership. Because the elite which spearheaded the independence movement coincides largely with the current governing group, this task gains added significance.

Movements for independence, directed toward replacement of an alien ruling power, mobilize sentiment by promising an era which will remove grievances and usher in a time of plenty for all. Public focus upon the tactics and episodes of the phase of seeking and capturing power often minimizes the importance of affirmative aspirations and problems. The expectation of a single dramatic resolution of difficulty—"Freedom"—if kept alive, contributes to an ultimate sense of disenchantment. After independence, sections of the people who have not found their condition materially bettered are now able to assert their own particular wills against the nationalist leaders. The latter, so recently revolutionary and change-oriented, now seek to maintain the new *status quo*, to consolidate its power, and to cope with the waves of protest and antagonism that tend to characterize the early post-independence period. It was to this end that Deputy Prime Minister Sardar Patel attempted to convince a Calcutta audience that the revolution was over, and now was the time for all Indians to "combine together and work in love and peace for the progress of their country."[1] But, as Prime Minister Nehru was to note on the same occasion, the people's despondency and impatience had become all too apparent.[2]

Much of the post-independence discontent was because of the generally low level of economic existence, but changes erupting in the social fabric for many decades prior to independence contributed to it. Tremendous dislocation caused by partition of the country also accounted for a whole series of socioeconomic problems. Leaders whose sacrifices during the agitation for freedom were celebrated, now occupied positions of authority and control and thereby made themselves eligible targets of the aggressions arising from frustration. The racial element also entered into the picture: the fact that one's own fellow countrymen now occupied the seats of power previously held by aliens made it appear less dangerous to express resentment. For despite all the hostility against the British, the long period of servitude had left a legacy of inferiority. It was relatively easy to believe that Indians were corrupt and ineffectual.

In the face of this grumbling and disenchantment the elite found it

[1] *Times of India*, January 16, 1950. (The following notes, unless otherwise indicated, are from the same source.)
[2] January 16, 1950.

useful to retain its link with the independence movement, and to attempt to reactivate the sentiments so successfully organized during the period of struggle. To call forth new sacrifices from the people in the name of the freedom struggle was to touch the sensitive area most amenable to manipulation. The Prime Minister, in a broadcast to the nation, spoke about unkind fates testing the survival of the nation. But he expressed confidence that the tests would be met "calmly and unflinchingly, remembering always the great master who led us to freedom."[3]

By utilizing the emotionalized memory of this struggle, the elite seeks to unify the people and so to mobilize their support of newer goals. Emphasis is now given to unspoken alibis for lack of total success. There is stress on the limitations of time and resources; and utopian fulfillment is pushed into the future. The Prime Minister notes that "five or six years is too short a time for judging a nation. Wait for another ten years and you will see that our plans will change the picture of India so completely that the world will be amazed."[4] Especially on ceremonial occasions, the elite reminds the masses of their historic struggle, and thus reactivates the feelings of pride, sacrifice, and unselfish devotion which characterized an era long since ended. President Prasad, in an Independence Day address to the nation, skillfully wove all these elements together by commenting on the "novel and noble" nature of the freedom struggle, and calling for renewed adherence to the ideals of that period.[5] Calls for political rededication appear to echo the purport and style of theological appeals. Note, for instance, the language and the key symbols utilized by the President in another Independence Day address, when he talked about rededication "in all gladness and joy to the great mission which we had undertaken when we set out on our journey to the temple of Freedom."[6]

Because Gandhian strategy and ideals embodied utilization of nonviolent means in the struggle against British rule, and since the transfer of power was effected by negotiated settlement, the elite has constantly stressed the "uniqueness" of the Indian struggle for freedom. Such stress has served to buttress the self-respect of the nation. A further stimulant to self-respect in a global context is suggested in remarks such as those of Nehru who indicated how "the unique Gandhian way" is used as a model for other nations struggling for independence.[7]

The stress on nonviolence even more directly serves the current interests of the elite in power. By implying that means other than non-

---

[3] January 1, 1951.
[4] May 1, 1953.
[5] August 15, 1952.
[6] August 15, 1951.
[7] November 1, 1955.

violent ones are somehow un-Indian, they attempt to dampen the
ardor of those intent upon securing change through direct and possibly
violent measures. On the occasion of the ninth anniversary of India's
achievement of independence, the Governor of Bombay, Harekrushna
Mahtab, invoking the blessings of Lokmanya Tilak and Gandhiji, called
upon the people to rededicate themselves to patience, tolerance, democracy, and nonviolence.[8]

But great as is the emphasis upon the nonviolent nature of the freedom movement, the elite cannot totally disregard those episodes rooted
in the politics of violence. It has had to take into account violent
revolutionary landmarks. The mutiny of 1857, often referred to as
India's first War of Independence, was one such occasion which could
not be lightly dismissed when its centenary arrived. Even the advocates
of nonviolent change were forced to note its importance. Another major
national revolt entailing violence against the British raj has also been
lauded. The Governor of Bombay Harekrushna Mahtab noted how it
was in Bombay that the slogan "Quit India" was first raised, soon to
spread throughout India and within five years to evict the British. He
also noted that in the same city the last battle for independence was
fought on August 8, 1942.[9]

Apparently, the leaders perceived no contradiction between stressing,
on the one hand, the violent revolts of 1857 and 1942, and, on the other,
the more frequently cited nonviolent struggles. It is evidently out of
the question for the elite to ignore or to openly deprecate incidents
which are heroic landmarks in the struggle for freedom. In no case in
our investigation was violent revolt condemned—provided that the revolt
occurred during the pre-independence era. Obviously, this is a contradiction, but political rhetoric need not defer to the canons of logic.

Although the top leadership continues to evoke the image of the
freedom struggle, it is well aware that political freedom is not enough.
The President reminded the Indian people that until all citizens had
attained a minimum standard of living and freedom from want,
political freedom was incomplete.[10] New social patterns had to and
were emerging, not least significant of which was, according to Nehru,
the revolutionary change in the position of women.[11] The Prime Minister
was all too aware that political freedom had to be accompanied by
socioeconomic freedom. This is vividly illustrated by his description of
the series of revolutions which India had been undergoing since 1945,
and from which she was now emerging successfully. In a sense, his

8 August 15, 1956.
9 August 15, 1956.
10 August 15, 1957.
11 December 15, 1957.

analysis of these revolutions neatly summarizes the major areas of stress in Indian society and the manner in which the elite has responded to them:

> The first was the peaceful withdrawal of the British from India. Although this rung down the curtain on the bitter memories of the past, India emerged out of it still friendly with Britain.
>
> The second was the *chutt putt* merger of the princely states through peaceful negotiations. Chronic injustice had clearly been done to the subjects of most of these states, but the second revolution was also consummated without ill-will or bickering.
>
> The government, in its turn, Nehru said, had been "more than generous in its gestures and compensatory provisions" as far as the former rulers were concerned.
>
> The third was in the sphere of land reform. The Prime Minister said that this was in the process of completion in most progressive states of the union.
>
> Here, too, he said, the abolition of zamindari, talukdari, and jagirdari rights was nearing completion, belying the pessimistic prediction of violence, bloodshed, and unrest made by critics of the government. India was now committed to bringing about its "fourth revolution" of a socialistic pattern of society. Her past successes and present political and legislative trends gave her reason and confidence to believe that she could achieve this in a reasonable period of time.[12]

THE INDIAN NATIONAL CONGRESS

Since the advent of freedom in 1947 the Congress party has dominated the Indian political scene. If Prime Minister Nehru was the most powerful individual in Indian politics, his political party, the Congress, was and remained the most powerful organization. It had operated on the political scene for nearly a century, and had been transformed from a group of loyal petitioners of the British raj to the largest mass-based political party in India. In the period covered by our study, the Congress party controlled the government at the center, and ruled the constituent states of the Indian Union for the most part alone, although in some instances with the collaboration of minority parties.

The Congress party's organization was not matched by that of any other Indian political party. Whereas the Congress party reached down to the villages, its political rivals scarcely were able to operate at the district level. Consequently, over vast areas of India the Congress was virtually unchallenged; the people knew of no other political party. Partially this strength could be attributed to the cardinal factor of

[12] November 1, 1955.

power itself. A ruling party inevitably attracts to itself the politically ambitious, especially when opposition parties are little able to offer rewards in terms of power and patronage. Furthermore, the Congress party, tolerating dissent within its ranks, demanded only rudimentary allegiance from its members.

The Congress has been in existence longer than any other political party. It was *the* national movement for freedom. Within it there was a place for the capitalist, the socialist, and the communist. Prior to 1947, to be associated with the Congress was simply to be on the side of those who wanted freedom from the British rulers. This has given the Congress a symbolic importance and advantage which cannot be minimized. It is illustrated by the fact that the national flag and the Congress party flag bear very close resemblance. Moreover, the Congress is the party of the father of the Indian nation, Mahatma Gandhi. Thus, a rich symbolic past provides strong support for the appeal and viability of the premier political organization in India.

It should be acknowledged that the organizational demands of a national liberation movement representing almost an entire nation are qualitatively different from those of a party which functions within an independent state where power must be achieved through the democratic process. The achievement of authority and control over the governmental apparatus by the Congress party involved an influx of new elements as well as an outflux of several ideologically dissident groups. During World War II the Communists had supported the war effort and opposed the agitational activities of the Congress party; they therefore had been cast out of the otherwise extremely tolerant Congress. After independence, the Congress Socialist party left the fold to operate independently and in opposition to the parent body. The lure of power, joined with genuine opposition to Congress policies, brought into being several ideologically distinctive parties, such as the Jan Sangh and the Swatantra. During the span of time covered by our study, political reverses in some of the states demonstrated that while the Congress was still capable of marshaling majorities, these majorities could no longer be regarded as automatic. Public opinion began to find new organs for articulating the diverse demands of a large-scale national state whose institutions were democratic.

As early as 1950 the Prime Minister was referring to the "present crisis in Congress history" when Congress suffered from "sickness in the body and soul" requiring "inner treatment."[13] Another Congress leader who early recognized the need for change in the party organization was the late Sardar Patel, Deputy Prime Minister of India. He

[13] August 14, 1950.

told West Bengal Congress party leaders in the same year that despite his poor health he had come to Bengal with the hope that he could "rejuvenate" the provincial Congress, so that it could inspire the Congress in other provinces to re-establish itself to better serve the people.[14]

Among the most significant problems Congress has faced is its inability to communicate with the people. This problem, as Sardar Patel noted, has been especially serious in rural areas. He expressed distress that district congressmen tended to lose contact with their village people once they came to the city and began mixing with other members of the party. He predicted such a pattern would destroy the Congress. He urged rural congressmen to apply pressure on urban party leaders to end this situation and thereby maintain popularity with the masses.[15]

In fact, the Congress party has consistently been able to depend upon the allegiance and votes of the rural areas where little opposition has existed in organized form. But in a metropolis such as Calcutta, capital of West Bengal, there is not only jockeying for power and patronage within Congress, but competition for votes from eager opposition parties. Although West Bengal has traditionally been one of the more stormy centers of Indian politics, whose population has possessed an especially lively political awareness, the picture painted of the West Bengal Congress party's problems by Sardar Patel could be applicable to the situation in most of the Indian states. Other top leaders of the Congress hierarchy did express similar awareness of the onset of organizational weakness; for, as Nehru candidly commented, "the Congress, as it is organized today, is a feeble instrument for carrying out the nation's work, more especially among the people."[16]

In addition to awareness expressed about the lack of effective communication with the masses, some members of the elite were cognizant of the lack of communication links between top Congress leaders and those at intermediate levels. This, plus absence of firm disciplinary sanctions, facilitated the gradual development of conflicting centers of power within the Congress. In a speech delivered in 1951, Nehru once again referred to the "disease" afflicting congressmen, the symptoms of which were "mutual dissension and faultfinding."[17]

General appeals for unity and concord can be only partially effective. For some, the past intrudes powerfully to contribute to cohesiveness; for others, the Congress has lost its purity of purpose and such appeals no longer have the intended effect. Factions and cleavages had existed under the umbrella of the Congress during the independence struggle,

[14] January 16, 1950.
[15] January 16, 1950.
[16] February 15, 1952.
[17] October 1, 1951.

but now, having achieved the overriding goal of independence, factionalism acquired a new meaning—orientation toward the capture of power, the influencing of policy, or sheer opportunism in the search for patronage.

In addition, there have been accompanying problems of corruption and nepotism. M. P. Mishra, Congress party member of Parliament from Bihar, noted in the House how official corruption on all levels was undermining public confidence.[18] And in the Punjab, Kedar Nath Sehgal, veteran hero of the national movement, and member of the Punjab legislature, expressed the following sentiments when he and his colleagues were expelled by the Congress party: "We feel relieved of the heavy burden of responsibilities of corruption, favoritism, and nepotism that we shared with those in power in the government and the Congress."[19]

It should be noted, however, that the Congress party has had strong national leadership and an abundance of talent at the very top. Nehru himself expressed awareness of the fact that there was "too much functioning on the top only."[20] This was a rather extraordinary admission inasmuch as he combined in himself, at the time, the official leadership of both the Congress and the government. Delegation of responsibility was always difficult for Prime Minister Nehru. But his colleagues in the Congress were equally to blame, for they profited well from association with his powerful name, and stressed his indispensability. Seth Govind Das, president of Mahakoshal Provincial Congress Committee, for instance, confessed that although he opposed, in principle, one man holding both the offices of prime ministership of India and presidentship of Congress, he felt Nehru was an exception.[21] On the other hand, S. K. Patil warned "it was time the Congress stopped basking in the reflected sunshine of Gandhiji, Sardar Patel and Mr. Nehru." He observed how the Congress was increasingly becoming a "party of delegated democracy." And he warned that unless the party stood on its own feet and became more truly democratic, it would "topple like a house of cards" after Nehru's retirement.[22]

Several reasons account for Nehru's own reluctance to delegate authority. Some of the revered colleagues of the Prime Minister were to him distastefully feudal and obscurantist in outlook. Nehru's acceptance of both the presidentship of the Congress and the office of prime minister illustrates his concern in this regard. At the time, an

18 February 15, 1953.
19 October 15, 1953.
20 February 15, 1952.
21 October 15, 1954.
22 May 1, 1955.

orthodox Hindu, Purshottamdas Tandon, was Congress party president. Tandon's parochial outlook is evident from his remarks in Parliament during the debate on the food problem, when he attacked the use of artificial fertilizers. He likened the latter to aphrodisiacs, and advocated instead cow dung, and, better still, human excreta and urine to increase productivity.[23]

The Indian elite focussed some attention on new recruitment policies which could help the Congress solve its organizational difficulties. The secretary of the Gujerat Provincial Congress Committee, Vajubhai Shah, noted a need for new blood infusion into the Congress "from the bottom up."[24] S. K. Patil similarly stressed the need for "new blood —young men and women from the colleges."[25] The conflict between the desire to maintain a mass base and the need for restrictive recruitment policies to ensure disciplined cadres is not new to political parties. Such vacillation between restrictive and incorporative tendencies has manifested itself in the Congress, but more on the verbal than the action levels.

The fact that the Congress party existed as a national movement for a longer period than it has functioned as a political party has created ambivalences regarding electoral policy. Prior to independence, Gandhi had recommended strongly that the Congress abandon its political functions and become a nonpolitical social-service organization. The death of Mahatma Gandhi and the events which have since followed have made this suggestion one of only historical interest. The Congress did assume political power during Gandhi's lifetime, and it has continued to function as a political party. Among those near to Gandhi, the decision to pursue political goals involved soul-searching. The hard core of devoted Gandhians, such as Vinoba Bhave and the circle of his disciples, have, indeed, carried out Gandhi's suggestion and withdrawn from the political scene to concentrate upon the removal of the social inequities rampant within Indian society. Others, such as Nehru, have had moments when the Gandhian mood projects itself; they feel a wistful urge to renounce politics and accept the traditional role of the unselfish guru or teacher who wants no power for himself but seeks only good for the unfortunate of his society.

While such renunciation of power was never an urgent temptation felt by Nehru and his close colleagues, their approach to winning power at the polls was not wholly conventional. Indeed, Nehru, at least, felt both the political necessity to advance the cause of his party and the urge to stress the altruistic ideals which, in the past, had so largely

23 July 1, 1952.
24 May 1, 1955.
25 May 1, 1955.

guided the Congress policies. Invariably, the politician dominated in Nehru; but we ought to note that Nehru also functioned, within the Indian context, as a teacher to the masses, educating them, chiding them to follow certain paths. In an address to Congress party workers, Nehru warned that he would leave the Congress if it became merely an election-fighting organization. He urged party workers to revive Congress's spirit, so that it was not reduced to the lifelessness of other parties.[26]

The very diffuseness of the Congress membership and its lack of any coherent ideology contributed to continuous charges that the Congress was largely a body of opportunists. Nehru expressed this concern for the reputation of his party when he told a public meeting in Patna that "he was not bothered whether individual congressmen were elected or defeated at the polls. What he wanted was that the fair name of the Congress should not be sullied."[27]

In this respect he was especially concerned about dissident congressmen who usually, because they had not been given a party ticket, were attacking Congress from behind the scenes. He preferred that such congressmen leave the organization and join other parties.[28]

It must be remembered that the first general election in India was held under rather difficult conditions—the world's largest free elections in which the electorate was nearly 80 percent illiterate. There were in many quarters serious doubts about the results of such an experiment in democratic elections, but Nehru, in a circular to party members, assuaged them. He said he was impressed with the intelligence, discipline, and discrimination of the electorate and their broad understanding of any issue properly put before them. He was especially impressed with the performance of the uneducated:

> Indeed, the so-called illiterate voter has probably taken this election more seriously than many of the literates. My respect for him has gone up and whatever doubts I might have had about adult suffrage in India have been removed completely. These elections have fully justified adult suffrage and the faith we put in our people.[29]

Some of the more enlightened Congress leaders in the period under consideration showed a lively appreciation of the dangers inherent in a one-party system in which opposition, while permitted, did not flourish. Prime Minister Nehru told a public meeting in Patna that the opposition parties should assume responsibility for ousting the Congress from

[26] April 1, 1958.
[27] February 15, 1957.
[28] February 15, 1957.
[29] February 15, 1952.

power.[30] On the other hand, from a practical standpoint, the virtual monopoly over political offices enjoyed by the Congress could be considered as a stabilizing influence over Indian politics at a time when consolidation was of primary importance.

But this monopoly of power also generated difficulties with respect to the attitude which the party could appropriately adopt toward the government with which it was largely identified. During the days of British rule, the relationship between the Congress party and the government was clear and direct: Congress opposed government. But the formation of the Congress governments in the various states and the capture of power in the central government demanded a new relationship. The question of the extent to which the party could influence government policy formulation arose almost immediately after independence. In this, as in so many other cases, the party elite looked for guidance from the British model, especially as exemplified by the Labor party. Prime Minister Nehru reflected that while the All-India Congress Committee should offer advice to the government, it should do it in a manner resembling England's Labor party, which traditionally laid down only broad policies rather than interfering in routine day-to-day matters.[31]

Another problem for the Congress party has been the vagueness of its ideology. The intentions of the Congress leaders need not be called into question, but their thinking on how to bring the fruits of freedom to the people were devoid of clear conceptions of strategy and tactics. Gradually, since 1947, the Congress party began to evolve, through considerable groping, a pragmatic approach to policy making. As opposition political parties grow in power, especially the parties of the right, the Congress will probably be forced to express its policies with increasingly greater precision and clarity. We suggest that the ideological haziness of the Congress cannot persist over a long period after explicit alternatives begin to manifest themselves. In fact, Nehru showed distress at the fuzzy thinking that characterized large sections of the Congress leadership, and in his circular to the active workers he called for military discipline and formation of "definite objectives."[32]

By and large, the Nehru wing of the Congress party was able to carry the organization behind its version of socialism which, in its intellectual

[30] February 15, 1957.

[31] February 1, 1951. This was, of course, a poor example for Nehru to cite: The influential role of trade-unions in the Labor party's policy-making process has no counterpart in India, nor do Indian parties resemble the Labor party in membership structure. And perhaps even more important is the fact that the power of the Labor party in the British party spectrum could hardly be compared to that of the Congress in India.

[32] February 15, 1952.

foundations, owed much to the Fabians and the British Labor party. But this is not to suggest that the Nehru wing had an easy victory—the nonsocialist elements in the Congress were and remain extremely powerful. Typical of the thinking of the latter was the late Deputy Prime Minister Sardar Patel, who criticized those who would clamor for nationalization of industries when neither men nor money was available to run them.[33] These nonsocialist elements, tradition-oriented and close to the Indian industrialists and landlords, have been against the state's interfering, to any great degree, on behalf of labor and peasant classes. This is not to imply that these elements oppose the workers and peasants; rather, they look with favor on retaining the kind of relationship between government and the people that was established by the British rulers. They have also tended to oppose those state measures which have appeared to favor the masses at the expense of the entrepreneurial group.

In addition to nonsocialists with definite leanings toward the private-enterprise system, another group within the administration has not always favored Prime Minister Nehru's approach: this is the highest echelon of civil servants and administrators whose outlook is essentially nondoctrinaire and aimed at achieving results. Their approach is typified by two Indian Civil Service (ICS) men who have played vital roles in the post-independence era. C. D. Deshmukh, Finance Minister in the government of India, told Parliament bluntly that although the public sector could not be expanded "ad lib," if private capital did not respond to the nation's needs it would be eliminated.[34] Another distinguished officer of the Indian Civil Service, G. S. Bajpai, expressed a similar view. He noted that the scope of the state's ownership and operation of industry would be largely determined by the behavior of private enterprise, not only with respect to their use of capital resources, but also with respect to their attitudes toward and treatment of labor.[35]

In the actual formulation of the policies of the Indian government, the Congress party's directives have furnished the broad guidelines; but specific policy has been greatly influenced by the core of former ICS officers who have actually manned the command posts in government at the center and in the states. The tradition of the Indian Civil Service has been that of an elite corps; its members have conceived of themselves as personifying Plato's Guardians. In outlook, they have not been averse to a paternalistic role for the state; and, consequently, although they might be averse to Nehru's ideological socialism, the ICS officers would probably find state control and regulation congenial.

The development of Congress party economic policy, from its initial

[33] January 16, 1950.
[34] March 15, 1951.
[35] March 15, 1953.

groping to a semblance of concreteness, can be traced through pronouncements of the Prime Minister. Early in the post-independence
period, he only cautiously claimed that "the Planning Commission had
met with far greater success than might have been expected."[36] But he
also warned the Federation of Indian Chambers of Commerce and
Industry that although he would not bar criticism of the government,
he felt it was neither "possible or right either for Chambers of Commerce or labor unions to tell government what they should do."[37] By
this time initial steps toward active planning by the government had
been taken; and the basis for orientation toward a planned economy
appears to have been laid. Therefore, in spite of antisocialist biases and
factions within the Congress, the Nehru wing apparently had scored a
major success.

By 1956 we note Prime Minister Nehru demanding action and active
cooperation with a still greater measure of confidence. In his address
before the All-India Manufacturers' Organization he said that socialism
would not come from mere expressions of good will for the down-
trodden: these expressions had to be followed up with concrete action.[38] The Prime Minister declared that centralization of heavy industries was inevitable; he said there would be some attempt to decentralize
consumer-goods industries, but these would be operated along cooperative lines; and the Prime Minister emphasized the importance of
agrarian cooperatives.[39]

By the middle of the 1950s the Congress party had also declared itself
explicitly in favor of a "socialistic pattern of society"; and this was, in
fact, merely a rubber-stamp approval of the policies pursued by Prime
Minister Nehru. The meaning of this "socialistic pattern" was never
completely clarified. Acharya J. B. Kripalani rather accurately assessed
the situation when he commented: "Is there anything in the world
that the Congress party does not stand for? The Congress is socialist,
Gandhian, and capitalistic all put together, and Mr. Nehru even admired communism 'minus its manifestations in the country.' The Congress is everything to everybody."[40]

Prime Minister Nehru's multifarious remarks tended to lend credence
to this assessment. To the Indian National Trade Union Congress, the
Congress party's labor union federation, he said that he refused to be
wedded to any kind of dogma despite his belief in socialism. Even the
principle of nationalization would not be approached in a doctrinaire
fashion: It was a question of whether or not it could aid India's

36 April 1, 1951.
37 April 1, 1951.
38 April 15, 1956.
39 April 15, 1956.
40 September 1, 1952.

economic development.[41] The Prime Minister admitted there was confusion over India's socialistic objectives when he addressed the Associated Chambers of Commerce three years later. He said that the nearest
definition he could suggest was the creation of equal opportunities for
all the people to progress. And, "with that accomplished, the next step
would be to raise the level of progress equally for all."[42] Occasionally,
however, Prime Minister Nehru enunciated more doctrinaire leftist
views. An example of this is Prime Minister Nehru's remarks in the Lok
Sabha wherein he declared that

> . . . in schemes of social reform and social engineering such as
> zamindari abolition or imposition of a ceiling on land holdings or
> slum clearance, it was neither possible nor proper to pay full
> market compensation. Payment of full compensation even if it
> were possible would be absurd when the underlined motive for
> the change was to narrow the gap between the haves and the
> have-nots.[43]

The only exception Nehru made was in the case of slum clearance.
He said that it was a crime to have slums and that no compensation need
be payable to slum owners.

Such a statement, delivered in a parliament by a Prime Minister, under ordinary circumstances would have been accepted as a policy pronouncement. Congress governments, however, tended to ignore many of
the implications of the Prime Minister's remarks. Landlords were
handsomely compensated for land, for instance; and slums, when cleared,
were cleared with compensation for the owners. In other words, the
Congress leadership in control of the government quite often has confused the roles of official responsibility and political irresponsibility. The
habit of extemporaneous speeches, acquired during the independence
struggle, has carried over into official pronouncements and has been a
major factor in much of the confusion which tends to follow such
pronouncements.

Aside from the group of nonsocialists mentioned above, socialism is a
creed to which almost every Congress party member—not to speak of
almost every Indian—pays lip service. Illustrative of this apparent
ideological commitment to socialism are statements from three of the
Congress elite. Jagjivan Ram, Minister for Labor in the government
of India, for instance, remarked in 1951 that labor could do without
capitalists but "capitalists cannot afford to do without labour."[44] And
N. V. Gadgil, a Congress M. P., remarked somewhat later that the

---

[41] January 1, 1954.
[42] December 15, 1957.
[43] March 15, 1955.
[44] January 15, 1951.

budget appeared designed to benefit relatively rich persons: it did not seem to be conducive to implementing Congress socialism. Gadgil felt that a ceiling on maximum income should be implemented immediately.[45] Tripathi, General Secretary of the Congress labor union, INTUC, told the Lok Sabha that it was simply pointless to compare private and public sectors. For whereas the private sector aimed at exploiting labor, the public sector was a model employer.[46]

From time to time the Congress party embraces within its ranks genuinely ideological factions. During the period of our study it was the Congress Socialist Forum. The remarks of U. N. Dhebar, the Congress president, reveal the party's attitude toward this group:

> So far as we know it is a forum and not a group. We do not want to interfere with the initiative of anyone and I am not sure they [members of the forum] are not thinking on group lines. If the particular phraseology they have adopted creates any such impression, I have no doubt that they will be the first to modify that phraseology.[47]

This group, a so-called ginger group, remained a small minority within the Congress, but it continued to flourish and even boasted of a periodical aimed at evolving a new brand of Indian socialism. Among its supporters were a few members of the central cabinet and a handful of high-ranking Congress personalities. In fact, however, the ideological gap was minimal between Nehru's approach to socialism and that of the forum.

In sum, the symbol "socialism" under Indian conditions meant for the Congress essentially the creation of a society in which greater socioeconomic opportunity will prevail. Since Indian tradition sanctions authoritative action by government, much of the burden for bringing about such equality of opportunity is left to governmental machinery. What the attitude of the Congress party will be in the future depends upon both the performance of the public sector of the economy and the political power of parties arising on the right and left. A further limitation, and an important one, is the extent of and the conditions under which India receives external aid.

THE INDIAN SOCIALIST MOVEMENT

During the period of our investigation, not only congressmen, but almost every educated Indian, called himself a socialist. Even many big-business interests expressed their faith in socialism. Political and non-

[45] March 1, 1955.
[46] April 15, 1956.
[47] January 15, 1958.

political groups who advocated lessening of governmental control advocated socialism. Antistatists and Gandhian anarchists also, in their own way, were socialists. To profess a belief in socialism has implied that one believes in a modicum of fair play, acknowledges that poverty ought to be abolished, and stands for a strong and healthy nation—this is, by and large, the meaning that socialism had come to embody in the Indian context.

There are, of course, many brands of socialism in the political market place of India in addition to that of the Congress party. The Gandhians, some of whom have remained within the Congress party, believe in a uniquely Indian brand of socialism which approximates the ideal of a nation of self-sufficient villages with either a cooperative or a communally-based economy. There are also "official" socialist parties such as the Praja Socialist party (PSP) and the Socialist party of India (SPI).

All these groups have sought to lay claim to the mantle of Mahatma Gandhi. Indeed, it was the Gandhian component in Indian socialism which many claimed lent the ideology its uniqueness. J. B. Kripalani suggested that Gandhi had introduced the element of morals into socialism, whereas scientific socialism as it had evolved in the West had been somewhat amoral, with ends more important than means. Kripalani also said that Indian socialists believed in devolution of power and decentralization, and advocated a new technique of resistance, *satyagraha;* this, too, was a contribution of Gandhi, and it distinguished Indian socialism in the world.[48]

The origins of Congress socialism, Gandhian antistatism, and the socialism of the PSP and SPI can be traced to the early 1930s when within the Congress party there emerged a faction that was increasingly attracted to the currents of Western socialism as they manifested themselves in Britain and Europe. In a sense, therefore, the present leaders are erstwhile comrades whose differences were bound to emerge with the disappearance of the unity of purpose brought about by the struggle for independence. Jayaprakash Narayan, one of the founders of the socialist movement in India (and now one of the band of Gandhians who have "renounced" politics in order to do "constructive work"), led the Socialists toward a program that was to "Indianize" socialism, divorcing it not only from the Congress party, but from the Communists as well. By removing the Socialists from the Congress fold, Narayan hoped that his party would be able to rally the democratic forces within India behind him and his party, and thus provide a viable political alternative to the Congress party. Another leading intellectual of the Socialist party at the time, Asoka Mehta, also viewed the party in this way. At the

48 September 1, 1952.

time of the first general elections, he noted that only two out of the hundred twenty parties had the courage to take a concrete program to the people: the Congress and the Socialists; all the other parties "would disappear as snow under the summer sun."[49] The leadership of the Indian Socialist party, especially since it had been so closely linked to Nehru, had the impression that it was natural for it to assume power, if not as a ruling group, at least as the major opposition. The frustration that results from remaining out of power without experiencing a sense of growth often leads either to a dilution of ideology or a tendency to break into sectarian groups. The Indian Socialists appear to have suffered from both these tendencies.

Jayaprakash Narayan also was largely responsible, first, for the Socialists' extremely close collaboration with the Communists throughout the united front of the thirties; and then, largely because of his disillusionment with this period, for the adamant refusal to allow any electoral collaboration with the Communists during the first election. A. K. Gopalan, a leading communist leader, insisted on the desirability of a renewed united front of the left, and suggested that even if the socialist elite did not wish it, the rank and file would collaborate despite them.[50] In fact, however, the Praja Socialists have had less and less contact with the Communists, to a point that the vocabulary of the Indian Socialists is largely composed of anti-communism in one shape or another. Instead of developing programs which would appeal to the intellectuals and the masses, the Socialists appear to have adopted a course in which little more than anti-communist diatribes were called for. Among journalists and other intellectuals whose life revolved around politics the Indian Socialists have not commanded serious attention. It is often said that the Praja Socialist party has leaders, no followers. A tragedy of the Socialists is that even the leadership is incapable of putting forth a viable platform and organizing a mass base. In terms of an original program one of us was told by one of the PSP's most respected intellectuals and a member of the Parliament that he had simply taken, without acknowledgment, large sections from one of Professor Robert MacIver's books (the distinguished political sociologist at Columbia University, New York) and incorporated them into the party's national program. There is intellectual sluggishness within the Praja Socialist party.

There is, in fact, a dearth of comment on socialist domestic and even foreign policy. Regarding the former, Asoka Mehta claimed that the Socialist party did not dangle a vision of a prosperous tomorrow. Hard work and sacrifice were needed, but the party could not ask the people

[49] October 15, 1951.
[50] July 15, 1951.

for these until a measure of economic equality had been achieved. The party program, according to Mehta, embodied a fair distribution of land and a narrowing down of the margins of income.[51]

Regarding foreign policy, the party initially advocated the creation of a "third force" which would stretch from Yugoslavia through the Middle East, passing through India on to Japan. Eventually, however, the Socialists, like most other political groups, had no alternative but to support Prime Minister Nehru's policy of nonalignment. But until recently criticism leveled at official policies took the line of Asoka Mehta's remarks at the PSP's National Convention, that India's foreign policy had never been less successful; that other Asian countries such as Burma, Ceylon, and Indonesia were afraid of antagonizing America and therefore India found herself at a critical period of history without any friends.[52] The Socialists did not fundamentally disagree with the official foreign policy, although they had been extremely cautious of India's efforts to befriend Communist China, and were active in leading protests against the Chinese annexation of Tibet. On South Africa, on the other hand, the PSP would see eye to eye with the Congress and the other political parties. As Purshottam Trikumdas declared: "Malanism would create perpetual cleavage between the white and dark races and . . . might lead to massacre in which the blood of white men and dark men would flow freely."[53]

The Socialist party, formed by Ram Manohar Lohia in the mid-fifties, was a result of supposed doctrinal differences within the Praja Socialist party. There exists evidence that this split within the socialist ranks might have had more to do with personality differences than with genuine political conflicts. The Lohia faction is composed of what has been often called the lunatic fringe of Indian socialism. Dr. Lohia advocated compulsively "original" theories among which one calls for "an approximation of mankind"—a plan which would rapidly merge the various races of the world. Dr. Lohia, a life long bachelor, expounded a variety of socialism which contains heavy doses of both overt and covert sexual symbolisms which remind one of the romantic exiles from Russia in nineteenth-century France and Switzerland.

ATTITUDES TOWARD COMMUNISM

When the government of independent India was formed, it was clear to observers of the political scene that Prime Minister Nehru represented the forces of the left within Congress, and Sardar Patel, Deputy

[51] October 15, 1951.
[52] January 1, 1954.
[53] January 1, 1954.

Prime Minister, represented the party's right wing. While both Nehru and Patel belonged to the avowedly non-communist Congress party, their respective views on the nature of communism and the activities of the Communist party of India diverged considerably. During the period immediately after independence, Nehru's remarks regarding communism were prone to be critical, while those of Sardar Patel were unambiguously hostile. Their differing views reflected the polarization on this subject within the Congress party (although we should allow for the fact that Sardar Patel as Minister for Home Affairs was responsible for internal security). After Sardar Patel's death Prime Minister Nehru's attitude toward the Communist party gradually assumed a harsher coloration.

During the early years of independence the Indian Communists had been attempting to challenge the authority of the government through terrorism. They had established their own version of Yennan in the Telengana district of Hyderabad where they managed to gain considerable support from the impoverished peasantry. Sardar Patel, at a public meeting in Ernakulam, warned the Communists that India would not become another China, and that the central government would not tolerate murder and dacoity. He asserted:

> Certain young men believed that a few bombs thrown on our own people, a few murders committed, and a few dacoities will convert this land into heaven which they think has come to China and will come to us. It will take a long time for China to build its own country. There is a considerable amount of devastation. Mutual slaughter and destruction would do no good to any country. It will never do good to India.[54]

Soon afterward, the Indian government adopted drastic measures and was able utterly to destroy the Communist bases. The insurrectionary activities of the Communist party of India were not repeated. Sardar Patel also warned Bengali Communist terrorists in a similar manner, suggesting that if they hoped to gain anything, "they were living in a fool's paradise."[55]

Nehru's intellectual development in the 1930s was decidedly influenced by Marxism. In general, his approach was a receptive one; although repelled by Marxism's rigidity, he was impressed by its scientific approach and methodology. Even in 1950 the Prime Minister was declaring that "if the Communists have any set policy, we shall certainly be prepared to consider it and see how far it is workable."[56] But by the mid-fifties his comments had become more consistently derogatory.

[54] May 15, 1950.
[55] January 16, 1950.
[56] January 2, 1950.

The most damaging charge that can be levied against any political group, and especially in a newly free nation such as India, is that it owes its loyalty to an alien power. This theme was not ordinarily utilized by Prime Minister Nehru except when he had been particularly incensed.

A dramatic example of extremely angry comments by Nehru is available from his electioneering tour of Andhra Pradesh:

> I read in the papers today that one of the Communist candidates for election here said at a public meeting that he was speaking with a loudspeaker in one hand and a gun in the other. It is an extraordinary thing to say. We are a grown-up country, mature country, civilized country, with 2000 years or more of cultural background. Are we going to tolerate this fantastic nonsense? I am astonished at the temerity of these people.[57]

In the course of this same speech, Prime Minister Nehru noted that a Communist candidate had called him a traitor. He said he did not mind, but regarded it as "a bit odd" coming from a member of the Indian Communist party.[58]

Equally significant are Nehru's comments on the nature of Communist ideology. Addressing the All-India Manufacturers' Organization, the Prime Minister declared:

> If Communists rely on Marx today, they rely on something which is out of date. Undoubtedly, he was a great thinker. But it is patently wrong to think that in the middle of the nineteenth century he could have told us what should be done in the middle of the twentieth century. That is true of all other thinkers of the previous century.[59]

These comments regarding the inapplicability of communism formed a theoretical assessment of the doctrine. Nehru went even further when he stressed the fact that as a crusading creed, world communism had lost much of its vigor.[60] Anchoring his assessment in these views, Nehru was able to account for the electoral success of the Communists in the state of Kerala by suggesting that their victory was not because of the electorate's response to their ideological attraction, but rather to the people's dissatisfaction with the previous state regime and the need for a change.[61]

[57] January 15, 1955.
[58] January 15, 1955.
[59] April 15, 1956.
[60] July 15, 1957.
[61] July 15, 1957.

In fact, despite his basic criticisms of the Indian Communist party, Nehru was still of the view, even during the insurgency phase of Indian communism, that it was better to take "the positive approach of removing the economic and social breeding ground of communism" rather than for the country to join an anti-Communist bloc.[62] Moreover, the Prime Minister urged adoption of some Communist strategy of development, such as state-directed planning. He was constantly defending this strategy as illustrative of his independence of mind and his true revolutionary spirit. He told the Indian National Trade Union Congress that the Indian Five-year Plan was "an essay in revolution," and that the very plan for development was a revolutionary event.[63] In this way he was able both to criticize Communist ideology and to counteract the considerable influence of the right wing within his own political party. Elsewhere he debunked those who would criticize the plan as communistic or authoritarian. He insisted that India had a democratic structure, and that in planning he would "take whatever was good from any quarter, be it Communist or anti-Communist."[64]

In contrast to the rational and critical views of Nehru, the two Gandhians in our study appear to regard communism benignly. Kumarappa, identified with many front organizations, is reported to have stated that communism and violence were not synonymous, and that it was both possible and desirable that the government establish communism in India—economic equality and social justice—through peaceful and nonviolent means.[65] Consider also the remarks of G. Ramachandran, of the Hindustani Talimi Sangh, who suggested that although the methods were different, the objectives of both Gandhism and communism were the same. He insisted that Gandhism was even more revolutionary than Marxism, which appeared rather narrow and outdated today.[66]

In fact, Gandhi and his followers have always been attracted to the ultimate goals of communism, but there are perhaps two fundamental differences: Gandhism forswears violence in all forms; and its version of utopia is not a highly centralized state, but decentralization carried to the point where every village constitutes a "republic." The latter point, however, has been reconciled with the "withering away of the state" of the Marxist dogma. On at least one occasion Gandhi had referred to himself as a believer in communism *minus* violence.

[62] February 1, 1950.
[63] January 1, 1954.
[64] June 1, 1955.
[65] June 1, 1952.
[66] June 1, 1952.

Similarly, statements of Gandhi's "spiritual heir," Vinoba Bhave, have contributed to the Gandhians' confused interpretation of Communist ends and means. This may be partially explained by the excessive zeal with which Gandhians attempt to reconcile apparently diverse points of view; it is a tenet of the Gandhian faith (reinforced by Hindu tradition) that the opponent, no matter how wrong he may appear, has some validity to his point of view. Similarly this reflects the essentially incorporative aspects of so much of Indian political rhetoric and style.

Our study reveals that comment from Communist leaders is not extensively reported. Most of the available comment is from the more moderate members of the Communist elite. T. V. Thomas, leader of Communists in the Travancore-Cochin legislature, did appeal to dissident Congress party members to join leftists to get their problem solved decently, instead of going back for support "to the bloodstained hands of Congress."[67] But this was atypical of the Communist pronouncements which reached the pages of the press during this period. More representative appears to be the comment of A. K. Gopalan, who noted that the Communist party would have a reasonable chance of forming coalition governments in some states and a strong opposition in others if elections were fair, and repressive measures (taken in connection with the Communists' recently abandoned terrorism) were withdrawn.[68]

It is not until 1955 that we again find references to Communist remarks. Hiren Mukerjee is reported to have advocated that British capital should be expropriated without compensation.[69] Again, his rather mild criticism of the country's foreign policy was alluded to when he "applauded Mr. Nehru's peace policy," but added that this was not consistent with the maintenance of the Commonwealth link.[70] Finally, a comment from Mrs. Chakravarty, a Communist member of Parliament, reveals another area of criticism: that new government projects—what Nehru termed "new temples"—should not be allowed to "hide corruption."[71]

By and large the Indian Communist party continued to follow its line of participation in the elections, democratically seeking to win power. Much of the earlier harshness seemed to be disappearing, as evidenced in the decline of symbols demanding violent overthrow of the existing order. The strategy of power through the ballot yielded notable dividends as the Communists were able to score legislative advances in nearly all parts of India.

[67] February 1, 1955.
[68] July 15, 1951.
[69] March 15, 1955.
[70] April 1, 1955.
[71] August 1, 1957.

COMMUNALISM

The term "communalism" in the Indian context refers to political action on behalf of a particular religious community. Usually the term refers to the Hindu and Muslim communities, but it has also been extended to other religious groups. The term "communalism," therefore, implies the opposite of secularism. Among the liberal intellectuals in India the word "communalism" has tremendous emotional significance—in a negative sense. The struggle for independence from the British raj and the resulting partition of the country into two states— India and Pakistan—are associated, in Indian minds, with communalism. Most Indians would contend that the British imperial policy of divide and rule was responsible for encouraging separatist tendencies. The alternate favoring of Hindus and Muslims, the separate and exclusive treatment given to Anglo-Indians, the division of Indians into martial and nonmartial races—all these policies, Indians hold, contributed to the eventual division of the nation into two states. The emotions that cluster around the term "communalism" can be understood best by noting the fact that Indians cite it as the cause of the partition of the country and the massacre and uprooting of millions of people in 1946–1947.

Insofar as the dominant ideology in India is concerned, communalism has been, in Nehru's words, the "greatest enemy of the country."[72] Such a position is adopted by all political groups, from the center leftward. The Prime Minister's condemnation of communalism at a public meeting in Ludhiana, in the frontier state of Punjab, typifies the position adopted by liberal and left intellectuals in India, when he noted how communalism has not only created class barriers but also led to India's enslavement.[73]

While organized Hindu communalism had been weak during the independence struggle, Muslim communalism had continued to grow until it achieved its goal of a separate homeland. The vast majority of the politically and socially conscious Indians in that period, however, were in the fold of the Congress party, which was strongly opposed to communalism of Hindus as well as Muslims. Since the achievement of independence in 1947, the major communal threat in India has come from the Hindus. While Hindu communalism is still only a minor force, it has continued to gain strength. Its forces are politically organized in the Jan Sangh and Hindu Mahasabha, and in para-military groups such as the Rashtriya Swayam Sevak Sangh (RSS). Simply stated, Hindu communalists believe that India is the homeland of the Hindus who, they

[72] October 1, 1951.
[73] October 1, 1951.

feel, ought to be considered as the only real Indians. Consequently, Hindu communalism is aimed primarily at Hindu supremacy and against the secular nature of the constitution.

While few Hindu communal leaders are represented in our investigation, the positions adopted by them provide us with some understanding of their belief patterns. In the Lok Sabha, for instance, Hindu Mahasabha leader N. C. Chatterjee strongly criticized a proposed amendment to the Constitution which would give the legislatures rather than the courts the power of compensation for property. He felt such an amendment might lead to arbitrary expropriation with a possibility of unjust compensation or none at all. He predicted this would "destroy the sanctity of property and pave the way for a totalitarian regime."[74]

The leadership of the Hindu Mahasabha and other communal organizations has been—and the pattern persists—tradition-oriented, although there are those within the leadership who combine varying degrees of modernity and traditionality. Since the communal leadership seeks the unqualified dominance of its ideas, its ideological position is at extreme variance with that of the secular-oriented Indian majority. There exists profound distrust, and barely concealed hatred, between the secular and communal elements. While the Hindu communalists, for instance, would seek to restore Hinduism to its past glory by an unambiguous equation between "Indian" and "Hindu," the secular-oriented would deliberately seek to underplay religious differences. The latter declare that religion and politics are private and public spheres respectively; that the making of modern Indian culture is the result of contributions made by the various communities which dwell on the subcontinent, and that the greatness and future of India lie in precisely such a rich blending.

Indicative of the distrust and hostility which the communal elements hold for the secularists is the characterization of the Prime Minister as the premier enemy of a Hindu India. Dr. N. B. Khare, president of the Hindu Mahasabha, described Nehru's efforts as resulting from the "desire of a dictator to enslave the nation."[75] Much of this resentment has arisen from the inability of the Hindu communalists to rally enough support for themselves. It is obviously frustrating for them to see the creation of a Muslim state carved out of "Mother India"; added to their feelings is the fact that India still has a Muslim population only slightly less than that of Pakistan. Finally, they are forced to face the historical reality that independent India does not profess to be based on Hindu supremacy. It is out of such frustrations that Hindu communalists have created their dreams of victory in the near future, when,

[74] April 1, 1955.
[75] September 15, 1951.

as Dr. N. B. Khare prophesied, "Hindu ideology would 'reign supreme' in the country in five years."[76]

Hindu communal forces are still politically weak. But they have continued to gain power under the leadership of the Jan Sangh. For whereas the Hindu Mahasabha is one of the oldest politically active communal parties, the Jan Sangh is organizationally one of the most successful political parties to arise in the post-independence period.

There is probably no great disagreement in India about Nehru's unqualified secularism. While Nehru lashed out against communalism in any guise, his special wrath was directed at Hindu communalists. He said that since the Muslim League no longer existed, communal organizations such as the Jan Sangh and the Hindu Mahasabha, which embodied the same spirit as the Muslim League, should be wound up.[77]

The Prime Minister vigorously opposed the Hindu communalists for their advocacy of a "United India"—for such an entity would arise only out of the annexation of Pakistan. He said that talk of a reunion was meaningless.[78] Some secular elements cherish the hope that in the future India and Pakistan may unite. For both communalists and secularists, however, such hopes are receding, as the legacy of suspicion and hostility continues to persist between India and Pakistan.

Secularists and communalists, given the tremendously differing conceptions of the self and the country, are inclined to consider each other politically misguided; they are also prone to question basic loyalties. So much of personal identity is at stake that anxiety appears to distort what, under more normal conditions, would be in the nature of a dialogue in the political arena. An especially good illustration of this is a commentary by Prime Minister Nehru, who suggested that Hindu communalists, by creating disunity and strengthening the ideal of a Hindu Rashtra (Hindu state), were actually unwittingly strengthening the Pakistani cause.[79] Furthermore, where the identity of the self and the nation is fundamentally challenged, political rhetoric is apt to be extremely emotional and uncompromising. Of Hindu communalist agitation in the frontier state of Punjab the Prime Minister declared: "This is goondaism, and the country will not be allowed to fall in the hands of goondas."[80]

To Indian secularists, the tradition-oriented communalists are seen as representatives of those very forces within Indian society which have

76 September 15, 1951.
77 April 15, 1958.
78 January 2, 1950.
79 October 1, 1951.
80 June 5, 1956. The word "goonda" refers to a person who is antisocial. The nearest English equivalent is "a bad character"—one most likely in the police files.

contributed to the decline of the nation. They are regarded as a major threat to any progressive changes within the society. And much of this harsh criticism of the communalists has a basis in reality. Because the modernizing elite is so acutely aware of the backwardness of the masses, it reacts with great insecurity to communal forces: it realizes only too well the seductive appeal which a combination of tradition, religion, and politics has for the mass of the people. Thus, beyond any threat to its personal power and influence, the secular elite is aware of the tremendous costs of communalism to Indian society. Prime Minister Nehru vividly characterized this attitude when he suggested that communal forces had "reduced Hindu religion to a 'kitchen religion.' For them, religion meant what one should eat and what not, and where and how."[81]

Although the official ideology is secular, and the Congress party controls the country with political strength which rests on popular support at the polls, there is a constant awareness that given the slightest opportunity, communalism can exercise its powerful appeal. The left wing in India has repeatedly charged that an appreciable section of Congress party leadership itself is not unfavorably disposed toward the idea of a Hindu India. Evidence to support this proposition does exist, although communalistic expressions are rarely overt on the part of these right-wing congressmen. In a sense, a comparison might be made with American counterparts, who, while fully realizing that the United States is a secular state, nevertheless would wish to identify Americanism with Protestant Christianity. The comparison is a weak one, however, since under Indian conditions such identification has graver implications in terms of national and personal identity.

We suggest that communalism in India will exercise a continuing appeal because of a triple threat. First, continuing hostility on the part of Pakistan tends to create insecurity for nearly 50 million Muslims within India who may be looked upon as potential fifth columnists. Second, the drastic changes that are being introduced in a tradition-based society generate anxieties which may be sought to be resolved in one of two equally drastic ways: either by equating Hindu society with all that is rotten in the social fabric or by regarding the newer social innovations as a threat to all that is precious in terms of the self. In both cases a crisis of identity is produced. Third, the presence of these two factors may subtly call forth a situation in which symbols of Hinduism will be partially identified with state rituals. Such a situation might tend to generate insecurities within the Muslim minority, and thereby perpetuate the presence of anxieties upon which communalism thrives.

[81] October 1, 1951.

PART II · THE
INNER
ARENA

UNITED STATES

CHAPTER 4 · THE
AMERICAN NATIONAL
IMAGE

The foreign observer of the American communication network is impressed by the preoccupation of Americans with their national image. One dimension of self-appraisal is in simple quantitative terms, such as that there are x percentage of people with red hair or that the number of hot dogs consumed by Americans each year could girdle such-and-such number of miles. The other dimension, equally lively, concerns itself with the public and private images of the individual—in both qualitative and quantitative terms: Is one meeting the standards of the community in terms of one's desirable image? Is one of the "right" height and weight as the fashion experts decree? In these and a host of other ways the American public is occupied with self-manipulation to alter personality and living conditions to meet the constantly shifting standards of excellence in style. The remarkable swiftness and detail with which styles and fashion manifest themselves all over the nation testify to the versatility of the American. The amazingly swift acceptance of diverse patterns suggests on the one hand a lack of strong emotional commitment to personal styles and on the other hand a remarkable capacity to learn and adapt. In things and in persons the American recognizes the significance of the first impression, the impact that an image conveys.

This eminently successful people is a confident one. The elite's statements exude the feeling that destiny has made them what they are. In the fervent tones of the Judaeo-Christian heritage, the Americans feel that some invisible and higher force can account for their being "the chosen people." This sense of uniqueness is often couched in openly religious terms; more often, in secular language. Even as sober

and careful an American politician as Adlai Stevenson did not hesitate
to refer to his people as "ordained guardians" of a faith reaching back
to Old Testament prophets.[1] While we must make allowance for the
fact that Adlai Stevenson's remarks are made in the context of a presidential election we ought to note, too, that their importance is not
alogether diminished by this circumstance. In lucid terms, he notes the
role of religion in American life:

> Religious faith remains, in my opinion, our greatest national
> resource. It animates the great majority of our adult people. It
> expresses itself in many ways although there are many who find it
> difficult to give formal expression to that faith.
> Yet it is a very real thing to most of us. We believe that there
> is a Creator who has given us life and the capacity and obligation
> to distinguish good from evil, to serve the good and oppose the
> evil. We feel under a constant obligation to measure up to the
> highest moral purposes we know, and that in the long run the good
> will prove to be the wise and the practical and the lasting.[2]

If we do not read too much into these remarks on religion as a force
promoting ethical conduct and solidarity, we can still draw attention to
its definition as a "national resource" which, with all its many manifest benefits, is also a "practical" matter.

Stevenson underscores the ethical function of religion in American
society. He notes in no uncertain terms the role of religion in promoting
a standard set of values men can live by: the nation's religious outlook
has protected it from moral confusion, moral nihilism, and the "blight
of moral relativism."[3]

During the same presidential campaign Dwight Eisenhower also issued
a statement to the *Episcopal Church News*. In less elegant terms, he described his personal faith in religion: "You can't explain free government in any other terms than religious. The founding fathers had to
refer to the Creator in order to make their revolutionary experience
make sense; it was because all men are endowed by their Creator with
certain inalienable rights that men could dare to be free."[4] And
Vice President Barkley tersely asserted his belief that "religion and
democracy go hand in hand."[5]

The source of almost all wisdom and certainly much of the credit for
the American "way of life" goes to the founding fathers. Many personal

[1] New York *Times*, October 15, 1952. (The following notes, unless otherwise indicated, are from the same source.)

[2] September 15, 1952.

[3] September 15, 1952.

[4] September 15, 1952.

[5] August 15, 1952.

preferences are subtly and unconsciously ascribed to them and their magical benediction is thereby obtained. President Eisenhower dwelt at length on the founding fathers:

> They wrote their religious faith into our founding documents, stamped their trust in God on the face of our coins and currency, put it boldly on the base of our institutions, and when they drew up their bold Bill of Rights, where did they put freedom of worship? First, in the cornerstone position! That was no accident. . . . Our forefathers proved that only a people strong in godliness is a people strong enough to overcome tyranny and make themselves and others free. Today it is ours to prove that our own faith, perpetually renewed, is equal to the challenge of today's tyrants.[6]

Adlai Stevenson also noted that America's continuing purpose had been "clearly stated for us in our founding documents. Lincoln defined it. He said it is 'that sentiment in the Declaration of Independence which gave liberty not only to the people of this country, but hope to the world for all future time.' It was that which gave promise that in due time the weights would be lifted from the shoulders of all men."[7]

A nation born in revolution, the United States is prone from time to time to divorce itself from the corrupted external world and to return to the reaffirmation of its revolutionary zeal. The valued past is a storehouse of precedent and allusion for mood. Stevenson's sentiments were not unique when he asserted that "from the dawn of the American Revolution the great men who had defined the ideas of our country had seen 'America as the Old World's Savior.' "[8] This is the role of Americans as the "ordained guardians" of the faith of their fathers.

The image of Americans as dedicated soldiers of freedom, tough and battle-hardened, ready to defend trampled liberties anywhere, is frequent in occurrence. President Truman in an address before the Boy Scouts at the Valley Forge Jamboree declared that America still had "the same unconquerable belief in freedom" which Washington's army had had at Valley Forge.[9] The strong sentiments that cluster around freedom are no monopoly of any party or association. President Eisenhower is interchangeable with President Truman, who asserted that Patrick Henry did not overstate the case when he said "give me liberty or give me death!" "This race will not die," said Truman. "It will live in liberty."[10]

Symbolic of American diversity and unity in the political sense is the

6 September 15, 1952.
7 September 15, 1952.
8 October 15, 1952.
9 July 1, 1950.
10 May 15, 1954.

national flag. Eisenhower notes that "his first belief about the Stars and Stripes was that it symbolized the spiritual basis of our civilization . . . the Stars and Stripes meant to him the devotion and courage of the men who had created this country; the gallantry of the men who had fought for freedom from Lexington to Korea; the sacrifices of the pioneer mothers and fathers, and today the symbol of the might of 156,000,000 Americans who had formed a nation from the children of many lands and cultures."[11]

More exclusive sentiments are represented in the remarks of Donald R. Wilson, a former national commander of the American Legion, who warned of the threat to the United States from the encroachment by international organizations such as the United Nations. He declared that "The Stars and Stripes are good enough to live under and die when the time comes."[12]

The appreciation of the doctrinal principles of the American myth took many forms. Lilienthal spoke of two great American principles: optimism and faith on the one hand, and the practical touch on the other.[13]

The autobiographical references of President Eisenhower illustrate the workings of these principles and the all-pervasive commitment to faith in the religious outlook. The former American President notes:

> It was part of the privilege into which I was born that my home was a religious home. My father and mother believed that "the fear of God is the beginning of wisdom."
> The Bible was a daily and vital influence in their lives. They tried their best to instill its truths and its faith into their six sons.[14]

This family, living in a religious atmosphere, guided by the Scriptures, reflected a sturdy faith and optimism. Despite business ruin, his parents remained hopeful because they "understood their American heritage too well to yield to despair."[15] The President asserted:

> there was nothing unusual about the way my father and mother raised their sons and sent them forth into the world. That was the main way American parents had been doing clear back to the families at Plymouth and at Jamestown. The history of our country is inseparable from the history of such God-fearing families. In this fact we accept the explanation of the miracle of America.[16]

[11] June 15, 1952.
[12] September 1, 1953.
[13] February 15, 1950.
[14] September 15, 1952.
[15] September 15, 1952.
[16] September 15, 1952.

These autobiographical fragments are neither suggested as uniquely characteristic of the Eisenhower family nor ought they to be taken as such. The myth of the promise of America and the sturdy faith and determination of its early settlers has enough factual content to make it one of the central beliefs of Americans. The language of self-reliance and the frontier still evokes strong sentiments. For many, the network of neighborly relationships and modes of behavior exemplified by the early settlers are still valid. Note, for instance, President Eisenhower's remarks on the occasion of his sixty-seventh birthday, when he transposed these sentiments to the world arena by suggesting that a "willingness to deal with neighbors next door, in the next state or section, or in countries far away would help to solve the United States' domestic and international problems."[17] These homilies are integral parts of the American outlook upon the world.

A measure of awkwardness is created when Americans consider their relationship to the outside world. As President Eisenhower had occasion to note:

> America has preserved its position as the friend of all . . . we have not been drawn into the position of being so completely on one side of a quarrel—any quarrel—due to emotion or sentiment or anything else that we are incapable of carrying out our proper role of mediator, conciliator, and friend of both sides when there is any possibility of settling a quarrel.[18]

On the other hand, Eisenhower also expressed the strongly felt notion that the United States has a mission in this world, a manifest destiny: "We of the United States are the center of the whole civilization that is depending upon the concept of freedom. So it is up to us. Nothing can hurt us except each of us."[19] The statement finds an echo in the remarks of Eisenhower's rival in the 1952 presidential elections, Adlai Stevenson:

> We are marked men, we Americans at mid-century point. . . . We have been tapped by fate for which we should forever give thanks, not laments. What a day to live in. What a flowering of the work and faith of our fathers. Who in heaven's name would want America less strong, less responsible for the future? Isn't this what we have always dreamed?[20]

But proud as Americans appear to be of the central position and role of their country, and arrogant as it often appears to non-Americans, there is often a discernible lack of militancy in their stance. It is not

[17] October 15, 1957.
[18] June 1, 1956.
[19] June 15, 1952.
[20] October 15, 1952.

unusual to discover pronouncements that seem to apologize for the overwhelming power of the American. President Eisenhower complained at a press conference that because of our strength we are badly understood, for the world seems to think we prefer to fight rather than go to the conference table; this, of course, was contrary to the truth.[21] The President insisted Americans were not military-minded; that the outset of past wars had found us poorly prepared, and for this very reason it was necessary to be better prepared in the future.[22] Dean Acheson, at a press conference in Vienna, also insisted that "the business of troops and occupation is something Americans do not enjoy" and wish to end as quickly as possible.[23] And General Marshall, speaking about the Universal Military Training Bill, complained that what constantly worried him was that the American people seemed to require some kind of catastrophe before supporting military measures.[24] This is again reflected in remarks by Senator Brian MacMahon, who asserted that, "like all Americans, I hate the hideous atomic weapons which our country has been forced to produce." The only trouble was that because of the arms race "we have no alternative."[25]

This apparent repugnance against affairs military would seem to characterize the nation as a whole. The military profession as such has never been ranked very high in terms of social esteem. And although military heroes have been celebrated and even called upon to lead the nation in times of peace, with very few exceptions these military heroes do not seem to have had the swagger and *élan* of the elites of violence in many other lands. The citizen-soldier is a more characteristic role in the United States.

American sentiments toward the military are ambivalent. There is some popular adulation of the martial and masculine qualities of the armed forces, especially the celebrated Marines. As the saying goes, "The Army will make a man out of you." But it may not be so much the utilization of violence that appeals to Americans; it may be the glamour of the uniform, the comradeship, and very often an appeal that is purely practical—"join the Navy and see the world," or "learn a trade." It is not, perhaps, a great exaggeration to state that as a people Americans are reluctant recruits to the armed forces. Reasons for such negative reaction may at least partially be explained by the economic factor, that is, it is not only safer to stay away from the

[21] October 1, 1953.
[22] May 1, 1953.
[23] July 1, 1952.
[24] May 15, 1951.
[25] June 15, 1952.

armed forces, it is economically more advantageous. In India, by contrast, the armed forces confer prestige and provide economic security to a much greater degree than the world outside; hence a career in the military is immensely attractive to both the educated and the illiterate.

When a protracted crisis does succeed in impressing itself upon the nation, there is a stout demand to "get it over with." The tremendous complications of modern warfare have, as Dean Acheson noted, brought out

> a tendency to feel that the more rapidly we appropriate billions and the more rapidly men are called into service, the safer we will be.
>
> I do not think the solution is so simple. We must not become involved by impatience or ignorance in an ill-considered overnight expansion which would smother well-considered methods and leave us in a dilemma of confused results, half-baked and fatally unbalanced.[26]

We find, as might be anticipated, that the American leaders take it upon themselves to exhort their fellow citizens to share alike in the responsibilities that face the nation. The definition of the "Fair Deal" was, to President Truman, that under the existing conditions "we all share—and share alike—the responsibilities and sacrifices of our defense program."[27] Similar in tone is the report to the President submitted by Director of Defense Mobilization Charles E. Wilson:

> Any person who is in a position to demand for himself a greater share of the limited supply of goods and services—and who enforces his demand, whether through unreasonable pricing, through strikes, or by other means—can only do so by taking those goods and services away from someone else. We cannot permit the strong to trample on the weak in this emergency.[28]

The members of the American elite, at least those in office, were firmly convinced that the danger facing the American people could no longer be met singlehandedly. Hence it was imperative to bring into being a coalition of nations capable of meeting the threat embodied in the postwar posture of the Soviet Union. In a sense, this was the recognition of the limits of American power. The emerging perspective is

[26] January 1, 1951.
[27] April 15, 1951.
[28] October 1, 1951.

reflected in the words of Charles E. Wilson, who identified "Three Keys to Strength—Production, Stability, Free World Unity."[29]

During the period of our study, the elite press continuously stressed the necessity of American involvement with the outside world. For the visible future there was little discussion of the possibility of withdrawal. America shared, in President Truman's words, a "common destiny" with the peoples of the world.[30] And the moral leader of the world's free people had to be America.[31]

There is a calculated effort to reassure allies and others that the United States is not a power-drunk giant; and that while fully aware of the immense power at its command, the United States is responsible, considerate, and compassionate. As Eisenhower stated it: "We are striving to make a better world for ourselves, for our children—that kind of world in which free men can live. I think it is just that simple and just that important."[32]

To fulfill this task, it was necessary to battle communism on a world-wide scale, and Eisenhower conceived of this in a fundamentalist manner: "What is our battle against communism if it is not a fight between anti-God and a belief in the Almighty? Communists know this. They have to eliminate God from their system. When God comes in, communism has to go."[33]

Nor is this orientation limited to any single type of American leader. The more intellectually oriented such as Adlai Stevenson asserted that most Americans expect their public servants to make "decisive distinction between right and wrong . . . not in our wealth, not in our productive ingenuity, not in our arms, but here in the religious conviction of our people is our stability for the future."[34]

Adlai Stevenson was representative of a group that welcomed initiative both at home and abroad. The *élan* of this group has been expressed by spokesmen of many old families and wealthy elements who are willing to take a directly responsible part in the American political process. The Roosevelts, the Harrimans, and the Kennedys, for instance, belong to sectors of this top elite in American society. Many of the most articulate members of this group have received their professional training in law; often they have come from the Eastern colleges, and subsequently pursued their careers in the East or in close association

[29] October 1, 1951.
[30] May 15, 1950.
[31] Adlai Stevenson, November 1, 1956.
[32] June 15, 1957.
[33] September 15, 1952.
[34] September 15, 1952.

with Eastern interests. Adlai Stevenson and Dean Acheson are excellent examples of the exponents of responsible participation.

It is not to be supposed that the social and educational differences fail to arouse tension and rivalry among members of America's political elite. There was more than a little acerbity in Eisenhower's reaction to Stevenson's first campaign, when the general accused Stevenson of using "smooth-flowing words with which to educate and elevate the American people."[35] This was a debating point that was used as part of Eisenhower's demagogic appeal to "the common man's" resentment against any display of erudition or refinement of expression which suggests that someone is trying to "put on airs." Authentic members of America's old families, such as Henry Cabot Lodge, are well aware of the jealousy of the "common people," and stoutly proclaim "there are no ruling circles in the United States unless it is the 62,000,000 citizens who voted in our last national election."[36]

The national image projected in the ordinary rhetoric of American elite figures is unmistakably uniform. There is no doubt that the value goals of the nation are compatible with the realization of human dignity at home and abroad. This means that the nation is committed to the ideal of widely shared rather than narrowly held social values. This value orientation is attributed by its spokesmen to the Christian tradition; in fact, it is strongly declared or implied that God has assigned a cosmic mission to the United States. Under these circumstances it is not much less than blasphemy to suggest that American confidence in its future greatness is exaggerated.

Power is not glorified as an end in itself. Rather, power is represented as an instrument of all values which human beings are predisposed to achieve. Power is to be democratized since the all-embracing demand for freedom includes the requirement of shared participation in the making of community decisions. In foreign affairs, where political and legal order is incomplete, America is seen as acting to defend the degrees of freedom thus far achieved in the nation-states of the globe. Peace is a positive aim; but peace must not be pursued at the price of acquiescing in tyranny.

The proper conduct of public affairs and the rational making of private choices depend upon freedom to give and to receive information. Enormous emphasis is laid on rectitude, on religious and ethical obligations to contribute to the public good. Differences in capacity do not justify exclusion from a voice in public policy, or from freedom of private choice so long as private choices do not restrict the similar

[35] November 1, 1952.
[36] February 15, 1957.

freedom of others. Elite members, for example, should be, and are, presented as eminent because of exertion in the competitive discovery of the common interest not because of inherited advantages. In some ways inherited assets are handicaps, although such handicaps may be surmounted by a fraternal style and by a devoted public service. However intense the American demand for achievement, the self system is seen as multivalued in character, compatible with a commonwealth all of whose members are enabled to develop their latent capacity into socially contributory skills.

THE PROPER SCOPE OF GOVERNMENT

The foregoing excerpts bring out the commitment of Americans to a public and civic order in which values are widely shared rather than narrowly held. Strictly speaking, every institutional practice—in economic, political, or any other sector of life—is subject to continuing appraisal according to its effectiveness as an instrument of the overriding goal. However, the ideology of Americans, in common with most ideologies, draws no sharp distinction between values and the specific practices specialized to particular categories of value or to particular phases of value shaping and sharing. Some institutions are widely treated as though they were as important as the value goals that they are supposed to be judged by. Institutions of free private enterprise, for instance, are sometimes mentioned as though they were synonymous with optimum freedom of economic choice in a modern interdependent economy. Obviously, such a claim is open to challenge. If freedom of choice is to be sustained in an interdependent society, established institutions must be subject to continuing reappraisal in terms of the fundamental policy goals of the body politic.

In no area of social life have problems of adjustment been more chronic and controversial than in delimiting the proper scope of government, especially in matters once left to private determination. The polemics over the scope of government are crisscrossed with controversies about the proper role of federal, state, and local government. There is no ground for denying that American tradition is both antisocialist and pro-local in articulate doctrine. Yet the plight of local government in an interdependent society has put many public men in the position of appealing to central government to use its authority to bolster the precarious financial position of primary units. This tends to happen when local government units appear reluctant to pass the appropriate legislation, as in the case of poverty, relief, and civil rights.

During the period under review, the conservatives were gradually adapting themselves to the idea of spending more public funds for measures in the field of education, health, and welfare. New specific proposals were almost certain to meet a barrage of invective from some set of conservative leaders who declaimed against "creeping socialism." Oveta Culp Hobby, secretary of the Department of Health, Education, and Welfare during the Eisenhower administration, branded a Democratic party "plan for free poliomyelitis vaccine to all children as a possible 'back-door' approach to socialized medicine."[37] Such a position strongly opposed any "free" assistance by governmental authorities. There is perceived to be something immoral about "getting something for nothing," and of "Uncle Sam being played for a sucker." On the more positive side, such an attitude affirms a sense of sturdy self-reliance and minimal dependence on government.

It would be a mistake, of course, to assume that conservative elements were unbending in their views and incapable of adapting their outlook to welfare policies. A few months after Secretary Hobby made her statement, President Eisenhower in a message to the Congress called for a "reinsurance" health program, for he felt that many Americans lacked treatment and preventive diagnoses because they could not afford the costs involved.[38] On this occasion the President met the situation with a simple statement of need, and left latent any bridge between distrust of government and the problem in hand. Other conservative spokesmen had already undertaken to find plausible justification for various health proposals. The chief argument has been in terms of minimum concession to the growing pressure in favor of government action. The late Senator Robert Taft in his address to the American Medical Association declared that the medical profession "should be thanked by everybody in this country who believes in the free economic system."[39] At the same time, in the course of his address, Senator Taft sought to justify the creation of the Department of Health, Education, and Welfare by the Eisenhower administration. This clear governmental assumption of limited responsibility in these sectors was not regarded by Senator Taft as a move which would hamper the medical profession in their attempt to maintain a "free" medical system in the United States. Rather, as Senator Taft noted in his address before the American Medical Association, this would "build up a philosophy to protect the medical profession for all time against intrusion of socialized medicine or anything else compulsory in the American free-enterprise system."[40]

When conservatives are confronted by what they conceive to be the need for government investment, they have been ingenious in adapting

[37] June 15, 1955.
[38] February 1, 1955.
[39] March 15, 1953.
[40] March 15, 1953.

doctrine to circumstances and in denying the ideological aspects of pertinent questions. Former President Herbert Hoover, for instance, in attempting to deal with critics of public development of water power, suggested that " 'more cement' and less ideology and emotion" was necessary to meet an urgent need.[41] In much the same manner, President Eisenhower, after prefacing his remarks by expressing his intense dislike of words such as "socialized" and "compulsory," and of any ideas which would threaten the free-enterprise system, declared that the medical profession would provide much better and needed services if the government were lending it its "cooperation and friendship."[42] Eisenhower might quip that "you can't run a farm in Texas from a swivel chair in Washington."[43] But he also seemed adjusted to the fact that government control, regulation, and welfare activities have become a part of the American way of life. In 1956 President Eisenhower, quoting from Alfred Tennyson's "Morte D'Arthur" at a press conference, gave a slightly edited version: "The old order changeth and giveth place to new, lest one good custom should corrupt the earth." He reflected that "Civilization moves in little bits of steps, makes little advances. We have gotten into the type of civilization now where the government must interest itself more in the old-age security, in unemployment insurance, and all that sort of thing, than it was once."[44]

In the face of this type of conservatism, and in order to defend private against governmental activity, traditionalists often would see themselves as targets of sinister conspirative influences seeking to destroy both America and freedom. Hence the defender of a vested private interest may skip over an avowal of his interest and present the issue in terms of the world ideological struggle. How dark the possibility of governmental intervention in the national health field can be made to appear becomes evident from the remarks of Dr. Louis M. Orr, president of the Conference of Presidents and Other Officers of State Medical Associations, who spoke of "politically inspired commissions, of sociomedical planners lurking in the background, and of advocates of socialized medicine who 'have simply made the expedient switch from the tactics of the frontal assault to the more subtle methods of infiltration and flank attack.' "[45]

It is interesting that even representatives of the liberal sector of American leadership, such as Adlai Stevenson, rather than countering such

41 July 1, 1955.
42 March 15, 1953.
43 October 15, 1952.
44 September 1, 1956.
45 June 1, 1953.

arguments on ideological grounds, sought to introduce "realism" into the political rhetoric of national politics. As candidate for the presidency, he warned that Washington exercised so much power over American lives because state and local governments were not meeting the people's demands. That was the reason the trend toward more centralization was apparently inevitable; and Stevenson conceded to the traditionalists that he also felt that such a state of affairs was undesirable from both the political and economic points of view.[46] The remedy lay, Stevenson suggested, in actually following the course suggested by tradition, that is, strengthening the powers of the states: "The states are the dikes which can build more strongly against the flood waters ever sweeping toward the District of Columbia."[47] This is, of course, arguing against a manifestly historical tendency in the United States. But the appeal to states' rights appears to be mandatory at some point in the language of a Democratic flag-bearer.

Stevenson was more obviously adapting to the new reality of the modern state when he took up the cudgels on behalf of "bureaucracy," a favorite scapegoat of all who are impatient with the scale and impersonality of the contemporary decision-making process. Stevenson told the convention of National Federation of Post Office Workers that Democrats "reject the language of those who sneer at civil servants as bureaucrats and talk of our public services as a part of the 'swollen bureaucratic monster of government in Washington'—and I am quoting President Eisenhower."[48]

Nor need one believe that the Democrats were so radically different in their attitude from the Republicans. Stevenson himself was not loath to criticize public administrators on occasion. Referring to their perfomance in public housing, he said he thought "our total governmental operation in this field is subject to indictment for confusion at the top, for apathy at the middle, and lethargy at the bottom."[49]

Concerning the long-term trend toward more government ("Big Government") in the United States, as in many other countries, the excerpts indicate the process by which elite perspectives incorporate the new without abandoning the old. Conservative elements meet new proposals with stout declarations of principle. Liberal leaders emphasize the importance of using the government, not as a matter of principle, but as the instrument best adapted to further the goals of the nation in the concrete circumstances under discussion. The conservative

[46] August 15, 1952.
[47] August 15, 1952.
[48] September 1, 1956.
[49] December 1, 1955.

leadership splits, as the most active element bows to political and social reality, and accepts particular policy projects. In this unacknowledged way the fundamental distinction between goal values and institutional practices is actually applied. The dialectic of politics calls for the incessant reappraisal of institutional devices in terms of the costs and benefits of all the policy options open to the body politic at the time of decision.

CHAPTER 5 · SELF-DOUBT: THE SHADOW OF INTERNAL DIVISION

During the years of our study the American body politic underwent a dangerous and rare experience. It was racked with self-doubt, suspicious of the loyalty of important elements of the community. There was fear that foreign-generated conspiracies would succeed in subverting the country, and ultimately destroy the independence, the unity of purpose, and the basic institutions of the nation. The leadership of the United States was singularly paralyzed for a time in the presence of a campaign initiated and prosecuted by a single member of the official elite, a senator from Wisconsin. We examine this episode in some detail in order to discover the way in which those who are identified with the American ideological system were momentarily rendered incapable of providing sure guidance to the nation.

If it is true, as Gorer has suggested, that in America one selects and earns one's nationality, and therefore is called upon to perform deeds that prove one's loyalty beyond reasonable doubt, we have a clue to a conspicuous feature of American political culture. A century ago Tocqueville, that most perceptive of foreign observers of America, had called attention to the "irritable patriotism" of the Americans. Reaffirmations of loyalty to the symbols of Americanism—the flag, the Constitution, among others—are commonplace in the United States. Observers generally agree that there prevails in America a degree of attachment and loyalty to the symbol "American" that is not surpassed by many other countries of the world. The variety of ethnic backgrounds that characterizes the American citizenry, and the fact that these backgrounds have, in most cases, been renounced as an act of choice, implies that there is lively concern for the new American identity. It is not farfetched to suggest that, lacking firm roots in the new American environment, anxieties may be experienced which are partially relieved by the unconscious expedient of projecting suspicion upon others.

It is also true that the United States does not possess minority groups which are as vulnerable to suspicion as the groups in many other countries. The location of such targets posed no problem for Hitler's Germany or the Soviet Union—the enemy was clearly defined. In countries such as India, Indonesia, Ceylon, and Burma, a specific minority can generally be singled out for suspicion and hostility. However, in the case of the United States, even during the McCarthy epoch, particular groups were rarely singled out as subversive. Ambiguity was the rule, perhaps because in a pluralistic democratic body, characterized so largely by multiple-group affiliations, political groups are able to enter coalitions to defend their interests.

In spite of the existence of numerous vigilante organizations and the House Un-American Activities Committee, there is little evidence that elite figures constantly indulged in coarse conspiratorial theories. Where such insinuations were made, the mode of attack and specification of the subversives was notably indirect. We find retired Admiral Crommelin, a supporter of Senator McCarthy, believing that since the end of World War II there had been "some hidden force or some hidden power or something that is influencing our people" so that United States policy had become "wishy-washy and appeasing."[1] Or we may occasionally find evidence of the emotions that might have characterized a loyal German citizen turned supporter of Hitler. Characteristic of this mode is G. G. Gurley, president of an oil corporation, who wrote to Senator William Fulbright: "We know there is some crackpot fronting for the Jews and we think it is you." He called Senator McCarthy "the greatest man in the Senate," and said Senator Lehman should be deported to Russia or Germany for "the gas treatment."[2] In general, however, if there is any clearly defined target for hostility it is associated with the term communism in its many varieties and gradations.

The sense of a political conspiracy directed against American institutions is by no means novel in American history. There have been numerous outbreaks of hostility against radical movements. In conservative circles suspicion has long existed that the American economic system is a continuing target for subversion, directed by radicals, indirectly and unwittingly assisted by liberal elements. The tendency to interpret increasing centralization within the United States as part and parcel of a grand design to transform American institutions is to be

[1] New York *Times*, November 15, 1954 (The following notes, unless otherwise indicated, are from the same source.)

[2] December 1, 1954.

found among a fairly large and articulate sector of the elite. Conservative political stances have been marked by a bellicose individualism
which seeks to identify Americanism with minimum central planning
or controls. An example of the reasoning that lies behind such thinking
is provided by the objections of Republican House leader Martin to a
report of the President's economic advisers. He asserted that the report was a plan which "in the name of the national crisis . . . would
transform America into a completely socialistic economy. The pattern
of control and regimentation which the council's report contains is
nothing short of a blueprint for socialism. . . . The touchstone in this
socialistic blueprint is increased taxation."[3]

This danger from within preoccupied many leaders. The danger of
subversion was felt at the highest quarters of the civil and military
elites. General Bradley, for example, talked about the threat from un-
dercover activity which was currently greatest in America's history, and
which was even extending to the schools, where children were being
taught ideas "contrary to our way of thinking."[4] Another member of the
military elite, General MacArthur, warned:

> It is not from threat of external attack that we have reason to
> fear. It is from those insidious forces working from within. It is
> they that create the basis for fear by spreading false propaganda
> designed to destroy those moral precepts to which we have clung
> for direction since the immutable declaration of our independence
> became the great charter of our liberty.[5]

It is instructive to note that in the same speech General MacArthur
suggested that "there are those who, believing themselves liberals, chart
a course which can but lead to destruction."[6]

These remarks of the military elite reflect their deep concern, and
also a decided ambiguity. The references to subversive elements are
sufficiently broad to embrace large segments of the American intel-
ligentsia. Reference to the dangers from the liberals provides an index
to the extent of their fear. Vice President Richard Nixon in an address
before the convention of the American Legion might assert that "the
only threat to this peace is the Communist conspiracy."[7] But, on lower
levels, administrators and bureaucrats, reflecting more the MacArthur
viewpoint, often interpreted the danger with a zeal that bordered on
panic or indiscrimination.

[3] January 15, 1951.
[4] April 15, 1950.
[5] June 15, 1951.
[6] June 15, 1951.
[7] September 1, 1953.

Dr. William Jansen, superintendent of New York schools, for instance, suspended teachers without pay for not answering questions that enquired into their political beliefs. Appealing to the patriotic sense of many Americans, he insisted that he was not enquiring into their beliefs, but merely "into their activities in an organization which advocates the violent overthrow of our government, which gives allegiance to an outside government . . . which teaches people to hate, and which teaches lying as a means of accomplishing its goal."[8]

Highest levels of the elite appear to have assumed, as a fact, the existence of an extensive subversive movement in the United States. Eisenhower declared that there was nothing extraordinary in Moscow wanting to subvert the United States but he did regard the Democratic administration's apparent indifference as extraordinary. He accused them of pretending that "every stolen secret, every disloyal official, is . . . just an unfortunate, almost insignificant accident."[9] Judging from Adlai Stevenson's remarks, however, the Democrats were far from indifferent. On the contrary, Stevenson felt that the Republicans were underestimating the Communist threat. He said the battle against communism in America was "an infinitely tougher and harder battle than most of the Republican leaders have ever admitted or evidently even understood."[10]

We can infer from these remarks: (a) The issue of subversion in the highest quarters of the government had become important enough to call for extensive attention during a presidential campaign; (b) there existed important elements within the United States who were prepared to utilize maximum penalties in order to suppress dissent; and (c) there existed serious differences within the American elite as regards the appropriate measures to locate and deal effectively with subversive elements.

President Eisenhower was vigorous in his criticism of the most extreme of these methods. He spoke about "would-be censors and regulators of freedom" who were dishonest, disloyal, and perverting a free society; although he did admit, rather benignly, that there were some among them who were merely misguided.[11] Eisenhower emphasized the need to avoid the censorial approach to the problem. He told students at Dartmouth College that communism was "almost a religion, albeit one of the nether regions." He then asserted that in order to fight communism one had to know about it, and he warned them: "Don't

[8] February 1, 1952.
[9] November 1, 1952.
[10] October 1, 1952.
[11] June 1, 1954.

join the book burners. . . . Don't be afraid to go to your library and read every book as long as any document does not offend our own ideas of decency. That should be the only censorship."[12] This same warning about book burning was echoed before a very different audience, the American Legion convention, by Richard Nixon.[13] The need for vigilance regarding internal as well as external threats to liberty was also voiced by Ralph Bunche. Very early in the period under study he warned of the dangers arising from those who would stifle protest, honest criticism, and traditional freedom in the name of fighting communism.[14]

It is quite another matter, however, when we come to consider reactions to the investigative methods of the government. Comment on Congressional committees is scant; and specifically, our study shows little direct attack upon such Congressional bodies as the House Un-American Activities Committee.

Indeed, there is stanch defense of the Congressional investigations. Vice President Richard Nixon told the American Legion that he could not agree with those individuals, however sincere, who believed that Congressional investigations of Communist infiltration into government should not be conducted. Moreover, he felt that refusal to testify before such committees should disqualify individuals from teaching in the public and private schools.[15] In a similar manner, Attorney General Herbert Brownell maintained that federal government employees who refused to testify (under their rights guaranteed by the Fifth Amendment) should be released from service.[16]

In fact, federal government employees—bureaucrats—in addition to diplomats, became the primary scapegoats against which anxiety-relieving aggression could be vented. During the Roosevelt era of economic depression, recovery, and war, the rapidly expanding role of government had threatened the interests of many powerful elements in the United States. The counterattack against innovation was deferred or diluted by the world war and then by the cold war. But the venom of the most conservative elements was intense, and the success of communism in China helped to focus animosity against the expansive executive branch of government.

Bitterness toward the bureaucracy was so deep that rhetoric took extreme forms, especially from the Republican leadership. Senator

[12] June 15, 1953.
[13] September 1, 1953.
[14] April 1, 1951.
[15] September 1, 1953.
[16] October 15, 1953.

Kenneth W. Wherry, Republican from Nebraska, demanded that President Truman "get rid of the alien-minded radicals and moral perverts in his administration."[17] And Senator Robert A. Taft, Republican party leader, asserted that under the Truman administration the Far Eastern Section of the State Department had "always been friendly to the Chinese Communists."[18] Even Eisenhower accused the Democrats of lacking the honesty and common sense to admit they had been deceived by the subversion existing within their administration.[19]

Easily drowned in the shrillness all around, voices of moderation appeared to whisper modifications to these views. Stevenson stated that the job of ferreting out Communists in the government was a job for "a highly professional, nonpolitical intelligence agency." He felt "it could be done without slandering innocent people."[20] But these remarks in themselves are concessions to the view that accusations by the McCarthy group were justified. A similar suggestion appears to have emanated from Secretary of the Army, Frank Pace, Jr., at a ceremonial presentation of the Four Freedoms, Inc., award to General Marshall. Like Stevenson, Pace, too, called for an impartial assessment of governmental institutions, not only to help improve these institutions, but also to "give the people more confidence in them."[21] Amid the pervasive atmosphere of tension and fear, Pace was particularly concerned about this loss of public confidence which had resulted in part, he suggested, from attacks against what were basically sound governmental institutions. One of the rare representatives of academic leadership who appears in the investigation also addressed himself to this problem in a moderate but clear manner. Grayson Kirk, President of Columbia University, noted:

> Alongside the timid, petty bureaucrat and the headline-hunting demagogues there must be a solid core, in elective and appointive positions, of men who are devoted to their country and who have an enlightened and farseeing conception of its true interests.
>
> As long as we have such men, our country will be safe and we need not worry overly much about the little men, however noisy they are. When men of the proper kind refuse to go into public office, then our worries properly begin.[22]

---

17 August 15, 1950.
18 September 15, 1950.
19 November 1, 1952.
20 October 1, 1952.
21 March 15, 1952.
22 January 15, 1954.

Of all the views on this subject revealed by our study, however, only one appears to have embodied with any degree of vigor a direct denial of McCarthy's accusations against government employees. President Truman, defending himself and his administration against charges bordering on treason, declared:

> They are trying to get us to believe that our government is riddled with communism and corruption—when the fact is that we have the finest and most loyal body of civil servants in the world. These slandermongers are trying to get us so hysterical that no one will stand up to them for fear of being called a Communist.[23]

Utilizing the very symbol appropriated by those whom he was attacking, Truman said that it was the duty of all Americans to stop such persons and make a "fight for real 100 percent Americanism." Actually, there is little evidence that the United States government was deeply penetrated by the Communist apparatus. If such evidence does exist, it has never been disclosed.

The hysteria which manifested itself over the issue of subversive elements within the internal bureaucracy extended also to Americans serving in the United Nations. And again no important traitors were ultimately discovered. This lack of evidence, however, appears to have had little effect on the general unanimity of perspectives shared by Democrats and Republicans alike. Senator H. R. O'Connor, Democrat from Maryland, lamented that it was "a sorry day" when Americans, working for an international organization, would not answer questions about their loyalty.[24] To Republican representatives Kenneth Keating of New York and Patrick J. Hillings of California there was no question about the disloyalty of these Americans. Representative Keating expressed concern about national security threatened by their presence.[25] And even more bluntly, Representative Hillings declared, with reference to the alleged American subversives, that it was "shocking that these Communists should be in the United Nations while we are fighting the Communists in Korea."[26] Even Secretary of State Dean Acheson, testifying before the House Judiciary Subcommittee, maintained that the alleged American subversives working for the United Nations had given "a black eye . . . blow to our prestige."[27] Yet it is significant that in the

23 August 15, 1951.
24 October 15, 1952.
25 January 1, 1953.
26 January 1, 1953.
27 January 1, 1953.

course of this same testimony Acheson also defended his aides and denied that they had been lax in screening the alleged disloyal Americans in the United Nations. Secretary Acheson declared that he would not "snatch the knotted cord from the hand of God and deal murderous blows to my associates."[28]

Why do we find such an apparent divergence of views between the legislators and the representative of the executive? Acheson and his associates evidently stood for something that aroused deep concern and hostility. Was it, perhaps, the sense of class-bound honor and loyalty that was associated with Acheson's "old-school-tie" loyalty toward Alger Hiss? Was there in this confrontation evidence of cleavage between the provinces and Eastern metropolitan culture? Were the sons of the immigrants, settled in the Middle West, asserting themselves against presumed aristocrats from old Eastern families to whom power and success seemed to come naturally and easily?

Answers to such questions perhaps can come more readily if at this point we explore in some detail the rhetoric of Senator Joseph McCarthy. Our study contains Senator McCarthy's comments from 1950 through 1955. McCarthy seemed to combine the techniques of the debater with the vocabulary of a successful car salesman. He would unqualifiedly assert that "the simple fact remains that the State Department had adopted the official Communist program in the Far East down to the last comma. If Mr. Lattimore was not the salesman for the Communist party, then I ask Mr. Acheson and his friends who did the selling job."[29]

This style and mode of expression are characteristic of much of middle-class American vocabulary: that is, the tendency to utilize the vocabulary of business for the discussion of ideas and personalities.

McCarthy displayed the technique of subtly insinuating that those who might oppose him were likely to be close to the conspirators themselves, if not a part of their group. When President Harry Truman unleashed his attack on the senator's tactics, for instance, McCarthy responded by depicting himself as the lone fighter against the nation's enemies. Questioning the integrity of even the President, he declared "it ill befits the President of this great nation to try to protect the dupes and stooges of the Kremlin by using his high office to attack—not the facts—but whoever attempts to bring the facts to the attention of the American people."[30]

Presenting himself as a representative of the people, seeking fear-

28 January 1, 1953. A State Department press officer said that this quotation was from William McFee, *Casuals of the Sea.*

29 May 1, 1950.

30 August 15, 1951.

lessly, against overwhelming odds, to report the true facts to his constituents, Senator McCarthy placed himself in the American tradition of muckrakers. Here was presumably a patriot pitted against a sordid conspiracy at the highest levels. By questioning the integrity of the President himself, Senator McCarthy was making a bid to become a tribune of the people. The style and sentiments reflect the classical pattern of demagogic mobilization of mass sentiment.

When McCarthy alluded to presidential protection of the "dupes and stooges of the Kremlin" the novelty lay only in the fact that he questioned the highest elected official in the land. The pattern of allegedly sordid relationships between criminals and the politicians in the city hall and at the state house, however, is familiar to all. The insinuations by McCarthy exploited a national proclivity to suspect all men at the pinnacles of power. In McCarthy, the inside dopester was combined with the muckraker to produce a formidable combination.

So pure and virtuous did McCarthy paint himself that in the Senate he charged that his accusers were either persons with ulterior motives or they were "unwilling victims of powerful pressure groups in the country who are best characterized as opponents of a vigorous fight against communism."[31] He contended that some of those senators who had supported a new anti-Communist resolution were "only interested in getting the stench from their skirts and mud from their hands."[32] He even characterized those who controlled the Democratic party as "the same group of men responsible for twenty dreary years of the Harry Dexter White type of treason."[33] It was perhaps the continuous sly questioning of the motives of those who dared question or oppose him that in the end contributed to his downfall.

Significantly, however, during the period 1950 through 1953, when McCarthy was at the height of his accusations and power, our study reveals only President Truman forthrightly denouncing the Wisconsin senator. Mincing no words, he publicly appraised McCarthy as a "pathological character assassin who needed no information to make accusations against others."[34] President Truman was also alert to the efforts of anyone else who attempted to stand up to McCarthy, and encouraged such persons, such as Senator William Benton, for having "stepped right up and tagged Joe McCarthy for what he is, when a lot of other people were running for cover—or were even doing a little sordid coat-tail riding."[35]

[31] September 1, 1954.
[32] January 15, 1955.
[33] January 15, 1955.
[34] February 1, 1952.
[35] June 15, 1952.

In fact, aside from these isolated examples it isn't until the very move to censure Senator McCarthy was brought to the Senate floor that the relative silence in the face of the McCarthy onslaught was broken. Even then caution was advised, as in the remarks of Senator Jenner, who warned that no law could make an unfair man fair, and that the Senate would be wrong to establish any rules which would "hamstring and destroy Congressional committees."[36] The censure move was a political action bound to alienate large segments of the public. More important, it meant one was liable to charges of being "soft" on communism. Senator Lehman identified this fear as the compelling force that made the Senate hesitant to deal with the McCarthy issue. In bidding for support of censure, in rhetorical exaggeration necessitated by the context, Senator Lehman exhorted his colleagues to "face the danger. Let us put aside this fear. Whatever the repercussions, history will honor us for a vote of censure, and, in my judgment, our constituents will, too."[37]

The fact is worth underlining that despite long years of acquiescence, at the terminal stages of the censure move no important figure is noted as coming to the defense of Senator McCarthy. It had finally become obvious that the junior senator from Wisconsin had most certainly stepped beyond the limits of commonly accepted decency. The Senate was used to fairly intemperate language, and Senator McCarthy's wild utterances could be matched with those of several of his distinguished colleagues. The point where Senator McCarthy most antagonized his fellow lawmakers was when he assailed the personal integrity of other senators. It is important to note, however, that rather than using the same invective technique in reverse, or even arguing on ideological grounds, the remarks on the censure motion, as revealed by our study, seemed much more focused on the issue of the preservation of our national institutions. Senator Flanders declared that he was "sure that of greatest importance to the maintenance of government and to its triumph over communism is that its spirit and form shall not be compromised or lost in any respect."[38] Senator Fulbright, eloquently pointing out that McCarthy's abuses "have recalled to the minds of millions the most abhorrent tyrannies which our whole system of ordered liberty and balanced power was intended to abolish," expressed anguish that McCarthy had "degraded and brought into disrepute the great and vital power of the Senate to investigate."[39] It was especially the reputation of the Senate which was at stake; as Senator Lehman phrased it:

[36] August 1, 1954.
[37] August 1, 1954.
[38] August 1, 1954.
[39] August 1, 1954.

"It is not the senator from Wisconsin who is on trial here before us. It is we who are on trial, we the Senate of the United States, on trial at the bar of public opinion in our own country, and of world opinion, too."[40]

The McCarthy era disclosed two important facts about the political leadership of the United States. In times of national insecurity enormous latitude will be given to a strategically placed individual, regardless of his excesses, if politicians out of office expect to gain from his insinuations. But these circumstances are short-lived. When the attacks continue, it is gradually recognized that the fundamental consensus of popular government is imperiled. And the elite acts to purge itself.

BELATED RESPECT FOR NEGRO AMERICANS

Ideological traditions of Americans were challenged by an accelerating set of problems relating to Negro Americans during the years of our investigation. The circumstances provide an exhibit of the way in which the American leadership seeks to preserve unity and continuity while making historically belated attempts to overcome discrepancies between proclaimed ideals of human dignity and the everyday treatment of a substantial fraction of the American people. The degree of success attending this as well as the concomitant, integrative process is perhaps best attested to by the absence of comment and concern about non-Negro ethnic groups.

Hubert Humphrey provides us with an appreciation of the dimensions of the general withdrawal of respect in American society and its effect upon national well-being when he notes that "many American citizens are today unable to contribute their skills and abilities to defense production solely because of their color, religion, or national origin."[41] But American society remains essentially an integrative society whose most conspicuous failure to date has been the slow rate of induction into the ranks of full citizenship of one-tenth of its population which is black.

One index of the lack of status of the American Negro can be inferred from the relative absence of Negroes whose elite status is recognized by the prestige papers of the nation. It is significant that those few Negroes who did command attention were likely to have confined their comment to issues which pertain to status. On other aspects of American society, Negro elite comment was conspicuously absent. Even on the issue of integration we find relatively few Negro spokesmen.

[40] December 1, 1954.
[41] January 15, 1951.

The most extended comment was evoked from Ralph J. Bunche, generally considered at the time to be among the most prominent American Negroes. Ralph Bunche's comments demonstrate controlled anger against felt injustice. Yet there is a ring of optimism. He observed in 1951 that the poll tax and other "classical Southern barriers against Negro suffrage were 'falling prey to enlightened legislation and judicial attrition.' "[42] Bunche linked the advance in Negro rights to the course of advancement of American democracy: "Louder voices and bigger men than Byrnes and Talmadge have seen their bigotries prove futile against the inexorable onward march of American democracy."[43]

Shrewdly, and correctly, Ralph Bunche connected the words and actions of the ruling elite of the South with the American image in the cold war. It was Byrnes and South Carolina who typified for the world the "American way of life."[44] We venture to suggest that this strategy of linking the struggle of the Negro citizenry with the "American way of life" was not only an appropriate invocation of the symbols of national identity, but that it was probably the only strategy that could be effective under existing conditions.

Only a few of the specific controversies in which the Negroes have struggled for their rights rose to the surface during the period under study. The general denial of the Negro in the courts, however, was cited by Thurgood Marshall, in his capacity as the counsel for the National Association for the Advancement of Colored People. His comments before the Supreme Court were an open and solemn declaration of a deep sense of wrong felt by the Negro. Marshall noted how it appeared that only in cases where a Negro was involved did the court attempt to postpone constitutional rights, or take a middle ground on their enforcement.[45]

There was also an attempt to indicate a relationship between the treatment of the American labor class and of the Negro. W. P. Randolph, vice president of the AFL-CIO, voiced his observation that the purpose of the South's White Citizens Councils appeared to be two-fold: to deprive Negroes of "first-class citizenship" and to weaken unions.[46] While it may be natural for Randolph, a labor leader, to link the rights of labor with the Negro, it is significant that Ralph Bunche, an intellectual and international civil servant, also perceived a connection between the two. In a different tone he noted that "Southern

[42] April 1, 1951.
[43] April 1, 1951.
[44] April 1, 1951.
[45] April 15, 1955.
[46] May 15, 1956.

anti-Negro bitter-enders like anti-labor bitter-enders" were currently making their "last stand."[47]

There is a rough parallel between the struggle of the Negroes in America and of the Muslim and other minority groups in India. The caste aspects of Hinduism, no doubt, accounted for much of the resentment that was politically mobilized and eventually resulted in the creation of Pakistan. Affronts to self-respect have a way of lingering on and provoking sentiments that demand total and indiscriminate release in hatred. But in the Indian case the minorities were demanding political solutions which the nation as a whole could hardly concede. In the American case, the individual Negro wished to participate rather than withdraw into a separate community cut off from American society. By participating in American society he can presumably share a high standard of economic enjoyment and can be identified with a formidable and powerful national state.

Turning to the comments of anti-Negro leaders, we note that they emanated almost exclusively from the Southern states. Negro spokesmen appear to have identified largely with national aspirations and goals; this theme is distinctly missing from the views of anti-Negro leaders. There is also a lack of self-assurance revealed in their comments, an indication that the power of the old Southern leadership is waning. Prosegregationist views are rather indirectly phrased. The tenor of anti-Negro remarks conveys the impression that Southern spokesmen realized that the nation at large no longer considered respectable the espousal of racially discriminatory policies. In any society, and especially so self-conscious a society as the American, this is a factor of great cruciality.

Bryant W. Bowles, founder of the National Association for the Advancement of the White People, declared: "When the Negroes walk in the whites will walk out. I'm sure of that."[48] But the very name of his organization indicates that his movement is essentially defensive and imitative. Once it is conceded that the Negro can organize and marshal support and thus bring overwhelming pressure to bear upon the South, a psychological breach is made in the racial armor of the South.

More representative of the "reasonableness"—and defensiveness— that had been forced upon the Southern leadership is the statement of Arkansas' Governor Orval E. Faubus after his meeting with President Eisenhower. Noting that changes necessitated by the 1954 Supreme Court decision on integration could not be accomplished overnight,

[47] April 1, 1951.
[48] October 15, 1954.

Faubus admitted that his personal opinion on this issue was irrelevant, and that the decision was "the law of the land and must be obeyed."[49]

Similarly, the *élan* of an elite in full control is missing from Senator Richard B. Russell's comments before a television audience. Declaring that the civil-rights legislation before the Congress was "very severe and un-American," he said its primary purpose was not voting rights but forcing the intermingling of races in the schools at bayonet point, if necessary.[50]

Senator Russell's further comment betrayed the feeling that all that the old Southern elite could do was to attempt to slow the pace of change and to put obstructions in the path of the execution of the Supreme Court decision.

Senator Russell suggested that the civil-rights legislation, backed by the NAACP and ADA, was "shot through and through with politics." This is, of course, a time-honored way of discrediting any measure, since in the American vocabulary the phrase implies that crooked deals underlie it all. What is more significant is that Senator Russell said he hoped the bill would be defeated, but he admitted that he recognized "the realities" of the situation—an indication of the acceptance of possible and impending defeat.

At the national level insistence on living up to the basic value demands which are part of the American creed seems to have registered itself with increasing force, as is evidenced by Eisenhower's address to a South Carolina audience.

> Equality of opportunity was part of the vision of the men who founded our nation. It is a principle deeply embedded in our religious faith. And neither at home nor in the eyes of the world can America risk the weakness that inevitably results when any group of our people are ranked—politically or economically—as second-class citizens.[51]

A crucial factor in Negro elite communication is the independent and forceful stance they seem to have adopted. There is no servility in Negro leadership comment but, even more important, the assertive and often aggressive Negro leadership position seems to be accompanied by an apparent lack of self-confidence on the part of the reactionary Southern elite. The demands of the Negro leadership to be admitted into the national life on the basis of equally shared values could not be postponed indefinitely. For where an oppressed minority has created its own spokesmen who can address others on an equal

[49] September 15, 1957.
[50] July 15, 1957.
[51] October 1, 1952.

basis, pressures are generated that force larger numbers into demanding dignity for themselves. Failure to induct such a minority into the national life at a rapid enough pace may very well set the stage for more extreme—and even violent—leadership. Our investigation suggests that the American scene was now prepared for the final resolution of the most depressing of all national issues.

CHAPTER 6 · PRESIDENTIAL ELECTIONS: THE PROPER LIMITS OF CONTROVERSY

In some ways the significance of the American ideology in operation is most explicitly revealed to the outsider by the quadrennial campaigns for the presidency. During the months preceding the party conventions the nominations may be hotly fought. But ranks typically close along two party lines since the American structure of government gives unmistakable advantages to a bipolar confrontation at the national level. At the same time the accepted position of the Congress is such that neither the occupant of the White House nor the senators and representatives are firmly in control.

During the discussion of the presidency and of the candidates, many indications are given of American perspectives toward authoritative figures and organs of government. Persons acquainted with other cultures are likely to be impressed by an open almost naïve candor in various comments offered to the people at large by top figures. Consider the reminiscences regarding the presidency offered by President Eisenhower at his seventieth press conference in 1955. Summarizing his experiences over the three years he had occupied the highest office in the land, President Eisenhower told the assembled newsmen that he "still didn't like politics" in its derogatory sense, but working with and influencing people in the cause of world peace was "a fascinating business . . . that would engage the intense interest of any man alive."[1]

There is a wide-eyed quality about these comments—a refreshing

---

[1] New York *Times*, June 1, 1955. (The following notes, unless otherwise noted, are from the same source.)

quality about the American character that is perhaps best embodied in the expression "gee whiz." There is a feeling expressed in Eisenhower's comment that plain politics is somehow defiling—a proposition accepted by large numbers of Americans; and that persuasion is entirely different from politics, which is sordid and full of callous deals from which the citizens are excluded. President Eisenhower was candid about his joy at meeting "interesting" people while in office:

> There are in this office thousands of unique opportunities to meet especially interesting people because the government here in Washington has become the center of so many things that, again, you have a very fascinating experience in meeting scientists, people that are leaders in culture, in health, in governmental action, and from all over the world.
>
> There are many things about the office and the work, the work with your associates that are well, let's say, at least intriguing, even if at times they are very fatiguing. But they are—it is a wonderful experience.[2]

There is undeniable charm about President Eisenhower's remarks. He would appear to echo honestly the sentiments that many Americans believe they would have in the office. The blasé tone is missing which is so often cultivated by men of effective power and recognized authority. Present is the democratic element in public communication which never departs radically from the fantasies of the "common man." It is as if an average American had suddenly been elevated to the highest office in the land. Yet President Eisenhower had enjoyed power and access to the highest circles in his postwar role as general at NATO headquarters, and prior to that as one of the top-ranking military commanders in Europe during World War II. To the non-American observer, in particular, it is remarkable that such innocent enthusiasm can be acknowledged by a head of state without in any way demeaning himself. We suggest that it is episodes of this order that testify to the pervasiveness of the democratic ethic in American society.

It is doubtful whether such a candid exchange could take place in public in a country such as India. An Indian leader would typically stress the burdens that the office implied. He would be likely to mention his tenure of office as a matter of honor, sacrifice, and dedication. Indeed, the symbols used would exhibit the difference between a society where status and class have traditionally been rigidly prescribed and a more truly fraternal system. The self image of a pinnacle figure in the American elite is almost certain to be that of a "first among equals," not of a "superior among inferiors."

[2] June 1, 1955.

Presidents Truman and Eisenhower often gave expression to the pervasive democratic ethos; their confidence in persuasion is an unobtrusive yet pervasive theme. As President Truman explained: "I try to influence people to learn for themselves and I think if they are well enough informed they'll come around to my way of thinking."[3] President Eisenhower in a speech delivered on the occasion of laying the cornerstone of the American Federation of Labor Building recalled what President Wilson had said on a similar occasion:

> If you will come at me with your fist doubled up, you will find mine up no less swiftly than you do yours. But if you come to me in the spirit of friendliness and negotiation, you will find that I will say, "Come, let us sit down together and there, I assure you, we shall find that our differences are far more imaginary than real!"[4]

As we have observed earlier, communication of this order is not only democratic in content but it also affords the opportunity for the whole society to be instructed about a set of rules and modes of behavior appropriate to a democratic system of public order.

The heart attack President Eisenhower suffered while in office provided an opportunity to re-examine the problem of succession to a disabled president. Stressing a need for teamwork between vice president and president, Eisenhower suggested:

> If a president later is suddenly disabled or killed or dies, it would be fatal, in my opinion, if you had a tense period on, not only to introduce now a man of an entirely different philosophy of government, but he, in turn, would necessarily then get an entirely new Cabinet.
>
> I think you would have chaos for a while. So I believe that . . . if there isn't some kind of general closeness of feeling between these two, it is an impossible situation.[5]

Few American presidents have expressed themselves with such fervor on the necessity of teamwork. Presidents Roosevelt and Truman were quite capable of functioning with essentially ordinary vice presidents. Indeed, the case of President Truman himself is often cited as an instance of the office transforming the man. It is of even greater interest to compare President Eisenhower on the subject of succession with Prime Minister Nehru. The Prime Minister destroyed any moves to nominate his successor. Nehru's belief was that India was great, and

3 April 15, 1958.
4 May 1, 1955.
5 June 1, 1955.

that his greatest gift to India was that it would be able to replace him without difficulty. Nehru took the problem so seriously (one might say dogmatically) that he compared the election of a deputy to him as tantamount to reverting to monarchy. Possibly the motives were more complicated, and one cannot ignore the strong probability of a hidden desire to refrain from sharing the limelight with anybody else.

The rhetoric of the campaigns of 1952 and 1956 provided ample opportunity to expose many assumptions underlying American politics. The strategy of a candidate is to emphasize the elements in American doctrine, law and lore which put him in a favorable light when comparisons are made with his opponent.

Adlai Stevenson, in the first formal address after his nomination as the Democratic party's candidate for the presidency, declared: "The essence of republican government is not command. It is consent."[6] There was a double meaning to the definition provided by candidate Stevenson, since the 1952 election was a contest between a military hero and a civilian politician. The general and the governor were candidates for the presidency of the United States not only as individuals but also as symbols. In a period of persisting mobilization, the shadow of a garrison state seemed not unreal. The choice between a military leader and a civilian posed questions which were sometimes raised in the open though more often left unstated.

Governor James Byrnes, when abandoning his party's choice, declared that he would rather have a professional soldier than a professional politician, especially inasmuch as it was necessary to avoid a third world war and end the Korean conflict.[7] It is safe to presume that Governor Byrnes was echoing the feelings of a substantial segment of the American citizenry. The magical attributes of the tough and incorruptible qualities that are generally the hallmark of the professional soldier were called into play. As Mr. Summerfield phrased it at the Republican National Convention: "I am proud to tell you that the man who organized the great Normandy invasion in World War II, the man who organized the great drive that brought Hitler to his knees, needs no lessons from anyone in the value of political organization."[8]

There had been enough of military and diplomatic defeats for the American public; domestically, the infiltration by enemy agents and ideologies had been impressed on the community at large. The splendor of a soldier cleaning up the mess, standing firm before the enemy— these must have been important components of the feelings of many who desired Eisenhower as president. The exaggerated claims made on

6 August 15, 1952.
7 October 1, 1952.
8 August 1, 1952.

behalf of the general also brought out into the open the dogma of civilian supremacy and capability. Some even thought that it was impossible for a general to become a good president. President Truman expressed himself on the disqualifications of a general for the office of the President of the United States, suggesting that when a man had spent forty years in the Army, and knew nothing about the economy, he would have learned only how to ask "how much can I get to spend?"[9]

While the military versus the civilian candidate provided one dimension of the 1952 election, there was another symbolic aspect to this contest: the intellectual (or egghead) versus the man of the people. We have referred before to candidate Eisenhower's sneer that Stevenson was using "smoothly flowing words" to presume to "educate and elevate the American people."

The outside observer of the American campaign scene cannot fail to be impressed by the uneasy balance between the attempt to manipulate the voter and confidence in the voter's good sense. The symbolic task is to present the self—the candidate and the supporters— as trying to submit facts and recommendations to the public, in whose judgment one has total confidence; and to present the rival—the candidate and his supporters—as attempting to poison the streams of public enlightenment by sly and sinister manipulation.

Gael Sullivan, the campaign manager for Senator Kefauver, appealed to the image of openness by strongly endorsing the utilization of television at the convention. Holding that it would then be impossible to have a "synthetic draft" candidate, he noted how millions would have "living-room rights" to the convention.[10] Senator Henry Cabot Lodge argued in a similar manner, suggesting that the best of American traditions would be violated if the American people were deprived of their right to exposure to convention proceedings which could be conveyed by radio, television, and photographers.[11]

The right of the American people to know is as popular a belief as the one that politics is a matter of smoke-filled rooms and deals.

The vocabulary of business and sport has also seeped into the arena of party politics, often in a pejorative fashion. Candidate Stevenson, on his part, in his first formal address after his nomination, ridiculed the opposition for the "doctrine of change for the sake of change . . . like buying a surprise package in a novelty store. Maybe the cigar is a good one, or maybe it will explode in your face."[12]

Alluding to Vice Presidential candidate Richard Nixon's appeal re-

[9] October 1, 1952.
[10] July 15, 1952.
[11] July 1, 1952.
[12] August 15, 1952.

garding his campaign funds, President Truman said that a soap opera was one of the "tried and true ways of selling soap. They had the traditional cast—a young veteran, children, tears, pathos—even a little dog. But they had very few facts about where the money went. And no reason at all for making him vice president."[13]

Vice Presidential candidate Richard Nixon described the strategy of the campaign in sporting terms. It must be "one of motion where you cover all the bases and go every place where the Republicans have a chance of winning."[14] Reminiscent of a football coach haranguing his team before the game, Nixon stated that he and Eisenhower are agreed on a "tough fighting campaign. . . . In this election we are not going to take anything for granted. I don't care what the polls say, or what the political columnists say. We're going to keep on fighting down to election day."[15]

There is another aspect of the campaign that might at first sight appear startling to a foreigner. We refer to the accusations which are hurled back and forth that sinister financial interests are holding the candidate captive. The very charges that Radio Moscow levels at the American political system are identically reproduced by Republicans and Democrats with what might appear to be alarming faithfulness. President Truman accused Richard Nixon of being "a young man of very limited experience whose expenses are paid by oilmen, real-estate men, and tax lawyers."[16] Vice President Barkley said that just as Remington Rand had taken care of General MacArthur, so he expected General Motors to take care of General Eisenhower after his projected defeat.[17] And President Truman, recalling statements of Senator Taft, also accused Eisenhower of having been selected by "New York financial interests and a large number of businesses subject to New York influence."[18] Lending credence to these Democratic charges, John D. M. Hamilton, former chairman of the Republican National Committee, and at the time Eastern manager of Senator Taft's campaign for the presidential nomination, merely asserted that everyone knew local Eisenhower funds were "from the deep vaults of Wall Street international bankers."[19]

Presidential campaigns also allege that candidates are captives of other types of interests: namely, factional political ones. Thus, Senator

13 November 1, 1952.
14 July 15, 1952.
15 August 1, 1952.
16 November 1, 1952.
17 August 15, 1952.
18 November 1, 1952.
19 June 1, 1952.

Henry Cabot Lodge, representing the Eisenhower group, assailed the Taft forces by alleging that a small group of men were undemocratically meeting in secret and arrogating "unto themselves the right to disfranchise thousands of American citizens who were cheated out of their votes."[20] From the Taft supporters came a counteraccusation: Mrs. Katherine K. Brown, national committeewoman from Ohio, declared that Eisenhower was in the "shackles" of the group fostering his nomination.[21] General Eisenhower might protest that "I have no political debts . . . I am strictly a no-deal man."[22] But, as might be expected, the Democrats accused him, in Truman's words, of having "surrendered, lock, stock, and barrel, to the Republican reactionaries, to Taft, and to all the rest of them."[23]

The Republicans also could allege political subordination of Democratic candidates. Richard Nixon, then candidate for the vice presidency, attacked "the myth of the independence of Adlai Stevenson. . . . He is a captive candidate and would be a captive president. . . . He's Jack Kroll's candidate. He's Jake Avery's candidate. And—this is his greatest handicap—he is Harry Truman's candidate."[24] A more extensive list of the organizations and individuals whose captive he was supposed to be was offered by Adlai Stevenson himself in his first formal address after the Democratic party nominated him for the presidency:

> They say I am a "captive" of the city bosses, and then the "captive" of the CIO, and then the "captive" of the Dixiecrats, and then the "captive" of President Truman, and then the "captive" of Wall Street, and finally I have been called the "captive of an organization called the ADA."[25]

If for no other reason, these charges and countercharges provide us with a most plausible list of the groups and men who are to be considered as powerful political forces within the United States. No doubt an instructive chart could be made of the ranking of these political forces by noting the frequency with which they are mentioned as the captors of candidates. Charges of this kind are often embellished for the amusement of the audience. It appears that biblical rhetoric, such as the following which issued from Vice President Barkley, is increasingly rare: "When I think of the so-called crusade by the Republicans, I wonder whose voice it is that will speak in the White House, a

20 July 1, 1952.
21 August 1, 1952.
22 June 15, 1952.
23 October 1, 1952.
24 August 1, 1952.
25 August 15, 1952.

voice that may sound like the voice of Jacob but the hand that will be extended will be that of Esau."[26]

More prosaic rhetoric appears to be the rule. The point is to talk in the language of the masses, an egalitarian attitude best typified by President Harry Truman. An example is his criticism of the candidacy of Richard Nixon where he asks his audience to engage in evaluating him along with himself: "And while you are looking, you might look at the Republican candidate, too. Ask yourself whether you want a man with that kind of unsavory financial record and that kind of a reactionary voting record as a potential president."[27]

In India it is not uncommon for a political leader to address the public in a language they may not even understand. Or, in a meeting in a remote village, an Indian political figure may very well give a discourse on the United Nations, Congo, and the Common Market. It is perhaps unfortunate that American political speeches seldom reach the sophisticated level demanded by some academic audiences, but the fact must not be overlooked that politicians in the United States are expected to be able to know a great deal and to be able to answer the queries put to them by the ordinary man. In India, on the other hand, class and status lines are as yet so rigid that reliance may be almost wholly upon such charismatic qualities as a reputation for wisdom suggested by opaque and presumably elevated discourse.

The American seeks also to indulge his audience; the Indian politician, on the other hand, is prone to self-indulgence. The American public figure seeks to project himself as "a regular guy." Indeed, he is terrified of being labeled anything else. The Indian public figure is much more likely to make unspoken demands on his audience for deference as an uncommon not a common man.

In India it is rather unusual to expound upon the qualifications of a candidate, to stress his particular fitness for the job. In the United States, by contrast, it is imperative that a candidate advertise his assets for the post to which he wants to be elected. Indeed, there is much discussion by the candidates themselves regarding their unique qualifications. Statements such as the ones made by Adlai Stevenson are rarely to be found during election time in a culture such as India's. Stevenson, in the first formal address after his nomination by the Democratic party, drew attention to his four years of experience and training in Springfield, which had "given me a unique opportunity to explore and, I hope, to master in some measure the means by which competing parties, competing branches of government, competing groups

[26] August 15, 1952.
[27] November 1, 1952.

in the community can be brought to common action for the common good."[28]

It was this actual experience in politics that accounted for his qualifications for the presidency, for as Stevenson observed in the same address: "It is easy to have bright ideas about the art of civil government in the abstract. But you never really understand government until you are confronted with the concrete pressures of the day-to-day operating responsibilities."[29]

Whatever the validity of Stevenson's assertions, it is unquestionable that by so addressing himself to his listeners he was advancing the political horizons of many in his audience. The art of civil government practiced in a democratic manner requires that the public be informed and reminded of the roles and functions of individuals and institutions within the society. Where politics and charisma are closely linked, the people are likely to have recourse to very little in the way of control over the decision-making process—except through revolution. One is left with the impression that the election process in the United States, despite its many defects, retains a definite educational function. In addition there is the ego gratification afforded the people at large who are addressed by the contestants in a manner that enhances their self-respect and caters to their demand to participate in the national decision-making process.

Even the manner in which candidates enter the political arena is an object lesson in the practice of democracy. Senator Taft, when informed that Governor Earl Warren of California was entering the lists, reacted with "the more the merrier."[30] And Governor Warren, seeking the Republican nomination for the presidency, stated: "with all humility, I have concluded to become a candidate."[31]

Presidential campaigns brings into the open the fraternalism which characterizes public life in a relatively mobile society. Elite members provide a model of interpersonal behavior even under the stress of electioneering. The practice of addressing candidates by the first name is but the most notable of these signs. Where in the United States political popularity might earn a leader the title of "Mr. Republican" or the affectionate and familiar Ike, in India Nehru becomes, at the most familiar, Uncle Nehru, and Gandhi in his lifetime was called *Bapu*, or father. In the one case, there is affection expressed in terms that one applies to equals; in the other case, the only mode available and

[28] August 15, 1952.
[29] August 15, 1952.
[30] November 15, 1951.
[31] November 15, 1951.

acceptable is that of incorporating the beloved leader into the hierarchical family system where all loyalties originate and remain.

We do not overlook the fact that during the closing days of a campaign, when fatigue and uncertainty take their toll, the good-fellowship images wear thin and occasionally give way. But this is a prelude to the ceremony of unity that is socially mandatory on winner and loser alike. In the 1952 campaign there was very little direct accusation on the issue of communism by the candidates themselves. The issue was, more subtly, indicated in several instances. Sometimes linked to issues entirely different, these accusations were nevertheless present. Adlai Stevenson, for example, in the later stages of the campaign, accused General Eisenhower of repeating "the Kremlin story," the Communists' "theme song" that American progress even in such fields as social justice had, for the past twenty years, been based on war and rearmament.[32]

In the closing days charges and counter charges often grow in acerbity. An example is provided by President Truman's attack on the integrity and the decency of General Eisenhower:

> In his desperate attempt to get votes, the Republican candidate would have you believe that General Ridgway, General Clark, General Collins, General Bradley, General Vandenberg, Admiral Fletcher, Secretary Pace, and Secretary Lovett are just not interested in saving the lives of American boys by building up the South Korean army.
>
> How far can a man go in impugning the character and patriotism of his former associates?[33]

Yet, in spite of this acrid campaign, when the Republican party won the presidency, a most prominent member of the Democratic administration, Secretary of State Dean Acheson, declared in his final official press conference that "now the roles of command and advice, the travail of alien knowledge which goes with it, pass to other hands. And our thoughts are with them. I ask for them something beyond good will and a fair chance."[34] The tradition clearly is that, publicly at least, one bows out of power with as much grace as the circumstances can possibly permit.

Some criteria of appraisal are so obvious to all, and so universally accepted, that political rhetoric is certain to be adapted to their requirements. Everyone agrees that economy, efficiency, and honesty are desirable, and that waste, inefficiency, and corruption are deplorable.

[32] October 15, 1952.
[33] November 1, 1952.
[34] January 15, 1953.

Everyone agrees that special interests should be subordinated to common interests. Hence the argumentative form of every campaign is predictable: Each candidate declares that he and his party are—and always have been—devoted in theory and fact to economy, efficiency, honesty, and the common interest, while the opposition is wasteful, inefficient, dishonest, and the servant of privilege.

At first glance it may seem absurd to find that candidates are saying the same old things in the same old way. But this overlooks two fundamental features of any political process. Discussion is possible only when there is agreement on the value goals, the criteria to be applied to public affairs. Hence the uniform dialectical structure of the argument in a free election is a sign of political stability. Second, general propositions are always uttered in a particular context in which the words are given relatively specific connotations. It is well known to students of comparative politics that a party which has been in office for a considerable period of time has probably been associated with at least a few public scandals of waste, inefficiency, graft, and special privilege. Having been out of office for a while, the challenging party has fewer specific incidents of this kind in recent memory. Such was the position of the Republican party in 1952, since for twenty years it had not captured the presidency. Candidate Eisenhower proclaimed a crusade on behalf of the positive virtues and the Republicans tried to keep alive the memory of the indictment against the Democrats during the Congressional election of 1954. Leonard Hall, the Republican national chairman, declared that this party deserved to remain in power, because it had "put an end to the Truman era of mink coats, deep freezes, and income-tax fixing."[35]

After the Civil War, when the Republican party was in control of the White House for many years, the party became identified in the minds of many labor and professional groups with the defense of big business. The Democrats have never been without important business support, but they have tried to keep alive the image of Republicans as the party of wealth and privilege. The Republicans, in their turn, have attempted to depict the Democrats as the instrument of new forms of special privilege, which was the point of the campaign references to the city bosses who had allegedly captured Stevenson. The defeated candidate did not allow the new Republican administration to remain unattacked. Stevenson described the situation in his first major speech after his defeat:

> There is always the tendency to mistake the particular interest for
> the general interest. There is always the possibility that the suc-

[35] November 1, 1954.

cessor of the New Deal will be the Big Deal, while the New Dealers
have all left Washington to make way for the car dealers. I hasten
to say that I do not believe that the general welfare has become a
subsidiary of General Motors.[36]

The Democrats have tried to keep a "folksy" touch, and to portray
themselves as humanely concerned with the people as a whole, including
the weak and inconspicuous. Senator Lehman struck a familiar chord
when he said that the Democrats see their function as one in which
"we must persist in our role of special protectors and special pleaders
for the underprivileged, for the men, women, and children at the bottom
of economic and social pyramids, and for the minorities, the oppressed,
and the victims of discrimination."[37]

The standard Republican image is concisely projected in Vice President Nixon's words: "It is appropriate that the party which was conceived in the cause of liberty in 1856 is now becoming the symbol of
prosperity, peace, and freedom for people everywhere."[38]

The 1956 presidential campaign added little of interest to the themes
and tactics of 1952. Adlai Stevenson, the Democratic candidate for the
second time, was unable to find a way to release whatever dissatisfactions
had accumulated during the first Eisenhower administration. The situation draws attention once more to the role of doctrine in the political
process. The words may read the same, the fundamental criteria may
stay unaltered; but the context of mood and image that makes for
collective change may be missing. Over the short range at least the
gigantic processes of American society were reaffirming in 1956 the
application of fundamental ideology which they had made in 1952.
It would again be "time for a change"; but that date was 1960.[39]

[36] February 15, 1953. The allusion was to a General Motors' executive who had become Secretary of Defense.

[37] February 15, 1953.

[38] December 1, 1955. This is standard in the positive symbols employed, but it
is unusual in emphasizing Republican interest in international opinion.

[39] Our sketch of the election has played down the standard foreign-policy images
connected with the two parties since they are covered in the chapters on foreign
relations.

PART III · THE OUTER ARENA

INDIA

CHAPTER 7 · THE AMBIVALENCE OF EX-COLONIALS

INDIA AND GREAT BRITAIN

The impact of the conquering upon the conquered is, more often than not, different from what either of them intend or imagine. In the process of domination both those who wield power and those who are the targets of power are transformed not only for their lifetime but for generations to come. The effects, especially from the viewpoint of the colonized, are deep and enduring—they have a way of being more pervasive than what appears on the surface. Much will depend, of course, upon the qualities that the colonizers and the colonized bring to the situation. Resilience, capacity to construct defenses against onslaughts, ego structure—all these are brought into play on both sides. The defenses are present, and necessary, not only for the colonized but also for those who have left their moorings to govern in alien cultures. Despite the complexity of this process it is possible to illuminate some of the dynamism involved by examining the comments regarding Great Britain that emanate from the Indian elite.

The conqueror inspires fear but he may also simultaneously instill respect. There are qualities about him that the conquered finds poignantly missing in himself. There is an inner necessity to find reasons that would account for the power of the conqueror. Inseparable from the adjustment are negative appraisals of the self coupled with unrealistic exaggerations about the fortitude of those who rule and control. It is not totally unrealistic, however, to ascribe superhuman qualities to the rulers if one understands that the process of assessment is an attempt by a sorely disenchanted populace to explain their subjugation.

It is, perhaps, the initial step toward liberation when somewhat ana-lytic appraisals begin to be made of the factors that account for existing conditions. There are, of course, approaches which manifest themselves in such activities as (a) total withdrawal, as if to deny the very existence of the rulers; (b) blind adulation, by which one associates the self with the conqueror and accepts the view that one's group of origin really does deserve to be ruled; and (c) activistic opposition, whereby the relationship is defined as one of ineradicable conflict. Finally, we have the analytic approach, expressed as an endeavor to seek self-respect on philosophical grounds, or to state an independent program grounded in an ideological position. After imperial rule has been stabilized, it is particularly difficult to arrive at an analytic assessment. By that time the personality of the ruled is, more often than not, a somewhat dam-aged system. There are moments of lucid evaluation of the self in relation to the external world, but these glimpses of reality are likely to be few and difficult to sustain.

From early years the self has been socialized in an environment where the manifest "superiority" of the rulers is all-pervasive. Any child grow-ing up in a colonial country has often heard remarks to the effect that in order to gain freedom his people must utilize the methods and the weapons of the rulers. This implies that his own people have not and do not presently possess the superior assets which the rulers have long had at their disposal. The rulers—who are most successful when they keep enough social distance to avoid being known as mere mortals—perpetuate and benefit from myths about their omnipotence.

It is to be borne in mind that much of the mythology of the ruler's superhuman strength arises not from deliberate propaganda but from self-excusing fantasies of the ruled. There are enough objective facts about the apparent superiority of the rulers to intensify feelings of inadequacy and low self-esteem and to nourish the sense that one member of the ruling civilization is actually equal to a dozen of one's own people. Lying in the background—and occasionally intruding on attention—is the ruler's monopoly over the instruments of violence. Indeed, when a colonial sees that the ruler is able to utilize fellow colonials in accomplishing his task of suppression, the damaging impact upon the colonial's perception of his own group identity is all too obvious. Such conditions are hardly conducive to calm and objective comparisons. The colonial mentality is often so severely warped that it is unconsciously self-derogating. Note, for instance, the operation of this dynamic in the speech delivered in Nagpur by Prime Minister Jawaharlal Nehru: "Making an earnest appeal to the people to bear their present difficulties with fortitude and courage, Pandit Nehru said that after his recent visit to England his admiration for Britons had increased. People in England had been putting up with much greater hardships than people in India in regard to food, housing, and clothing. But then in that country he did not hear loud complaints from the public 'as we do here in India.' This was an example for the Indian people to copy with profit, he said."[1]

While exhortations to greater fortitude and to emulations of worthwhile behavior anywhere are commendable, the patently misleading remarks of the Indian Prime Minister, in suggesting that the average Briton was putting up with greater hardships than his Indian counterpart, cannot be accounted for on rational grounds. Although a triumphant ex-colonial by this time, vestiges of the colonial outlook lingered on.

The absurd lengths to which such comparisons can go is illustrated by another example, this time from the remarks of Dr. T. R. Naravane, Deputy Minister for Prohibition, in the Legislative Assembly of Bombay: ". . . the whole world was slowly turning in favor of prohibition. It would be a retrograde step for Bombay to think of giving up the prohibition policy. . . . He said that in the neighboring countries there was a growing feeling in support of prohibition. He read out a Reuter news item, published in the *Harijan* some time ago, that men in the British Army and the Air Force were now turning to tea and lemonade, and that in the Navy there was an astonishing increase in the consumption of milk. If those facts did not convince the people of how the attitude toward liquor was changing in other countries, perhaps nothing else would."[2]

Examples from nations and peoples other than Britain do not readily come to the Indian elite. In part, this has to do with the familiarity with British patterns of behavior. More significant are the characteristic features of a colonial and recently liberated style of discourse. We note: (a) The tendency to involve the self so emotionally that exaggerated statements do not appear as such to either the speaker or the audience; (b) a disposition on the part of elite members to make careless and relatively condescending communications to any audience which they perceive to occupy an even slightly lower status; (c) on controversial issues, conclusions or arguments involve maximum assertion and minimum evidence; (d) certain familiar authoritative patterns occur in the style of pronouncements of traditional village leaders and also the rising national elite; but (e) the elite of liberation sufficiently cognizant of both colonial and cosmopolitan language to adapt their styles—even when rational and objective in tone—when communica-

[1] *Times of India*, January 2, 1950. (The following notes, unless otherwise indicated, are from the same source.)

[2] October 1, 1955.

tions are directed at influencing the elites of the great world outside the local area. In sum we are led to explore the following proposition: *Political elites in liberated India (and in tradition-oriented societies in general) have not, as yet, perfected a language of politics that is simultaneously democratic and rational; hence the language reflects discontinuities in the life styles of both elite and masses.* During the transition phase the absence of a suitable language of political discourse encourages misunderstandings and stimulates mutual suspicion.

When the Indian elite speak in what it considers to be an appropriately modern idiom it follows the British style consciously or unconsciously. Admiration for the British style permeates large sectors of the national elite. Dr. S. Radhakrishnan, when representing India at UNESCO's fifth general conference in Florence, praised the British, stating not only that he had considerable respect for the sagacity of the British type of mind, but that he felt "the way in which they dealt with India will always stand to their credit."[3] Appropriate as these sentiments might have been, this is hardly the type of statement one would expect from the representative of an ex-colonial supposedly revolutionary government. We suggest that this admiration and adulation, while they give evidence of the capacity to accept and to learn from advanced models, nevertheless permeate so deeply that in many cases they are to be understood as expressing the sense of identity indicated by the rather opprobrious term "a brown Englishman."[4]

This uncritical introjection of the British model is undoubtedly harmful for the healthy development of Indian identity. There appears to be a lack of discrimination which arises from the superficial manner in which, in one's own opinion, the self has been "Westernized." It would be more accurate to say that ego has been partially "Anglicized."

Some of the more prominent qualities which Indians tend to associate with the British model of behavior are (a) haughty reserve, (b) punctuality, and (c) status consciousness. Despite the fact that (b) is in opposition to the concept of time in a nonindustrial society, the acceptance of the British model is heightened by the fact that (c) and (a)

---

[3] June 1, 1950.

[4] The tendency to emulate the British can cause an acute crisis of identity; in one such case, a prominent Indian writer, Nirad C. Chaudhuri, in the dedication of his book, *Autobiography of an Unknown Indian*, asserted that all that was best in India was made manifest and was quickened by the British raj. The writer Ved Mehta and the poet Dom Moraes, of a younger generation, write about their homeland in terms that are more exotic and alien than if a Canadian or a Swiss were to write about India. The undertone throughout is one of seeking to deny, by subtle ridicule, one's inherited cultural identity. We note further the persistence with which Americans during the period under study were ridiculed and looked down upon, a practice as widespread as the automatic deference that was offered to anything or anyone British.

coincide with the status consciousness of a traditional and imperial society. Clearly the incorporation of the British model does not signify as many radical departures for an Indian as one might initially assume.

The enviable status enjoyed by the bureaucracy during the British raj and the retention of these civil servants in independent India conspired to perpetuate the ways of the sahib. Repetition doubtless inhibited innovation and operated as a brake against the creative task of adapting rules, procedures, and styles to the emerging needs of India. Telltale signs are to be found in formal modes of address, in the names and the responsibilities given to governmental commissions, in rituals of state. While verbal homage may now be paid to the glorious traditions of India, members of the elite continue to study and follow British precedents. This may, of course, add stability to the process of governance since the British are notoriously hesitant to alter established forms.

The important question (and one most difficult to answer) is: Would India have been in a better position today had her elite been bold, innovating, and self-confident? In retrospect, all that is possible to say is that the manner in which the British transferred power was masterly, an act that displayed shrewd understanding of the character of the Indian leadership. Independence was handed to the Indian elite at a moment when revolutionary fervor was rising to the point at which it would have wrested it from colonial rulers. By this one act the British were able to create a favorable image that continues to yield rich dividends. The negative traits of the British were glossed over by the leaders to whom power was transferred. As the national elite they were now able to convince the masses of India that the British gesture was indeed a noble one.

A key role in retouching the conception of the ex-colonial ruler was played by a few individual Englishmen and Indians. Among the British there were outspoken partisans of Indian freedom at all levels of British society. Some of these Britishers, against tremendous odds, came to India and worked within the Congress party, for instance, C. F. Andrews and Mrs. Annie Besant. The intimate ties of the new national elite to these British subjects made it impossible to marshal unqualified hostility against the raj. It is important to observe, however, that when the full account of the Indian struggle for freedom is written, the crucial moderating influence of Harold J. Laski, Lord Pethick-Lawrence, and other leading figures of the Labor party will also stand out. While these anti-imperialists were working at home for the severance of colonial ties, they also exercised a moderating influence on the rising emotions of the Indian nationalist elite. Much of the pro-British bias of the Indian leadership can be traced to the aid and comfort given by this small band of Englishmen during the years of struggle and transition.

There has been a very widespread rumor in India that the Congress party accepted the partition of the country—against the avowed pledges and against the wishes and feelings of Mahatma Gandhi—because of the influence exercised on Prime Minister Nehru by Lord and Lady Mountbatten. While gossip, simple and malicious, is characteristic of all peoples—perhaps especially of nonindustrial societies—and while much too much might have been read into the informal press photographs of the Prime Minister and the last British Viceroy and his family, we have it on the authority of one of India's most respected national leaders, Maulana Abul Kalam Azad, that the Mountbatten family did exercise an amazing amount of influence upon the Prime Minister's decisions at the time of the transfer of power.

The perpetuation of pro-British perspectives and modes of living is also to be attributed in part to the educational system inherited from the British. The Indian universities remain factories for producing clerks and imparting a tolerable acquaintance with the English language. The upper and middle classes increasingly send their children to what are commonly referred to as "English schools," that is, schools run by missionaries or by the Anglo-Indian community. These schools neither provide a well-rounded education nor do they tend to promote a sense of national identity. These third-rate counterparts of Eton and Harrow give their students a good grasp of the English language and inculcate a rather superficial sophistication marked by an arrogance congenial to a tradition-directed and status-conscious society. From the schoolrooms of these establishments come recruits to the armed forces and the administrative services.

In some ways India's ties with Britain are stronger than ever. More Britons reside in India today than previously; and Britain has a larger group of Indians than at any time in history. British firms in India are probably doing more business than they ever had before. The major opposition to these expanding ties comes from Communists such as M. P. Hiren Mukerjee, who noted that "British capital and mines which had yielded huge profits already should be expropriated without compensation."[5]

Among the many chains that continue to bind India to Great Britain is the Commonwealth of Nations. This link has been described by the Prime Minister as "helpful to the cause of world peace."[6] And, as regards its functioning, Nehru has noted that "we function as independent

5 March 15, 1955.
6 October 1, 1954.

countries. Nobody interferes with our policy. Whether Conservative or Labour is in power our policy continues what it is."[7] The elite does not describe the implications of the Commonwealth link for Indian foreign policy. The organization of the Commonwealth of Nations is so loose that sufficient clarity and data are not available. We note with interest, however, that our study includes two criticisms of the Commonwealth association, both voiced in the lower house of Parliament. Acharya J. B. Kripalani, the leader of the Praja Socialist party advocated severance from "a Commonwealth of empire and colour bar."[8] And Hiren Mukerjee, the Communist member of the Lok Sabha, celebrated Nehru's peace policy, but added that this was not consistent and suffered from contradictions such as the Commonwealth link.[9]

When, initially, India decided to remain in the Commonwealth there was a great deal of criticism from all quarters. But as time passed the Commonwealth link was only sporadically assailed on occasions such as the Suez crisis or in connection with the discrimination by South Africa against citizens of Indian descent. It would not be too farfetched to state that Indian membership in the Commonwealth is no longer an issue that calls forth either enthusiasm or resentment.

Retention of Commonwealth membership was represented by the elite as a careful, realistic decision. Many grounds were asserted to justify India's position—it was necessary to rely on British sources for armaments, trade preferences, and to obtain the preferential treatment accorded to citizens of the Commonwealth. Above all, as Nehru often maintained, the Commonwealth was a device India could use to influence, via Britain, the course of world affairs. These considerations aside, a series of questions pose themselves: Why did India choose to retain Lord Louis Mountbatten as the first governor general of India? Was this necessary? Does one account for this as one more indication of the large-hearted generosity that Indians perceive as one of their own worthier traits? Was it magnanimity or was it a calculated gesture to demonstrate to the British and the world the purity of the Indian soul, the greatness of the leadership that had struggled against the British rulers? (If this was a symbolic act, why not adopt an untouchable girl as the first head of free India—a dream cherished by Mahatma Gandhi?) Or was this, as we suspect, an unconscious gesture of deference that was made to appear realistic at the conscious level? We note the rejection of the Commonwealth link by Burma; why not by India? It can be plausibly argued that India justified the link by maintaining a

[7] January 16, 1950.
[8] October 1, 1954.
[9] April 1, 1955.

steady rate of progress since independence. But the point is not to be dismissed out of hand that continuity was excessively provided for, and that Indian development is retarded in a deeper sense by failure to achieve a clear-cut sense of identity as a separate political culture from the raj.

THE DILEMMAS OF AID AND INDEPENDENCE

How does a proud elite, newly liberated, reconcile its independent *élan* with the imperative necessity of seeking assistance from those from whom one demanded freedom? It has become commonplace for dependencies to expect, almost as their birthright, economic assistance from erstwhile rulers. Pride no longer enters into the picture—at least, not on the surface. The emerging nations not only demand assistance; they receive it from all manner of sources. The changing structure of international relations should not allow us to forget that this pattern, now seemingly established practice, was quite new when India gained independence from the British in 1947.

For India, and especially the architect of Indian foreign policy, Prime Minister Nehru, it must have been difficult to reconcile the declaration of political independence with the crying need for foreign economic assistance. Since the Prime Minister was fully cognizant of the economic bases required to maintain independence, this task of reconciliation must have been especially painful. The first few years of independent India were marked with suspicion of foreign capital—the neo-Marxian simplification that postwar, capitalist America could be expected to seek investment markets abroad was pervasive enough to find echo in official pronouncements.

There was no doubt a desperate need for foreign capital. But, as we noted, there was tremendous fear of neo-colonialism, too. Such fears were only gradually dispelled, and less by reassurances from capitalist America, which appeared to have been the inheritor of the erstwhile British supremacy, than from what must have appeared as a most amazing lack of any overt American desire to seek out India as a dumping ground for its surpluses. Apparently, the economic advisers to the new government of India failed to realize that the United States had an expanding domestic economy starved for consumer goods, that Latin America offered good investment opportunities; and that the rehabilitation of war-devastated Europe would more than absorb America's industrial capacity. A survey of the earliest speeches and conference records shows that the Indian elite confidently expected attempts at economic domination from the United States. To some of these assertions Americans often reacted with surprise.

The responsibilities of office and the necessity of improvisation called forth in the process of administering a vast country under adverse circumstances favored the discovery of a formula whereby desperately needed foreign capital could be brought into India. The eclectic nature of the ideology of the Indian elite facilitated this. We must note, however, that suspicions, many of which were related to pride, could not immediately be subdued.

The early suspicions, natural enough in newly independent India, have since given way to a maturer understanding of the role of foreign economic assistance. Addressing the Indian National Trade Union Congress, a labor-union federation sponsored by the Congress party, the Prime Minister said India was prepared to accept foreign economic aid for development, and he was grateful to such friendly nations as Great Britain and the United States who had given such aid. Nonetheless, he felt India must depend primarily on her own resources: "If foreign aid stopped, did it mean India should cease to carry out the Five-year Plan?" he asked.[10]

The vision of a great and powerful India implies self-sufficiency. It means that India is not dependent on external assistance for her development. As he had told labor, the Prime Minister made clear to the All-India Manufacturers' Organization: "No country could be really free if it depended on other countries for its essential requirements."[11] On another occasion he noted that improperly utilized foreign aid tended to become a kind of disease which could sap initiative and vitality from the recipient; an overdose of foreign aid caused indigestion. Nehru emphasized that "foreign aid could be accepted only to the extent it conformed to the nation's dignity and self-respect."[12] If it were at all feasible, the Prime Minister preferred to see his country pull herself up by her bootstraps. In an address before the Swadeshi League he said it was better that India depend on her own resources and learn by even making a few mistakes than to "go abegging for foreign aid, as if it was a cure-all."[13]

If India were to have depended completely upon herself, it would have meant that radical measures would have had to be taken, increasing the role of the government in the economy and, along with this, stifling interest groups and limiting political freedom. The magic formula of nationalization apparently had not worked in Great Britain; the costs of following the Soviet model appeared too great and too

---

[10] January 1, 1954.
[11] April 15, 1956.
[12] June 1, 1956.
[13] June 1, 1956.

crass for the sophisticated Prime Minister. In fact, India was committed to a mixed economy.

There has, of course, been no surfeit of foreign aid. Indian representatives have been active in foreign capitals appealing for more aid. The process of rapid industrialization has involved almost the total depletion of foreign-exchange reserves. The need for foreign assistance became so great that drastic cuts were instituted in imports and even foreign travel was restricted.

Economic dependence upon foreign nations has also served to introduce an especially sobering note in Indian foreign policy. The United States Congress, in making its annual appropriations, closely examines India's international role. Cuts in foreign aid to India have been threatened by the United States Congress because of the Indian stands on Goa and Kashmir. More recently, the Indian government negotiated with the Soviet Union for MIG aircrafts to be manufactured in India. Under normal circumstances, the source from which India makes her military purchases is solely her private business; but these moves on India's part have elicited adverse reactions in Washington and London. The Indian elite realizes that under the prevailing circumstances it is hardly profitable to alienate the Western powers who supply the bulk of economic assistance for her developmental projects. If economic assistance from the Soviet bloc rises in magnitude, India will have to walk an even tighter rope. From the theoretical realm India has passed into the practical and political realm of bargaining; hence purity of motives and action are no longer passionately advocated by New Delhi.

These contradictions and dilemmas posed by the changing world configuration are vividly brought out in the issue of foreign aid. In 1957 the Prime Minister stated that "he did not approve of aid being tied to a military policy. Any aid linked with a military policy affected the aid itself."[14] While this statement was made in reference to the Eisenhower doctrine, its relevance for India is without dispute. Insofar as it has been possible, India has not entered into any military pacts in order to gain economic aid on a larger scale. However, the reverse is true. For instance, India extended massive economic aid to Nepal and provided all manner of military assistance. More recently, when the Nepalese took a leaf from the Indian handbook on diplomacy, New Delhi felt particularly embarrassed. Similarly, the linking of economic and military assistance to the Himalayan kingdoms of Sikkim and Bhutan goes against every public pronouncement of India in regard to economic and military assistance. These contradictions are only gradually becoming visible; and we foresee more shifts in Indian policies and

14 June 15, 1957.

perspectives in regard to aid. The direction, of course, will not depend altogether on New Delhi.

THE BANDUNG CONFERENCE: THE PERSISTENCE OF A DREAM

Until the coming of the British, India had been able to absorb all types of diverse religions and nationalities. Even the militancy of Islam had been tempered, and a synthesis between Hinduism and Islam was emerging. Emperor Akbar, the mystic saint Kabir, and the religion of Sikhism were testimonies to this emerging synthesis. The new rulers, however, were aloof. Instead of settling in India as conquerors and becoming Indians in the process, the British maintained strong ties with a land thousands of miles across the seas. They preserved their social distance much in the manner that the Brahman observed his distance from the untouchable. Economic factors also played a highly important role in these developments. To colonize a civilization thousands of miles away is a matter of prestige *and* profit. The changing economic constellation hastened or retarded, and in turn was affected by, changing identities, redefined value goals, and revised maps of expectation regarding past and future.

The rise of nationalism in Europe also partly accounted for the behavior of the British. Experiencing their new identity, they perhaps wished to maintain this identity and prevent it from merging with an alien one. It is possible to see Englishmen in the relatively empty lands of Canada, Australia, and the American colonies asserting themselves as Englishmen, and in the process creating new or partially new identities. But in the alien and totally opposed context of India, to associate with the local populace (provided that was easy) and thus be at one with it was considered neither feasible nor desirable. The British appear to have set the stage for the emergence of opposites: on the one hand, they, with their European identity; on the other the Indians, who at this period were slowly evolving their newly discovered bonds of common aspiration with other Asian peoples.

Indians, who are possibly a people with the least sense of history, were now being exposed to the riches of their past via translations and interpretations made by European scholars, especially by the Germans who to this day are regarded in India as the leading Sanskritists in the world. Hence, even at a time when a sense of shame and guilt was resulting from alien conquest, new pride was being manifested in the Indian past. As the Prime Minister was to remark in retrospect, Indians were now discovering that for six thousand years they had made great strides in art, literature, administration, and religion; "wherever one went in Southeast Asian countries one was overwhelmed by the great impress which India had made in these countries."[15]

In the context of this growing awareness, the independence movement had very early begun to anticipate the proper role of a free and united India. Gradually her horizons were widening to include areas and people outside the scope of the traditional relationship between subject Indians and the ruling British. The triumph of Japanese arms over Czarist Russia had prepared the stage for wider identifications. Later the Turkish crisis, since it involved the future of the caliphate, affected the Muslims of India; through the Khalifat movement, pan-Islamic aspects were incorporated into the Indian nationalist struggle. World War I demonstrated how dependent Britain was for Indian arms to maintain her empire. Meanwhile, "foreign-returned" Indians, that is, Indians who had received their education in the West, were bringing in a new mood which connected India to the rest of the colonial world. During the period between the two world wars Nehru and others attended anti-imperialist conferences in Europe and made contacts with nationalists elsewhere in Asia. The Congress party passed resolutions on Ethiopia, Spain, and China. To Spain, India contributed its mite to the Loyalist regime; but special attention was given to China. All over India "China Day" was celebrated and large contributions were sent to the Chinese nationalists. A medical mission was also sent by the Congress party to China; and the story of this mission was subsequently portrayed in the motion picture Dr. Kotnis ki Amar Kahani (The Immortal Story of Dr. Kotnis), which elicited great sympathy for the Chinese people. In sum this rapid succession of widening areas of concern and the ensuing enlargement of focus contributed to the creation of an identity which had not previously existed—the identity of being an Asian.

It was in the thirties that Nehru and others talked and dreamed of concepts such as a Greater India, to include India and large portions of Southeast Asia; and an Asian Federation, which would stretch from Afghanistan to China. The common struggle against imperialism was a bond that enabled the nationalists to think in such inclusive and ambitious terms. One of the first measures in this direction was taken by the interim government of India when an Asian conference was convened in Delhi. The lessons of this conference demonstrated that Sino–Indian rivalry was a factor to be reckoned with. India and China each seemed to patronize the other as a younger brother. Following this conference, the government of independent India called a second, to discuss the Indonesia issue and to exert all possible pressure to help Indonesian nationalists. But cooperation among Asian nations now ap-

[15] December 1, 1957.

peared a diminished possibility—questions of equality and national importance were persistently raised. Some resented what they felt was India's bid for leadership of the Asian continent. More important, the cold war was beginning to extend its presence; and internally India's problems began to claim her overwhelming attention. Disenchantment started to set in.

The Bandung Conference, convened by Indonesia, displayed more diversity than unity. Yet, for the Indian elite at least, maintenance of a semblance of an image of conference unity was regarded as an emotional necessity. The Prime Minister called upon the Lok Sabha to endorse the Bandung declaration, which for India would be but "another step in the fulfillment of her historic destiny."[16] He spoke about Dr. Soekarno's "inspiring" opening address which had "proclaimed to the world the spirit of resurgent Asia."[17] And he detailed the implications of this conference:

> Bandung proclaimed both the political emergence in world affairs of over half the world's population and the capacity of new Asian and African nations for "practical idealism." Secondly, it underlined the basic unity of these countries with apparent diversities. Thirdly, it represented a breakaway from the existing belief that Asia had to rely exclusively on the non-Asian world for financial and cultural cooperation. Fourthly, the Bandung decisions had strengthened the United Nations and forced Asia and Africa to play an increasing role in the conduct and destiny of that great world organization.[18]

This is, we suggest, largely political rhetoric, based upon a minimum of reality. Most of the sentiments were wishes which were once cherished, but which perhaps even Prime Minister Nehru knew were no longer possible. Yet so great was the degree of involvement with these fantasies that it became impossible to disavow them publicly. There are many ways of dealing with a wish that is not possible of fulfillment. Prime Minister Nehru chose to rationalize the importance of Bandung by suggesting that the goal of the forthcoming conference would support India's expressed ideology. He said the "real message" of Bandung was Gandhi's "message of peace." This had been epitomized in India's Panchshila (Five Principles) agreement with China; and now it was to become "Asia's challenge to the world."[19] The vagueness and incoherence of Nehru's formulation of this function of the conference find an echo in his analysis of the Bandung conference after it had been

[16] May 1, 1955.
[17] May 1, 1955.
[18] May 1, 1955.
[19] April 1, 1955.

held. "The most important decisions of the conference, Mr. Nehru said, referred to world peace and cooperation. He said that the substance of Panchshila or the Five Principles enunciated in the Sino-Indian Treaty on Tibet had been embodied fully in the Bandung declaration."[20]

One Congress member of the Lok Sabha, K. Raghuramiah, "hoped that Bandung would spell the end of colonialism and racialism."[21] But such sentiments, although they tended to linger on as visions, appear to have been little reflected in practice.

The image of a united Asian front still evokes a great deal of emotional response. But hostility between Indians and Pakistanis is as great as it has ever been, and India and China can scarcely think of themselves as brothers any longer. Whispers of Indian and Chinese imperialism continue to permeate communication networks of most Southeast Asian countries. Economic and cultural cooperation within the region is minimal, not only for political reasons, but also because most Asian nations look to the West for technological knowledge and cultural cues. Indeed, one might say that an Indian intellectual had more in common with a Britisher and an Indonesian intellectual more in common with his Dutch counterpart than the Indian and Indonesian had with each other. Much of this can be accounted for by the centuries of isolation between Asian countries. The myth of Asian unity has been a hollow one to date since it has relied on emotive factors with little practical content to lend it meaningfulness.

If we project ourselves into the future, we foresee rather futile attempts at closer collaboration. However, most of the newly emerged Asian nations have an emotional stake in "Asianess" as long as they are in a relatively disadvantaged position with reference to the Western nations. The concept will lose its significance when Western and Asian countries grow closer to one another and regard one another with a greater degree of mutual respect. When the question of self-esteem no longer is one of fundamental importance—as in the case of the relationship between contemporary Japan and the West—the new identity will undoubtedly be cosmopolitan and not provincial. Under existing circumstances, an Asian identity is actually provincial. Collaboration in a far-removed arena such as the United Nations may lead to regional collaboration for particular purposes. The sense of "Asianess," although mainly a mirage, will continue to be invoked from time to time when encounters between an Asian nation and the West take place.

[20] May 1, 1955.
[21] April 1, 1955.

ANTI-COLONIALISM IN ACTION:
THE STRUGGLE FOR GOA

The formal incorporation of the Portuguese colonies in India was achieved by military measures. Goa and the other enclaves had been described as "pimples" on the face of India, removal of which was originally attempted through nonviolent action. That it was deemed necessary to utilize the armed forces of India in order to remove the last vestiges of colonialism is significant for the future course of Indian foreign policies: (a) It had to be admitted that moral persuasion in the guise of nonviolent action such as satyagraha could fail when opponents were capable of totalitarian methods; (b) military methods could achieve national objectives in which there was intense interest; and (c) India would utilize, when necessary, armed might in order to achieve strategic objectives.

An image had been created that presented India as wedded to a policy which renounced force. This image was much better established outside India than within the country. Partly this may be attributed to wishful thinking on the part of Indophiles who were prone to construct an India in which spiritual values and the gentle philosophy of Mahatma Gandhi were state policies. India's constant and often eloquent appeals for the renunciation of force as an instrument for settling international disputes between the two major powers were hastily assumed to be fixed strategies of India's own policies. In either case, faulty intelligence was responsible for the shock experienced in many quarters when Indian troops liberated Goa.

On July 1, 1955, the *Times of India* carried the speeches delivered in Bombay at a public meeting convened in order to launch a satyagraha against Portuguese occupation of Goa. The list of speakers covered the entire range of political opinion. Considering the fact that some political differences between the Jan Sangh on the right and the Communist party on the left are immense, the uniformity of expression on Goa was an impressive example of national solidarity on the issue of anti-colonialism. As Nath Pai, member of the Goa Liberation Committee and Praja Socialist party leader, pointed out this was the first time that all the political parties of independent India had been brought together over a single issue.[22]

Presiding over the meeting, Dr. Lanka Sundaram, an Independent member of the Parliament, appealed to the Pope to issue an encyclical "warning Salazar not to go further with his brutalities and not to

[22] July 15, 1955.

quote the Bible."[23] Waxing philosophical, he exhorted his audience that "man lives but once, and we will all live only once. But let us live honorably. The doom's day of Portuguese rule in India is not far away."[24] In this nonviolent campaign against alien rule in Goa Dr. Sundaram suggested that every satyagrahi, whether or not he was a member of Parliament, would be on equal footing: "Among them there would neither be leaders nor the led."[25] Another M. P., Dr. V. B. Gandhi of the Congress party, viewed the struggle as "merely an extension and continuation of the nonviolent struggle which India had launched against the British."[26] A. K. Gopalan, leader of the Communist party, also evoked symbols of martyrdom from the independence struggle: "Jallianwalla bagh and O'Dwyer had not been able to stem the tide of India's freedom movement. Therefore, the brutalities of little Portugal would not cow the spirit of the people."[27] He said that of all imperialisms the Portuguese was the most barbarous. Endorsing the satyagraha, Gopalan declared: "Let the Portuguese beat us. We will suffer the beatings until either Goa is free or we are dead."[28]

Emotional appeals to action rise in importance when sensitive political issues are the subject of a politician's remarks. The Goanese struggle had already produced one martyr, Amirchand Gupta, and his name was invoked in heart rending terms: "Dr. Pundalik Gaitonde, speaking in Konkani, quoted Dr. Salazar as saying that Goa was a beacon of Western culture in the East. What did Western culture represent? It represented liberalism, enlightenment, and refinement. But what did one find in Goa? The late Mr. Amirchand Gupta was not merely beaten. When he fell, the Portuguese danced a devilish dance on his prostrate body with the result that several of his ribs were crushed. Did such atrocities constitute Western culture, he asked?"[29]

V. B. Gandhi repeated a familiar theme when he declared "let it be known that the martyr's blood is never shed in vain, and Amirchand's blood has not been shed in vain."[30] And T. B. Cunha, in an emotion-laden *non sequitur,* said that "Amirchand Gupta had made the supreme sacrifice of his life for the honour of India, providing proof that Goa was part of India. His death must be avenged soon."[31]

[23] July 1, 1955.
[24] July 1, 1955.
[25] July 1, 1955.
[26] July 1, 1955.
[27] July 1, 1955.
[28] July 1, 1955.
[29] July 1, 1955.
[30] July 1, 1955.
[31] July 1, 1955.

Finally, we note the remarks of Purshottam Misra, a leader of the
right wing Jan Sangh. He was the speaker at the all-party rally who
brought into the proceedings a hero of his own political party, thus
deftly linking his party's "martyr" with the new martyr of the Goa
liberation movement. As Misra noted: "The supreme sacrifice of Dr.
Syama Prasad Mukerjee had united Kashmir with India. Similarly, the
sacrifice of Mr. Gupta would united (sic) Goa with India."[32] Along
with the names of martyrs, the symbol of the flag was invoked, and
pledges to avenge the insults inflicted by the enemy were made. Nath
Pai promised that "when the Indian tricolor would fly over Panjim—
the time for it was not far away—the people would demand that those
who insulted the tricolor must answer for their actions."[33]

Satyagraha is a method of struggle that has become universally
accepted in India. Blessed by the success against the British overlords
and possessing moral overtones congenial to Indian conceptions of character, it has been repeatedly invoked, especially by opposition parties.
But in theory it is unconstitutional, and the Indian government often
finds itself in a position of having to oppose this action—especially
when it is directed against itself. In the case of Goa, initially, at least,
the official position also was to refrain from supporting the proposed
satyagraha.

It was not that the Prime Minister opposed the eventual merging
of the Goanese colony with the rest of the subcontinent. On the contrary, he expressed his firm commitment to the idea that India would
not tolerate "the existence of any foreign bit of territory." He emphasized that the Goanese—including a majority of Catholics—wanted to
merge with India. He said that, like Pondicherry, once merged, "Goa
would be maintained as a separate democratic unit in conformity with
its individuality and historical background." And he took great pains
to assure especially the Catholics that they would "enjoy a full freedom,"[34] a pronouncement, we might add, which suggests that this
religious group perhaps lacked enthusiasm over the prospect of union
with India. The conversion to Catholicism made some Goanese more
attached to Portugal than to India, tending to confirm the allegedly
subversive impact of Christianity in non-Christian lands.

Nehru also allowed his latent suspicion of the intentions of the West,
in general, to rise to the surface. He said that "the tentacles of NATO"
had come to Goa via Portugal. He remarked: "That did not do much
good to the prestige of NATO. It showed that behind its laudable

[32] July 1, 1955.
[33] July 1, 1955.
[34] June 1, 1955.

objectives NATO had some objectives which were not so laudable and which could be used for other wrong purposes."[35] The West is still considered devious and capable of menacing the nation's development. When Western powers are either extremely cordial in their behavior or are extending needed assistance, such suspicions rarely are expressed: distrust and other psychological legacies of colonialism are manifested in private. During a period such as the Goa crisis, and whenever indifference or opposition is perceived, these barely concealed hostilities tend to surface in public. These latent resentments and suspicions are important components of the Indian political predisposition.

Despite these feelings, however, and Nehru's special abhorrence for what he termed the "barbarous" attitude of the Portuguese authorities, he continued to counsel "patience and calm."[36] He insisted that "despite the non-cooperative attitude of Portugal, India would adhere to her basic policy of effecting a peaceful settlement of the question."[37] He did not appear to rule out satyagraha, but did emphasize that "satyagraha without any internal strength was not a potent weapon. The question was, therefore, one of disciplining the movement, and striking at the right time."[38]

It was also apparent that despite deep-seated resentments against the West on this issue, Nehru still did not wish to lose sight of India's position in the world arena. He hoped until the very last that pressure could be exerted upon Portugal through the machinery of international organizations. One such organization was the Commonwealth. And it was in this connection that Peter Alvares, a Praja Socialist leader and president of the Goa National Congress, warned Salazar to open negotiations with Prime Minister Nehru while the latter was attending the Commonwealth Prime Ministers' Conference:

> The date line of patience is the Commonwealth Prime Ministers' Conference. We shall then not hesitate to let loose unbridled forces for freedom in Goa, albeit, nonviolent, and to invite the participation of Indian nationals—in spite of the desire to the contrary of the Prime Minister.[39]

By the time of the all-party conference in Bombay, however, it had become clear that no nation or organization outside India would or could help. Although the official stand regarding the use of both violence and satyagraha remained the same, the consensus of the con-

[35] April 1, 1955.
[36] April 1, 1955.
[37] June 1, 1955.
[38] October 1, 1954.
[39] January 1, 1955.

ference appears to have been expressed by Nath Pai; namely, that "no internal or external opposition would stop us . . . nothing will stop the committee from having a mass satyagraha on the Independence Day. We shall not be persuaded or (sic) we shall not be coerced to give up the satyagraha."[40] The satyagraha movement was to be launched against the Portuguese colonialists, but, as S. M. Joshi declared, if the government of India were to stand in the way, the satyagrahis, against their own desires, would deem it necessary to utilize the same methods against their own government.[41] When moral righteousness becomes the basis of political struggles, the conventional limits within which political battles are fought no longer hold. It has been precisely this highly charged moral element in nonviolent resistance which has caused so much annoyance and confusion in contemporary Indian politics.

Moreover, no secrets were made about the strategies to be adopted. A clear statement of purposes is usual in Indian political life. In the fight for one's rights one is expected to be open and honest about purposes and methods. Prior to leading a band of 2000 Praja Socialists who were going to offer satyagraha in the Portuguese colony of Daman, Ishwarlal Desai declared: "We have no back-door methods. Our plans are quite clear."[42]

The Goan satyagraha was held as scheduled. The result was that the Portuguese authorities exercised all the instruments of coercion at their command and were able to crush the movement. They ruthlessly shot down batches of satyagraha volunteers who sought to enter Portuguese enclaves unarmed to protest against colonialism. The brave sentiments of the satyagraha leaders evaporated and the Indians found themselves falling back on pious hopes and a smoldering indignation. Morarji Desai, then Chief Minister of Bombay state, in a broadcast exemplified this:

> Though we had no major trouble during the last year, situation in the Portuguese possessions of Goa, Diu, and Daman caused us anxiety. Despite the provocations and atrocities, including killing of nonviolent satyagrahis by the Portuguese and strong popular resentment against their acts of barbarism, India had exercised restraint while adopting all possible measures to reinforce the stand that foreign pockets on Indian soil would not be tolerated.[43]

This seemingly infinite patience in the face of provocation, defeat, and degradation was a characteristic of the leadership that arose during the

---

[40] July 15, 1955.
[41] August 15, 1955.
[42] August 15, 1955.
[43] August 15, 1955.

independence struggle. An essential element was absolute self-confidence in the morality of one's cause. One suffers righteously, therefore one must triumph eventually: such is the doctrine.

Although the Portuguese enclaves posed no military threat to Indian security, their major significance was, of course, assessed in terms of national self-respect. Reflecting his frustration, Nehru articulated his distress in the presence of visiting Soviet leaders Bulganin and Khrushchev when he "condemned the silence of certain countries over this issue . . . such evasion amounted to cowardice if not deceit." He declared that "the issue is a touchstone by which peoples and professions for freedom will be tested."[44] In the end, it was R. Jaipal, Indian representative on the United Nations Trusteeship Council, who stated the situation perhaps most tersely and directly: "As far as we are concerned, Goa is a Portuguese colony established by force, initially by piracy, and later by conquest."[45]

The solution to the problem, finally, resulted from recourse to armed force. Patience, the Portuguese discovered, has its limits even for the Indians. The Indians, surprisingly enough, had discovered an easier and more workable way in which to solve collective political problems. Such a successful departure from declared sentiments of nonviolence can have far-reaching effects on the internal and external politics of India. It may well mark the end of an era in which moral sentiment was predominant in India's political style. The coming generation of political leaders will be far enough removed from the independence struggle to pay homage to satyagraha, while utilizing more conventional modes of conflict resolution.

THE WORLD ENVIRONMENT

The prestige press of India devotes considerable attention to the international news. The *Times of India* faithfully reflects this concern in its pages. However, what foreign nations and events come to the focus of attention is at least as important as the volume of foreign news. Our study reveals that the focus of attention is highly selective and many of India's most important neighbors are largely ignored or afforded little attention. In Asia, the premier industrial state, Japan, we would have imagined, should have received greater interest than in fact it did.

In this section we note the briefer references to foreign nations made by the Indian elite. The paucity of comment may indicate a lack of

44 December 1, 1955.
45 February 1, 1957.

interest, but in many cases it isn't interest that is lacking but adequate press coverage. Some of the issues we refer to below are emotion laden, others are of vital significance to the security and unity of the nation, and still others are only of passing significance.

Africa. The explosion with which this continent made its entry on the world was noted more carefully in London and Washington than in India. While several large communities of Indians live in Africa and a considerable amount of travel takes place between Africa and India, if we were to rely on the Indian press, the existence of this continent seems scarcely to have been noted. This finding of our study reflects what we impressionistically felt to be the real situation. Until very recently, with the exception of South Africa, there has been little interest in that continent. While public opinion has been largely silent, the government of India took one notable step. It sponsored several hundreds of African students for advanced study in India.

In 1952, Prime Minister Nehru made a reference to the African continent which illustrates the vague and sweeping nature of the Indian interest. To the Prime Minister, Africa "had all along remained in bondage and slavery. If she went on the path of violence it would be harmful to the progress of the Africans. . . . A big continent, like Africa, could not long be kept under bondage."[46]

Each year, however, in its foreign-policy resolution, the Congress party made references to South Africa. India has regularly brought the South African issue before the United Nations. Here again India has been able to do little besides severing all diplomatic relations. Historically, the discrimination against the South Africans of Indian descent was the experience that forged satyagraha as a political weapon. In fact Morarji Desai, before the All-India Congress Committee, protested that satyagraha had no place in a democracy, but it had been "justified in South Africa where 6 million people were subjected to unjust and discriminatory laws."[47] More in keeping with articulate Indian public opinion on South Africa are the remarks of Purshottam Trikumdas, at the Praja Socialist party's national convention, who expressed his apprehension that Malan's racial policies endangered world peace and "might lead to massacre in which the blood of white men and dark men would flow freely."[48]

It is not possible to state what role India played in the eventual exit of South Africa from the Commonwealth of Nations. We know little of the nature of India's relations with other African nations, inside and outside the Commonwealth. What is instructive is that India

[46] November 1, 1952.
[47] September 15, 1952.
[48] January 1, 1954.

has repeatedly advised Africans of Indian descent to align themselves
with local nationalist movements and aspirations. The fact that most
of the Indians in Africa are engaged in business and form the ambiguous
group between the ruling white population and the majority of Africans
has led, from time to time, to attacks on the Indian community, often
accompanied by violence. It is of interest that few important Indian
leaders have seen fit to visit Africa. There has been a great deal of
speculation, however, that the Indian action in Goa was, in part,
triggered by the tremendous pressure of Angolan and other nationalist
movements in Africa.

West Asia.   The Middle East is referred to as West Asia by New
Delhi. Predominantly Muslim, the West Asian countries are objects of
special attention by foreign-policy planners since their close ties with
India can serve to emphasize the secular nature of the Indian government, and afford occasions to neutralize or isolate Pakistan. Much
comfort was derived in India when Pakistani attempts to create a Pan-
Islamic federation were received coldly by Middle Eastern nations; and
when Egypt refused to allow Pakistani troops under the United Nations to patrol the Gaza region. Lack of support on the Kashmir issue
served to demonstrate to Pakistan that bonds of religion were not
quite so vital as had been supposed. In the words of Prime Minister
Nehru, India regards the nations of the West Asian region as people
"who, like ourselves, have recently established their national freedom
and sovereignty."[49] This view echoes one of the main assumptions
behind India's original aim of creating a belt of nations which would
form "the area of peace." The Prime Minister felt that West Asia
would not go Communist—"communism had no place in feudal countries." But he also emphasized "that any conflict over communism or
otherwise should be avoided in West Asia and he offered Panchshila as
the only policy that could guarantee peace."[50]

A great deal of elite attention has been focused on Egypt. This
opinion is well represented in the remarks of Dr. Anup Singh, a member of the Rajya Sabha and leader of a four-man good-will delegation
sponsored by the Committee for Asian Solidarity. Acknowledging President Nasser's popularity, Dr. Singh said it was based not only on
"his line of action during Egypt's crisis, but also on his reform measures,
including the distribution of lands to the landless and starting of
developmental centers."[51] We might note that while India recognized
the existence of the state of Israel she did not establish diplomatic

49 August 1, 1956.
50 July 15, 1957.
51 March 1, 1957.

relations with that country. The reasons for this have never been spelled out in great detail, but the general impression is that it is necessary to remain at a distance from the Israelis in order to cultivate ties with West Asian countries. The ostensible justification is, of course, that India can best serve the interests of peace in West Asia by retaining a somewhat detached position.

South Asia. To date, India has not been able to establish smooth relations with her immediate neighbors. With Pakistan there has been an uninterrupted feud; with China there are quarrels over northern frontiers. Little has been achieved in India's relations with Ceylon regarding the position of the large Tamil-speaking Indian minority in that country. To the north, India cannot claim to have created particularly strong ties with the Himalayan kingdoms. Within her own borders, the question of Nagaland has been a persistent irritant. Since comment on Pakistan and China is dealt with in other sections, we note here the few references that were made to the smaller countries surrounding India.

President Prasad, addressing the third session of the Parliament referred to the refuge of the King of Nepal in the Indian embassy in Katmandu in 1950:

> Nepal is a country with the closest relations with India and a treaty of friendship was signed between India and Nepal only a few months ago. It has been and remains my government's desire to respect the independence of, and to maintain friendly relations with, Nepal, and to see that her people achieve political and economic progress.[52]

The coup, reputedly engineered by the Indian embassy in Nepal, against the rule of the ranas and the eventual restoration of the powers of the king did not, as expected, in itself resolve all problems. The Nepalese king fully exploited the peculiar position of Nepal as a buffer between China and India. Since Nepalese policies are geared to assure maximum flexibility, looser ties with India have resulted. Even though rebels operate from Indian territory against the Nepalese government, this has had little effect on the newly asserted independence of Nepal. Nepal received more than sporadic attention only when the king sought actively to play China and India against each other.

Regarding Ceylon, again there is little comment and no resolution of the outstanding question of the Indian minority. Our sole reference comes from Nehru, who, in addressing a public meeting, said "it was stated that the recent disturbances in Ceylon were financed by foreign

[52] November 15, 1950.

countries. These were countries which wanted to see a weak India, too."[53]

The Far East. China is the only major power in the Far East that has received much attention. Japan is notably absent from the focus of elite comment. Regarding other nations in this region, brief references are available on two countries—Korea, where India played an important role, and Indo-China, where India has also been active under the auspices of the United Nations (furnishing the chairman of the International Control Commission).

President Rajendra Prasad referred to Korea in his Independence Day message by noting that "we look back with satisfaction that our humble efforts in the cause of peace have begun to show signs of success, particularly in Korea."[54] Three years earlier there had been an equally vague reference to Indo-China by the Prime Minister. He stated that "we are generally opposed to any foreign armies functioning in Asia. . . . That is a general proposition. . . . Our policy in Indo-China is to watch events and not to make any commitment."[55] Indeed, India's policy in this entire region has been largely passive. Extensive Indian communities are to be found in this region, especially in Burma, Malaya, and Singapore; but the early activistic policy with regard to Burma and Malaya has largely simmered down. Even though Indonesian pilots have been trained in India and the Malayan military establishment has had Indian advisors, this activity has hardly matched that of the Chinese.

Europe. (Other than Great Britain and Portugal.) Germany has had a peculiar role in Indian history. Her famed Orientalists have evoked admiration among Indians. From a distance, Indians have felt that Germany's utilization of the Aryan symbol provided a bond of kinship between Germans and the Indians, many of whom consider themselves as the original and only "pure" Aryans in the world. (The fact that Hitler considered the Hindus only slightly less despicable than the Negro is a fact not known to most Indians.) Germany enjoyed an enviable reputation for its technological and scientific skills. Above all, the hospitality afforded to Indian revolutionaries by the Kaiser, and later by Hitler, was a factor that predisposed Indians in favor of that country.

Free India, however, has not been overly enthusiastic about Germany. Facsism and nazism are still terms of abuse to the Indian intellectual. India has been cautiously developing good trade relations with both Germanies; West Germany, especially, has been quite active on the Indian economic scene, both in the public and the private sector.

[53] June 15, 1956.
[54] August 15, 1953.
[55] January 16, 1950.

Our study contains only a few and ambiguous references to Germany. Prime Minister Nehru's comments in regard to German unity (at a press conference in Bonn) are too vague to call for analysis. He simply stated "I presume the German people desire unity. The question is how it can be attained by peaceful negotiations."[56]

Algeria and France, again, are issues on which Indian elite comment has been sparse, reflecting a cautious approach to such issues. Asked at the same Bonn press conference if he planned to offer help in ending the fighting in Algeria, Nehru responded: "If people want us to be of help, we do not wish to stay away."[57]

Finally, we note a peculiarly Indian tendency, fairly widespread among the older generation as well as present-day Gandhians. Their conception of the world is indeed a unique one: it embodies no particular suggestions, only wishes. For instance, present-day Gandhians go around Indian villages and in lieu of the popular Indian greeting "Jai Hind" (Hail India), advocate that villagers should greet one another with "Jai Jagat" (Hail World). Our sample contains a choice example of this type of thinking in the remarks of the old Indian revolutionary, Raja Mahendra Pratap. In the Lok Sabha he suggested a novel way to meet threats from Pakistan with his inquiry as to "whether as countermeasure an Aryan federation should not be started."[58]

[56] July 15, 1956.
[57] July 15, 1956.
[58] August 1, 1957.

CHAPTER 8 · THE ANXIETIES OF POWER IN A DIVIDED WORLD

THE FUNDAMENTAL APPROACH

A question of great interest in the analysis of the world political process is the degree of contradiction or concordance between the ideology of a national elite in dealing with inner and outer affairs. In previous chapters we have outlined the Indian conception of the self with particular reference to the aftermath of the struggle for freedom and the political problems of internal cooperation and solidarity. The present discussion will provide indications of how the leadership conceived of its role in international politics as a whole, and how this self-perception was disciplined in the light of success and failure.

We noted how the elite sought to unify the disparate elements of the new nation by insisting upon the vital necessity of peaceful, non-violent negotiations. The same emphasis is prominent in matters pertaining to the arena of foreign affairs. In a sense, the international scene was felt to mirror the disorganized state of Indian society with its multiplicity of divisions and tensions. Intergroup antagonisms within the country were, at first sight, not considered very different from the frictions inherent in a bipolarized world with a still ambiguous set of neutrally inclined states. The resources of this world, like the resources of India, were not mobilized for the benefit of all. The key to solving these problems lay not so much in more advanced technology as in the development of a "civilized" outlook. As Nehru stated:

> Let us hope the world will become gradually civilized. It is not really civilized today. It is highly advanced technologically and scientifically, but it is not civilized. It will become civilized when

this technological advancement is used for human betterment and not human destruction.[1]

The architects of Indian foreign policy felt that it was they who had responsibility for providing sane counsel to an otherwise insane world. Indian leaders were confident of their own moral superiority in a world of unnecessary division and exploitation. The President, for example, expressed the hope that humanity, craving for one world and coexistence, would soon be in a position to say "we are copying India."[2] The Prime Minister expressed an identical sentiment during the course of a farewell speech for Bulganin and Khrushchev:

> Some people may not like some of our ways. But this feeling is bound to be a temporary one as our hearts are clear and with our eyes open we are looking around to befriend all. Any misunderstanding, therefore, in other people's minds about us will also disappear. What I mean is that our path is the path of truth and friendship for all.[3]

On another occasion Nehru declared that if Indians had a message of love for themselves and for others then "our power will be greater than any other power and we will be able to save our own country and the world."[4] Nehru felt that the moral approach—an emphasis upon love and persuasion—was not only of significant help in the achieving of desired goals, but it also could thereby strengthen a nation's self-confidence.[5]

The steadfast holding to moral values, moreover, represented the ultimate in courage. Not merely the established elite, but much of the opposition shared this view: there was, as it were, a consensus among large segments of the population. Note, for example, the appeal of the Praja Socialist leader, Asoka Mehta, "for the development of moral courage for, in the final analysis, that was the last arsenal on which human beings could depend."[6] And even the political style of Communist leaders was influenced by such dominant themes in the culture. Radical departures from traditional symbols in the communication process between the leader and the masses may isolate the leader or fail to mobilize the masses.

The moralizing note in Nehru's discourses obtruded on many oc-

---

[1] *Times of India*, October 15, 1957. (The following notes, unless otherwise indicated, are from the same source.)

[2] August 15, 1957.

[3] December 15, 1955.

[4] November 15, 1954.

[5] November 1, 1955.

[6] January 1, 1954.

casions in the foreign-policy field. There was also, however, the awareness that one had to maintain some degree of humbleness in one's
posture. Replying to critics who accused him of adopting a double
standard on the Kashmir issue, the Prime Minister said: "It is difficult
for me to know my failings, but I am not conscious of any double or
separate standard. If I deliberately judge the Kashmir issue by any
double standard I will stand condemned not only before other countries, but even more so before myself, my mind and heart."[7]

This manner of approach is illustrated repeatedly. At a public meeting where Premier Chou En-lai was present, Nehru referred to Chou's
comment that the Chinese could learn much from India. Nehru said
"that observation only showed the Chinese Prime Minister's regard for
us. But we must not become conceited or proud. Let our achievements
speak for themselves. We should only try to overcome our weakness."[8]
Moral exhortations were in this way tempered with a realization that,
convinced as one might be about one's rightness, there is the possibility
that the opposing side, too, has a measure of validity in its argument.
The situation was almost never presented as a polarization of right and
wrong, good and evil.

It is worthy of note, however, that whether it is the Gandhian, up-
holding tradition, sometimes for its own sake, or the established elite,
injecting traditional symbols into foreign-policy pronouncements, the
emphasis has always been on morality rather than on religion or the
role of supernatural forces. As the Prime Minister declared: "Our thinking has now to be of the fourth dimension . . . the ethical dimension."[9]

INDIAN PERSPECTIVES TOWARD VIOLENCE

The world image of India at the time of independence gave particular
emphasis to Indian attitudes toward violence. To a large extent this
theme is also present in India's self image. In particular, there is stress
upon the supposedly nonviolent nature of the Indian struggle for
freedom.

In dealing with a central problem such as violence, we shall give
special attention to recurring themes that emphasize cultural distinctiveness. Often the exhortations in regard to moral conduct are reminiscent of a wandering mendicant or Brahmin, and, in a few cases, of
the voice of a prophet.

The term "violence" includes physical manifestations of violence
and perceived threats of a serious character to the prevailing order.

[7] February 1, 1957.
[8] December 1, 1956.
[9] October 15, 1957.

In considering the specifically Indian context it is necessary to point out that traditional Indian culture includes both nonviolent and violent elements in images of ideal behavior. The great Hindu epics, *Mahabharata* and *Ramayana*, concern themselves not only with the desirability of peace and morality in interpersonal relationships; they repeatedly stress that when and if it is necessary the forces of evil should be met with all the violence required to conquer them. In the *Ramayana* we note the war waged by Prince Rama against King Ravana of Ceylon: victory achieved in that war is celebrated annually in India to this day as the triumph of Good over Evil. And in the key dialogue between Lord Krishna and Prince Arjuna in the *Mahabharata* Krishna impresses upon the indecisive and perplexed prince that there are situations in life when for the sake of *dharma* (duty) one must take up arms even against one's kin. Similarly, history and folklore celebrate militant heroes such as Rana Pratap and Shivaji. Along with Buddha and Emperor Ashoka, the Indian reveres Rama and Krishna. Consequently, it is of no small importance to see which particular tradition is stressed at what times by the new elite of contemporary India.

The expectation of violence—at home and abroad—was not overlooked in the language of Nehru and his colleagues. At times, however, suggestions would be made which would carry the belief in exemplary morality and nonviolence to an extreme. An eminent Gandhian leader and socialist, Acharya Kripalani, seriously suggested in a Lok Sabha debate on foreign affairs that India should "form a 'nonviolent army' as an example to the world."[10]

The Gandhians represented primarily by Vinoba Bhave and his group have repeatedly made suggestions of this order. Note, for instance, Bhave's idea "that women alone could establish a new social order—a 'Kingdom of Kindness.' He, therefore, appealed to women to take an active part in organizing a *shanti sena* (peace brigade), which aimed at self-defense through nonviolence. So long as violence was regarded as necessary for self-defense, women would continue to occupy a secondary place in society."[11]

Gandhi had remarked on occasion that the free India of his conception would be nonviolent to the extent that it would dispense with armed forces. Yet pacifism *sui generis* was not inherent in this approach. The Mahatma supported and blessed the despatch of Indian troops to check the Pakistani invasion of Kashmir. The transition from essentially nonviolent resistance against the violence of the British raj to the control of the violent apparatus of an independent Indian state posed similar dilemmas for the Congress. The Prime Minister reflected that

[10] October 1, 1954.
[11] June 1, 1958.

because India was not entirely free of either external or internal danger, it was necessary to have a modern army, navy, and air force. But he would have preferred "to save these armed forces for the development of the country's economy."[12]

This theme has many variations; and there are indications that violence cannot be morally justified. But there is also the realization that necessity dictates that conventional modes of self-protection cannot be discarded without peril to the existence of the nation.

One of the more persistent issues that called for continued exercise of violence at home was the revolt by sections of the Naga tribes. Military operations against these tribal Indians agonizingly brought home the painful lesson that a sovereign and democratic state is often forced to utilize instruments of violence against its own nationals. Indeed, one of the more amazing contradictions of independent India has been the passionate advocacy of nonviolence as a technique of conflict resolution and the reality of frequent, and often indiscriminate, resort to the instruments of violence. Possibly the most poignant case is that of the Nagas, large sections of whom are Baptists; it illustrates only too well the frustrations experienced by Prime Minister Nehru and his associates but it also provides a vivid example of the determination of the Indian elite to preserve national unity at any price.

The Naga independence movement has continued to defy the Indian government for more than a decade. Armed attempts to quell the rebellion have not been very successful, and the leader of the Naga independence movement, Phizo, has been at liberty in London. The entire area of Nagaland is sealed off to outsiders, including Indian citizens, and oddly enough had been under the control of the Ministry of External Affairs. In an address before the Nagas, Prime Minister Nehru said that he was "least concerned on account of India's defense. The country can look after itself but I am sorry that you are being misguided into a wrong course of action."[13] Nehru termed the demand of the Nagas for independence "absurd" and stated that their claim to nationhood was a "fairy tale." He chose to characterize their cry for a separate and sovereign Naga state as an "attempt to reverse the wheels of history."[14]

President Prasad, addressing a special session of the Parliament in 1950, declared: "It has been India's policy not to submit to aggression, for submission to aggression, in any part of the world, is to invite its repetition in other parts and thus to imperil peace and freedom."[15] But

12 April 15, 1950.
13 January 1, 1952.
14 January 1, 1952.
15 August 1, 1950.

a few weeks later the President spelled out in greater detail India's attitude toward the problem of aggression and his own sense of regret: "While aggression has to be met and evil cannot be condoned, it has to be remembered that war itself is an evil which brings even greater evil in its train. The peace that we seek and that is worth preserving is a living peace and not the peace of the grave."[16]

India was unable to ignore the international tensions that impinged upon her, especially in view of the gravity of tremendous domestic socioeconomic problems, including resettlement of millions of refugees in the greatest migration known to history. In 1950, the Prime Minister eloquently observed that the first half of the century had brought neither peace nor the promise of peace: "As we stand on this New Year's Eve on the sword's edge of the present, darkness seems to envelop the future."[17]

There was constant fear that involvement in the cold war could lead India into a shooting war, thereby diverting her resources and energies from development of the well-being of a population with one of the world's lowest standards of living. Because India's effective power radically to alter the world around her was limited, the leaders of the nation sought to penetrate beyond the boundaries of their country and to affect world public opinion. We find the Prime Minister drawing some comfort from the belief that

> ultimately it is human beings that count even in this atomic age and nearly 1600 million human beings—about two thirds of the world's population—in Asia and Africa must count. This staggering mass of humanity, if properly handled, could become a tremendous force in favor of peace.[18]

Krishna Menon also suggested that "the greatest weapon of survival . . . was the pressure of world opinion which was asserting itself against the armament race and stockpiling of nuclear weapons."[19] The over-all assumption behind suggested principles of strategy was, according to him, that "the lowering of tensions is a snowballing process, and we are all making efforts to better the world."[20]

The Indian elite conceived of India as being an important part of this world opinion, but it also acknowledged there were certain externally imposed limitations to the role which she could play. In 1950, referring to anti-Indian propaganda abroad, the Prime Minister noted

[16] November 1, 1950.
[17] January 1, 1950.
[18] January 1, 1955.
[19] September 15, 1955.
[20] June 15, 1955.

that "the mere fact that India counts, and it is rather an important entity in international affairs, makes other countries try to prevent India having her full weight."[21] Six years later, addressing a public meeting, he observed that some foreign powers "did not like to see Asian nations grown strong. They spent money to encourage things which would spread chaos in these newly independent nations and thus weaken them against these powers."[22]

Such an attitude might in part be the result of India's prolonged struggle against alien rule; but perhaps it reflected in some measure a basic fact of international life, the automatic play of the power-balancing process in a divided world. The general tenor of these pronouncements suggests that despite much moralizing the Indian elite was aware that it could not substantially effect changes in the policies of the two great powers, and this was a source of considerable frustration.

Our study reveals a great deal of comment on the specific issue of nuclear armaments, although it is limited almost wholly to statements made by the Prime Minister and his foreign affairs adviser, V. K. Krishna Menon. There is little reference to the danger of nuclear weapons from any of the opposition leaders or from the second levels of the ruling elite.

The major portion of comment on nuclear weapons appeared during the years 1955–1958, with a steady increase year by year, reflecting heightening anxiety. The first statement was by Prime Minister Nehru in 1955, when he noted in the lower house of the Parliament that "the world had reached a stage of 'atomic saturation' in respect of armaments, when any attempt by either bloc to develop greater military strength than the other was meaningless."[23] In his speech before Hong Kong's Indian community he seems to have evoked the imagery of an international system gone berserk:

> Yet, while all these people hanker after peace and peaceful developments, we see this terrible race in weapons of war going on—atomic weapons, hydrogen weapons, and ballistic weapons— which is an extraordinary sight, and sometimes I wonder if we have not somehow rather lost the habit of thinking logically. All this seems to me so illogical, so much without meaning.[24]

The Prime Minister commented on the absurdity of the space race, with its score charts of who got there first. He noted having read "about this so-called satellite moon thrown out into outer space from the

21 January 2, 1950.
22 June 15, 1956.
23 April 1, 1955.
24 October 15, 1957.

Soviet Union. What does all this mean? It means, I have no doubt, that very soon you will have one, two, three, or four more satellite moons from the United States."[25] This kind of scientific competition was felt by the Prime Minister to indicate a serious lag:

> The fact of the matter is that war, big war, is out of date today in the modern world. But the difficulty is that most of our minds are out of date. Science progresses, technology progresses at a record pace, but the power of our minds remains behind, unable to catch up with it. We still think in terms of a past age though sometimes we have glimmerings of the future.[26]

More compactly and directly, continuance of nuclear tests by the Great Powers led Nehru to reflect "how our thinking has become . . . divorced from every moral, ethical, and human principle. What has this nuclear test to do with human welfare? It is a direct violence on human welfare."[27] He also felt that scientists had a responsibility to enquire into the possible consequences of their inventions.[28]

In fact, while Nehru felt a power race was perhaps inevitable, he also observed that the leaders of the Great Powers poorly comprehended the consequences of this race, which was of such a radically different complexion from the armament races of other times. The nuclear factor had altered for the present, and perhaps for all time, the nature of international rivalry. The fate of mankind was at stake. Nehru said little, however, to condemn conventional armaments, perhaps realizing their necessity under some present conditions. It is, therefore, not a wholly nonviolent position that was adopted, but rather one in which emphasis was placed on the new magnitudes of war disaster.

Considering India's vital need for development, the degree to which the moralistic sentiments expressed by the Indian Prime Minister were reconcilable with the national interest is significant. Nehru's capacity for flexibility and realism becomes evident from the position he adopted when C. Rajagopalachari, a former governor-general of India, suggested that India exert all possible pressure upon the United States to suspend unilaterally the manufacture and testing of hydrogen bombs. The Prime Minister disagreed. He said he greatly admired Rajagopalachari's "highly moral stand," and for his own part would like to see hydrogen-bomb manufacture end completely. But he expressed displeasure at "linking it up with the offer and acceptance of American aid. Such an approach would reduce the issue to a political

25 October 15, 1957.
26 October 15, 1957.
27 October 15, 1957.
28 January 15, 1957.

one."[29] Considering the fact that Nehru rarely in his public utterances separated moral and political elements we can with some justification characterize his reasoning in his own frequently used word—"extraordinary."

Occasionally the Prime Minister would engage in wishful thinking when in an otherwise dreary picture he would grasp a ray of light and make too much of it. On one such occasion he observed that there "was a growing realization by everybody, and particularly soldiers, of the implications of a nuclear war. He cited the example of General Douglas MacArthur and said this was a welcome instance of the change that had come over the people's thinking."[30] But in general the Prime Minister maintained a rather pessimistic view of the nuclear race, and attempted to create an impression that his was perhaps the lone sane voice in a mad world.

We pass from the Prime Minister's views on nuclear weapons to those of V. K. Krishna Menon, often stated to have been the Prime Minister's alter ego, foreign-policy adviser, and closest comrade.

The first impression that strikes one in comparing the speeches of the Prime Minister and Menon is the rambling, philosophical, and almost wistful nature of the Prime Minister's utterances in contrast to the clearer, more policy-orientated, and informative comments of Menon. There are also echoes of Nehruisms to be discovered in Krishna Menon's language, however, such as in his speech delivered before the India-China Friendship Association. He noted that there was a lot of talk these days of so-called "ultimate weapons," but the only really "ultimate weapon was the determination to survive."[31] But concerned with specifics, Menon used his caustic tongue to good effect when he remarked:

> We are not in possession of these weapons today. But we have a fair idea of what is going on in the world. We were surprised but not horrified, partly amused, and partly disturbed by the demand made at Ankara for the possession of atomic bombs. I wish there was someone at Ankara who realized that atomic radiation does not respect frontiers.[32]

At this time Menon was able clearly and without any reservations to make the policy declaration that although India had the capacity to make nuclear weapons, she would "not use atomic power for destructive purposes."[33]

[29] June 1, 1955.
[30] February 15, 1955.
[31] February 1, 1958.
[32] February 1, 1958.
[33] February 1, 1958.

This highly moral and commendable gesture on the part of India was not sufficient, however; for the Defense Minister proceeded to call on China to make a similar declaration, and contribute "a moral gift to the world." The following remarks are fairly representative of the tone which marks Indian foreign policy in general—a tone perhaps best described in terms of an appeal to the moral conscience of the other, as if an appeal to the goodness inherent in the other could yield satisfactory results. "The Defense Minister said that China, in spite of the fact that she had been 'badly treated in the comity of nations' and the fact that an armada equipped with atomic weapons was not far away from her shores, should take courage to make the declaration not to use atomic weapons. She should take this step forward even if it meant 'some risk' for her."[34] It should be recalled that this exhortation of China was made at a time when India's concern regarding Tibet had been rudely rebuffed and the Chinese had been aggressively encroaching upon Indian territory.

We would suggest that the tenor of this extraordinary request of China was meant quite literally. Appeals to others to emulate one's sacrifice are a feature of the dominant Hindu culture. The tenacity of the distinctive rhetoric of the language of Indian politics—even in the face of deprivational experiences in the arena of world affairs—suggests that the perspectives of even the most Westernized of the elite had indeed been profoundly shaped by traditional doctrines. Much of India's relationship with China can be explained with reference to this cultural trait—the appeal to the perceived goodness in the ally or adversary. It, along with other such traits, has contributed to much confusion in the assessment of Indian moves and the motives that underlie them.

The possibility of utilizing nuclear energy for domestic development was also often stressed in Krishna Menon's pronouncements. On one occasion he suggested that if both Russia and America would dismantle three or four atomic bombs, this would not only be a step toward disarmament, but the material could be diverted to peaceful uses.[35] Again we ought to note that this belief in a token move toward the reconciliation of views of two differing parties forms a basic element in a particularly Indian approach, articulated by the elite and sanctioned by the culture.

One of the more direct solutions to the question of the nuclear-weapons race was contained in the Indian elite's exposition of the concept of "coexistence." As embodied in the Panchshila and Gandhian philosophy, coexistence is asserted to be not only useful to India and

34 February 1, 1958.
35 July 1, 1956.

an inherent part of her ideology, but also, in Nehru's words, "the
only way of survival in the immediate future."[36]

The concept of coexistence seemed to exemplify the tremendous emphasis upon the need for demonstrations of mutual trust in an atmosphere which the Indian elite characterized as one of fear. The following
quotation from the Prime Minister speaks for itself:

> I know you cannot be absolutely sure of trusting everybody. But
> I say that the mere fact of accepting right principles creates an
> atmosphere in the world which makes it difficult for people to break
> off these principles, and if any country breaks them it goes against
> world conscience. Anyhow, a right principle is a right principle.
> It is all right to say that we will not accept right principles because
> somebody else does not accept them. That has no meaning. It
> amounts to saying, "We don't speak the truth because somebody
> else may tell a lie." It is absurd, but absurd as it is, it is oddly
> enough the way in which world problems are being dealt with.
> Why? Because countries are afraid of each other, because of fear,
> and oddly enough fear grips the great powerful countries.[37]

Krishna Menon also spoke almost benignly about this distressing
climate of opinion. He said that neither the Soviet Union nor the
United States desired war, and he believed that all their continuous
endeavors to find ways to suspend nuclear tests and to disarm were
"sincere." But unfortunately, at the same time "they were accumulating
deadly weapons out of fear."[38] On another occasion he remarked that
it was "strange that the stronger a nation, the more afraid it is."[39] It
was, therefore, as if the Indian elite felt that the drawing up of
principles and avowals of coexistence and friendship could change this
atmosphere. The Indian Prime Minister was not naïve enough to
believe that mere acceptance of the Panchshila constituted a guarantee
of proper and ethical behavior. The point rather seems to have been
that acceptance of these principles, in itself, constituted a step in the
right direction.

The Panchshila originated in a Sino-Indian treaty, and Nehru's comment on China's acceptance of the principles of coexistence is significant
in this regard. Nehru held that "the acceptance by China of the principle
of coexistence is a good indication that she does not want to intervene
in the problems of other countries."[40] But the Prime Minister was also
aware that agreement in principle did not always lead to action based

[36] August 1, 1956.
[37] October 15, 1957.
[38] September 15, 1957.
[39] February 1, 1958.
[40] November 1, 1954.

on the accepted principles. At a public meeting in Delhi, where the Chinese Premier was present, Nehru said he was "pained that the people who talked a great deal about the Five Principles did not always live up to them. He was, however, conscious of the fact that a number of difficulties arose when a government sought to implement the principles. But it was of the greatest importance that people did not allow themselves to be swayed by their passions. India wanted to be friendly even with those countries which were not well disposed toward her."[41]

At a farewell banquet for the visiting Soviet leaders, Khrushchev and Bulganin, Nehru spoke in a similar fashion:

> We want to befriend every country so that our circle of friendship may grow and become wider, and cooperation and peace may thrive.
>
> What kind of friendship is that which envisages enmity with others? We should befriend all and stretch out our hand to all.
>
> For this reason our coming closer to this great country, the Soviet Union, is very important. But this does not mean that we have drifted away from another country. This is neither the position nor will it be at any time in the future. We have always wanted and we will want cooperation among the countries of the world to increase and world peace to be strengthened.[42]

But what if differences should arise? The Prime Minister's answer is rather ambiguous on this count: "In these circumstances, the two should tolerate each other and develop affection for each other. We have kept this example before others. I feel that its effect will be good not only on our country, but also on other countries."[43] As the Prime Minister himself knew well, it was quite impossible for him or for that matter any other Indian to develop "affection" when differences arose between India and Pakistan or India and South Africa. This, however, did not necessarily negate the possible validity of the Prime Minister's recommendation, nor need it be interpreted cynically. Manifestly this formulation is ambiguous, but the very assertion of such a belief had repercussions of its own.

Moreover, there was something more than sheer expedience in the advocacy of coexistence as a national policy. An extremely vital aspect of national pride and self-assertion appears to have been behind it. Nehru, at the unveiling of the statue of an Indian hero, Shivaji, delivered perhaps his frankest admission of this pride and its inextricable relationship to foreign policy. Despite all of his stress upon affection and

[41] December 1, 1954.
[42] December 15, 1955.
[43] December 15, 1955.

friendship, he asserted that "we do not bind ourselves to other nations with military pacts and then allow ourselves to be dragged along like camp followers."[44] For a person prone to understatement, this comment vividly illustrated the contempt in which he held unequal alliances. Prime Minister Nehru also declared that "India would never accept foreign military aid in any shape or form, nor allow foreign troops to land on her soil . . . any attempt at aggression by any country would be resisted with all its might by India."[45] It is to be observed, however, that at the time of this statement a considerable part of Kashmir was occupied by Pakistani armed forces. And since then several thousands of square miles of Indian territory have been invaded and occupied by Chinese troops.

It is rarely realized outside of India that the ruling Indian elite has never considered its country's foreign policy one of neutrality. The preferred designation has been "nonalignment." That labels incorrectly ascribed can lead to errors in assessment should be apparent, especially in India's case. As the Prime Minister pointed out at a press conference in Bonn:

> I thought the word neutrality was used in war. I do not under-
> stand neutrality in peacetime. To use the word neutrality in peace-
> time gives it a warlike significance.
> We [in India] do not think in terms of war and, therefore, the
> word has no significance to us. If one country wants to impose its
> policy on another country, that is domination.[46]

In a bipolar world it has often been suggested that India seeks to form a third bloc, a bloc of so-called neutral nations. In fact, prior to independence, the idea of a federation or bloc of Asian powers was indeed prominent in Nehru's thinking. Scattered through his autobiography and other writings are references to a free India as part of a great Asian federation. But the attempt to establish semiformal collaboration with sister Asian states after independence was a disillusioning experience. Some states accused India of seeking leadership, and the resulting ill feeling and suspicions presumably played a major role in the abandoning of a cherished notion of an Asian bloc. As one of the more authoritative sources on Indian foreign policy, Krishna Menon clearly asserted in Bombay that many people mistakenly believed India was seeking to form a third bloc: this idea was "ridiculous and suicidal." India wanted "freedom from blocs."[47]

[44] December 1, 1957.
[45] January 1, 1954.
[46] July 15, 1956.
[47] September 15, 1957.

In sum, not neutralism, not withdrawal, but selective participation has characterized Indian elite comment on international affairs. It is, in fact, reasonable to assert that Indian foreign policy was as activistic as possible under the circumstances. There has been, of course, the restraining force of the moralistic interpretation given public affairs by the governing elite; more pertinent has been the realization that India's power is essentially potential rather than power-in-being. In comparison with nations of West and East Asia, India has been a great military and industrial power; but her military capacity has compared unfavorably with that of the major powers. India can have little realistic hope of enforcing particular policies in the region surrounding her. But we ought not to conclude from this that policy preferences have been lacking. We have noted the intensity of feeling that resulted, as Nehru stated, with regard to the conclusion of the military pact between Pakistan and the United States: "We are generally opposed to any foreign armies functioning in Asia. . . . That is a general proposition."[48]

India would have preferred nations to her east and west to be insulated from direct entanglement with the cold war. The major part of this region, however, at one time or another, has been the arena for cold and hot war contests. There was evidence of Chinese, Russian, and American military assistance in Indo-China while Indian activity was limited essentially to diplomacy and serving on United Nations international commissions. This can be partly explained by the limited nature of India's military power, but perhaps also by the self-defined non-militaristic nature of Indian foreign policy. The Indian elite considered it impossible for India to enter into a military pact of assistance with Cambodia when the fundamental basis of Indian policy had been to condemn military alliances everywhere. There have been, however, contradictions even on this count. India played a vital role in the defense policies of her small northern neighbors, Nepal, Bhutan, and Sikkim—the last two being, indeed, her protectorates.

[48] January 16, 1961.

CHAPTER 9 · FANTASY AND REALITY: ORIENTATIONS TOWARD PAKISTAN AND KASHMIR

Perhaps the most continuing, if not exasperating, test of India's moralistic orientation toward politics, internal or external, arose in reference to Pakistan and Kashmir.

THE STRUGGLE FOR KASHMIR

Soon after India and Pakistan were created as separate and sovereign dominions in the Commonwealth of Nations there took place a conflict which persists to this day. The conflict over Kashmir is so deep that nearly two decades of negotiations and conferences have yielded little result. Indeed, under existing circumstances it is difficult to imagine how any settlement on Kashmir is possible which would be mutually satisfactory to the parties to the dispute.

On Kashmir, Pakistan and India each feel that virtue is on its own side alone. It must be recalled that when the Muslim League achieved its demand for Pakistan, it had gained what was to be a homeland for the Muslim minority in undivided India. Yet, even though Muslim-majority areas in the west and east of the subcontinent became constituent parts of the new state of Pakistan, a large Muslim population in India still remained. Indeed, India retained within its borders a Muslim minority only slightly smaller than the number of Muslims in newly created Pakistan. Whereas Pakistan was an Islamic state, India chose to remain a secular, pluralistic state and took deliberate steps to avoid any identification with the Hindu majority. Whereas Pakistan came into being as a testimony to the validity of the two-nation theory, the Congress party in India accepted the creation of Pakistan only as a necessity in order to gain independence. At no time, before or after the achievement of independence, did the Congress party accept the two-nation theory. The idea that the Muslims of India constitute a separate nation has never been conceded by the dominant political party in India. The Congress party continued to proclaim that India was the land of many religions and the independent Indian state would be built upon a strict separation of church and state.

When the British decided to quit the Indian subcontinent, it was agreed that the nearly half thousand princely states were to be given a choice that allowed them to opt for either of the two states or, theoretically, to remain independent. Geographical contiguity was a major consideration for the princes, khans, rajas, and chieftains in their decision. Of all the princely states, Kashmir posed the greatest difficulty. It was ruled by a Hindu maharaja whose population was, however, largely composed of Muslim subjects. To complicate the issue still further, the Congress party had been a major force in opposing the corrupt and venal rule of the maharaja of Kashmir. Indeed, the strongest political movement against the maharaja of Kashmir was led by Sheikh Abdullah, a political associate of Jawaharlal Nehru. Sheikh Abdullah was in the maharaja's prison as the ruler bided his time, not sure whether it would be a better bargain to opt for Pakistan or India. He had managed to delay joining either of the newly independent countries until the decision was completely taken out of his hands. Pakistani tribesmen and regulars swooped down into the Kashmir Valley, pillaging and looting until they were at the gates of Srinagar, the capital of Kashmir. It was at this time that the maharaja asked India to come to his assistance. Calling upon Indian aid to repulse the invaders, the maharaja signed the instrument of accession to the republic of India. As such, legally, the ruler had exercised his choice and opted for India. In the meantime, Sheikh Abdullah was released from his incarceration and installed as the premier in order to mobilize the people against Pakistani invaders. In the democratic zeal of the moment, Prime Minister Nehru held out a promise to the Kashmiri people that once the invaders had been repulsed, they would be afforded the opportunity of deciding their fate by the ballot box.

At a public meeting in Madras Prime Minister Nehru explained in retrospect the circumstances prevailing during that period:

I know how troubled I was at that time. With a background of nonviolence and peace it was a difficult thing for us. . . . Fortunately, at that time Gandhiji was with us. I did not want to take his name in this matter. However, I ran to him as usual for some lead and advice. Himself a man of peace, he told us that it was our duty to go to the aid of Kashmir. When we went there we found not mere raiders but the Pakistani army.

Whatever arguments you may use or have about India's right to use or have troops in Kashmir, there was absolutely no argument to justify Pakistan's sending troops. There is no doubt that it was aggression by Pakistan. We could have entangled Pakistan in a large-scale war and we were stronger. But we did not. We went to the Security Council to avoid war with Pakistan.[1]

The offer to the Kashmiri people of a plebiscite to ratify the accession to India was, indeed, unique. No other princely state, in Pakistan or in India, had been given such a choice or opportunity. It was most likely a gesture made out of democratic emotions at a time of much tension. The origins of this gesture are shrouded in mystery and will someday provide the historian with ample opportunity to calculate the confusion caused by this emotional outburst by a prime minister. It seems that Prime Minister Nehru had leaned over backward in order to prove to the world, and to himself, that the newborn Indian state could command the freely-given loyalty of its Muslim population. At the time Nehru made this offer the Kashmir Valley was overrun by Pakistani marauders, and their record of terror and pillage had been enough to frighten the local populace. More than this, however, the Kashmiri population was, by and large, mobilized in political support of the movement led by Sheikh Abdullah, a colleague and friend of Prime Minister Nehru. Hence, it was reasonable at *that* point in time to expect that a plebiscite in Kashmir would be in India's favor. Had an election taken place at the time, the Indian Prime Minister would have emerged not only as a statesman and a prophet, but he would also have shown the world the falsity of the claim put forward by the Pakistanis in creating their state. In retrospect, it was a generous and noble gesture on the part of India; but it is equally obvious that it was also a shortsighted and emotional one. It was a gesture that ultimately served Pakistani pcrposes better than those of India.

We must bear in mind that at the time the Indian government accepted the accession of Kashmir the ruling elite had just come to power after waging a long and bitter campaign against the two-nation theory upon which Pakistan was created. The ideals which moved the

[1] *Times of India*, February 1, 1957. (The following notes, unless otherwise indicated, are from the same source.)

Indian leadership were lofty; it was in this mood that India took the case of Kashmir to the United Nations. The point is that India herself made a case out of Kashmir where none ought to have existed. Legally, Kashmir was Indian territory, and aggression had been committed by Pakistan. If Indian troops repulsed the invaders, they had ample justification for doing so. Actually, Indian military might was much greater than that of Pakistan. As the record shows, Pakistani forces were being inched out of Kashmiri territory when the United Nations called for a cease-fire. Had India treated the Kashmir problem with less emotionally charged sincerity, there is ample evidence for asserting that the "problem" would have been solved.

Yet such is the myopia of ideals and emotions that Prime Minister Nehru fretted about the possibility of the Kashmiri conflict spreading into a third world war. Hence he took the Kashmir problem to the United Nations. There, Prime Minister Nehru hoped, the enlightened delegates would see the progressive nature of the Prime Minister's belief in a secular state, and reject the medieval and religion-obsessed grounds upon which Pakistan lay its claim. To Prime Minister Nehru it seemed clear that since Pakistan acted aggressively, the United Nations would call for the evacuation of all aggressors. The outcome was disenchanting.

The Indian delegate to the United Nations, M. C. Setalvad, addressed himself in appropriately dignified terms when he stated:

> India is anxious to settle the Kashmir dispute quickly and peacefully. It is no less to our interest than to the interest of Pakistan, indeed to the interest of the world, that these two countries, which have so much in common, should live side by side in complete amity, each fully and wholeheartedly cooperating in the pursuit of the common tasks of peace and prosperity.[2]

These lofty sentiments were undoubtedly part of the genuine outlook of Indian elite members. We must not, however, ignore other components of that same system of belief. The latter were rarely expressed in public, although they received passionate expression in private. The private belief was that Pakistan was born out of hatred for India, and that a guiding principle of Pakistani policies was to destroy India's secular statehood and to re-create the glories of a Muslim empire on the subcontinent. The views of Prime Minister Nehru, it appears, were, in part, conditioned by an intense desire to prove that the Indian subcontinent was civilized, progressive, and advanced—all in terms of Western democratic thought. The Prime Minister was evidently determined to act in the image of a progressive and responsible statesman; so determined, in fact, that he unconsciously, if not deliberately, under-

[2] February 1, 1950.

played the aggressiveness and maliciousness of Pakistani policies. It was not sufficiently realized by Nehru that the progressive circles to which he addressed himself were perfectly willing to listen to him, and also to accept the simple Pakistani contention that Muslim majority areas appropriately belonged to Pakistan, since Pakistan is a Muslim state and India, on the other hand, is a Hindu state. India's spokesmen could not deny the fact that India's population was largely Hindu and Pakistan's Muslim. This hurdle was never crossed by the Indian leadership. Secretly many among the so-called Western believers in pluralistic democracy were never quite convinced that such a system was suited to "backward" peoples, such as inhabited the Indian subcontinent. Nehru's error, humanly pardonable, diplomatically unforgivable, was to read into his international audience a potential majority of reasonable and altruistic friends. For this the subcontinent of India paid dearly and continues to suffer domestically and abroad.

This desperate desire to see and to evoke trust and good faith in others, to achieve, as it were, a transformation in others by the act of fully placing one's trust in them, even to find oneself made a martyr—this, as we have already noted in Indian attitudes toward China, has been a dominant theme in Hindu character as well as Indian foreign policy. Yet, while this may work elegantly among the Hindus themselves, there is no inherent logic that dictates it must be operative when dealing with nations outside one's cultural orbit. The "generosity" of such a culturally sanctioned process often works in ways that are not intended. For example, consider the treatment of Sheikh Abdullah by India. As a political leader and friend of Prime Minister Nehru he was elevated to the ranks of a near equal of the Indian Prime Minister. He was made into the embodiment of the secular basis of the Indian state. So much faith was invested in him that little allowance was made for Abdullah's only too human tendency toward personal power. Hence, we find that soon after assuming power in Kashmir, Sheikh Abdullah referred to the desirability of an independent Kashmir. The Kashmir Chief Minister Abdullah was called the Prime Minister of Kashmir. Kashmir was given special considerations and rights; and Indian citizens were denied rights and privileges in Kashmir that were theirs in other parts of India. Here again we note the operation of the mentality that seeks to incorporate the other by allowing unreasonable latitude. Indeed such a degree of liberty is permitted that when it is actually taken advantage of and used, there is a feeling of hurt and distrust. The incorporator now sees himself as betrayed.

As early as 1950, Sheikh Abdullah, as head of the Kashmir government, was expressing himself in unmistakable tones of power and equality. The "Prime Minister of Kashmir pleaded for a compromise which would give his state an independent status supported by the leading powers."[3] Yet, instead of removing Abdullah immediately as a secessionist, the Indian government permitted him to retain his title and powers as "Prime Minister" of Kashmir.

While Sheikh Abdullah wanted *both* India and Pakistan to evacuate Kashmir, Indian policy aimed at seeking the peaceful withdrawal of Pakistani forces. As Pandit G. B. Pant, one of the most powerful Congress party leaders, declared at the Indo-Pakistani Goodwill Convention held in India: "Pakistan should withdraw her forces from Kashmir and thus greatly improve the relations between India and Pakistan."[4]

The statements of Pandit Pant and Sheikh Abdullah appeared on the same day and illustrate how differently each viewed the problem. Yet, it is a testimony to Indian patience (or fantasy?) that Sheikh Abdullah continued to occupy his office for some time to come.

Following the statements of Sheikh Abdullah over a period of time, one notices that his willingness to commit the Kashmiri people to India was less than warm. During the regime of Sheikh Abdullah, the Kashmiri people were able to elect their own constituent assembly. It is significant that no other of the nearly half thousand princely states had had such an institution of its own. Only the sovereign republic of India had its own constituent assembly. Its creation in Kashmir was but another of the host of extraordinary concessions given to Kashmir. The clearest statement on the purposes and prospects of the Constituent Assembly of Kashmir was given by G. M. Sadiq, then serving as its president. Commenting upon the new constitution for Kashmir, Sadiq declared "it would be a democratic constitution where more emphasis will be laid on the economic aspects of our democracy."[5]

Sadiq referred to what he called the "peculiar position of Kashmir" and said that "the bonds with India should be strong; and at the same time we must be in a position to function according to our own program as well as the demands of the situation without outside interference."[6] To put the situation most cautiously, there existed at least a decided ambivalence among the leaders of Kashmir regarding the future of their state. In providing ample scope to the Kashmiri leadership to develop its political stature, the Indian government was playing a dangerous game. There was little in the way of firm control and decisive leadership on the part of India. Rather, it was by default that the Kashmiri leaders were allowed to develop grandiose notions of independent nationhood where there was no precedent for it.

[3] May 1, 1950.
[4] May 1, 1950.
[5] April 15, 1952.
[6] April 15, 1952.

The ambivalence of the Indian government was nowhere better demonstrated than in the sentiments and official statements of Prime Minister Jawaharlal Nehru. During a one-day debate on demands relating to the Ministry of External Affairs, Nehru as the Minister for External Affairs declared in the Lok Sabha that "he would be meeting the Pakistan Prime Minister, Mohammed Ali, in New Delhi on May 14. There was no doubt that the leaders and people of Pakistan favored a settlement of Indo-Pakistan problems. Yet, these problems had not become easier with the passage of time. It was difficult to 'unwrite' history. These problems would have to be considered in a realistic manner. Kashmir was the outstanding issue. But Kashmir had a soul of its own and could not be bandied about between India and Pakistan, irrespective of the wishes of the people of that state . . . the government of India would not come in the way of the state government if the latter wanted to publish certain correspondence that had passed between Sheikh Abdullah and various Indian leaders, including himself, in 1952 and 1953."[7]

Opponents of Nehru's Kashmir policy might take serious issue with his attribution of a "soul" to Kashmir and his denial of such a supernatural quality to other regions of India. This special concession to Kashmir, we suggest, accounted for much of the confusion in Indian policy relating to Kashmir. Here was a classic case of the private predilections of a decision maker interfering with the discovery of policies in support of the national interest.

When the Indian and Pakistani prime ministers did meet in New Delhi, the results of the conference were described to be as follows: "Referring to Kashmir, Nehru said that the Pakistani Prime Minister was friendly and constructive. They kept away from the 'old dead wall' approach and cut new ground. He, however, felt it was not fair to disclose details of the new approach for reaching a satisfactory settlement of the problem."[8]

In spite of the hopeful note struck by Prime Minister Nehru, the years to come did not bring the Kashmiri problem any nearer to resolution. It appears that the Indian position was a curious mixture. At first Kashmir was not considered anything of a "problem." Kashmir had acceded to India, and Pakistan had clearly been an aggressor country. At the second stage negotiations were conducted with Pakistan to resolve an outstanding dispute on the "problem" of Kashmir. Evidently the lack of policy clarification contributed vastly to the deplorable state of affairs.

In his address before a mass rally in Madras, Prime Minister Nehru

[7] April 1, 1955.
[8] June 1, 1955.

tried, as honestly as possible, to meet some of the accusations that had been hurled at him for his handling of Indian policy on Kashmir. Answering those of his critics who accused him of having a double standard on Kashmir, he replied that he was not conscious of such, but if it were so, he would stand condemned both before the world and himself.[9] One need not accuse Prime Minister Nehru of having deliberately and consciously adopted a double standard. Indeed, his entire life history and record would bear witness to his consciousness of a "gentlemanly" approach to political problems. From his statements one can only infer that other factors were at work than those on the threshold of consciousness. Nehru was obviously extremely distressed over the charge that he had not been "fair" in regard to the Kashmir issue. At the public rally in Madras he noted that "if he was convinced that he had not honored any international commitment about Kashmir, 'I shall honor it or resign from office.' " He was distressed by the charge. "If Pakistan alone had made that charge he could understand it, because Pakistan was in the habit of making the most irresponsible and even untrue statements. But it pained him when others repeated that charge." Nehru encouraged his countrymen to consider the Security Council decision as "a challenge to us from the world," and asserted: "Do not be excited or get cold feet. We have stout arms, calm minds, and sound heads to deal with the situation."[10]

When Prime Minister Nehru approached the last few weeks of his life in the middle of 1964, Sheikh Abdullah was released from prison. He was a hero to the Kashmiri people, and descended upon New Delhi almost as a messiah about to bring the reconciliation of India and Pakistan. There was little doubt that Prime Minister Nehru died with the Kashmir problem at a most dangerous and crucial point.

INDIA AND PAKISTAN

There is more comment by the Indian elites on Pakistan than on any other country in the world. Deep and disturbing emotions are elicited by the very name of Pakistan. The creation of Pakistan meant the truncating of the Indian state, the displacement of several millions, the murder of several hundreds of thousands.

For the leadership of the national independence movement, the creation of Pakistan made the independence of the country particularly bitter. To Hindu nationalists, Pakistan's existence meant that Mother India's holy body had been severed. To students of Indian history, Pakistan was a living reminder of the tragic cycle in which India had

9 February 1, 1957.
10 February 1, 1957.

been caught—the internal division at the expense of which foreigners had ruled the nation for centuries. Coexisting with these sentiments were the fears aroused by militant Islam in its repeated threats once again to bring the faith to the heathens, and to fly the Islamic banner on Delhi's historic Red Fort. The anxieties stimulated by Pakistan in modern India have been no less real than those primordial fears generated by the names of Aurengzeb, Genghis Khan, Timur Lane, and a host of similar marauders. As we noted, the creation of Pakistan was for its founders a triumph of their theory that two nations inhabited the subcontinent, Hindu and Muslim. For the secular leadership of the Congress party, Pakistan's creation was the price that *had* to be paid for gaining national independence. In a peculiar twist of fate, the creation of Pakistan left only slightly fewer Muslims in India than in the newly-created Islamic state of Pakistan. Both India and Pakistan chose to remain within the British Commonwealth of Nations, thus displaying a generosity toward former rulers that they did not have within themselves for each other.

The saber rattling of Pakistanis actually culminated in the year of independence with the invasion of Kashmir, the birth of Pakistani friendship with the Portuguese, and the increase of pressure upon the small Hindu minority within Pakistani borders. Such was the pitch of hatred and distrust against Pakistan that it is not unreasonable to speculate that a war against Pakistan might have been a very welcome release for the Indian public. It was to this militancy against Pakistan that Prime Minister Nehru addressed himself time and again. He described suggestions of war against Pakistan over the mistreatment of the Hindu minority as being " 'childish and irresponsible' . . . a 'mature' country like India does not think lightly along these lines."[11] And he noted that "many wrongs" were being done and "false cries" raised in Pakistan. Even persons in responsible positions talked in a similar vein, but the people of Pakistan desired to live in peace.[12]

The progressive, modern, secular wing of the Congress party had for decades preached unity among India's peoples, especially among Hindus and Muslims. So emotionally had this commitment been made for so long that it was not easily dismissed. Prime Minister Nehru especially placed such stress on this theme that extremist Hindus regarded him as the prime example of Muslim appeasement. The more conservative among Congress leaders were also affected by the pristine vision of a united India, irrespective of religion. Sardar Patel, referring to the Pakistanis as "brothers," said that "those friends who were with us until

[11] November 1, 1952.
[12] November 1, 1952.

yesterday had now become foreigners today. Artificial boundaries could not separate them from us. Our relationship and economic and political ties could not be broken."[13] It was difficult for the Indian nationalist leadership to accept the "foreign" nature of Pakistan. After all, they thought, Pakistan was carved out of a whole which had only one historic meaning. It was a well-known fact that the vast majority of Muslims had been converted over centuries from Hinduism to Islam. Nehru's remarks reveal unmistakable anguish when he related how he was "emotionally attached to the Pakistani people and had not conditioned himself to thinking of them as aliens. He reiterated his belief that nothing was more desirable than close and cordial relations with Pakistan."[14]

There is an inherent irony in Indo-Pakistani relations. For Indians to appear as friends, stressing common historic ties of brotherhood, has been to deny the essential distinctiveness of the Pakistanis. The incorporative predilections of Hinduism, no doubt, also facilitated the Indian elites' insensitivity to differences. When Hindus are most secular —as viewed by themselves—they appear to be precisely the opposite to Pakistanis.

Among the more responsible Indian elites there was a fear that history might repeat itself if India and Pakistan did not cooperate with each other. They felt that if cooperation failed, chaos and destruction would inevitably follow. Speaking at a Martyrs' Day meeting in 1950, Nehru appealed to all Indians to "work wholeheartedly for a 'faithful implementation' of the Indo-Pakistan agreement.

"The only alternative to the agreement is war which will not only destroy both India and Pakistan but is sure to engulf a good part of the world."[15] As Dr. Sita Ram, India's High Commissioner in Pakistan, in a message to the Indo-Pakistan Goodwill Convention, asserted, "United we stand, divided we fall, is the truth which holds good for India and Pakistan."[16]

It was no simple matter to maintain the civic peace in India in a manner creditable to the secular character of the Indian state. Indian leaders were aware of the fact that Hindu minorities in Pakistan were being liquidated. And as refugees flowed into India from Pakistan it was but natural that there be repercussions in India. The insecurity generated among the Indian Muslims is evident from the remarks of Mohammed Taher, a member of the Bombay Pradesh Congress Committee, who presided over a meeting of Bombay Muslims. As a Muslim,

[13] January 16, 1950.
[14] April 1, 1958.
[15] April 15, 1950.
[16] October 2, 1950.

he felt compelled to attest to the fact that "we will never act the role of fifth columnists and let not anyone be under the delusion that we Muslims profess dual loyalties."[17] To maintain a secular state meant, above all, to provide for the safety and well-being of nearly 50 million Muslims residing in India. Sri Prakasa, then the Commerce Minister in the government of India, told the Indo-Pakistan Goodwill Convention that "maintenance of peace and good will between the two countries was ultimately the responsibility of the people, because government could not provide police protection to each and every member of the minority community."[18]

It was especially difficult to maintain domestic peace when the voices from the political opposition were strident, even militant. N. C. Chatterjee, the Hindu Mahasabha leader, denounced the government in no uncertain terms. He accused the Indian government of "cowardice" regarding Pakistan. And he held that the Kashmir issue be considered closed, and the Khulna district of East Pakistan be annexed because of the large influx of Hindu refugees into West Bengal.[19] Others, such as Supakar, Member of Parliament, criticized the government on issues such as the dispute with Pakistan on canal waters. He advocated policies embodying a sterner mode of behavior. He stated that India's policy on the canal waters dispute with Pakistan "should be revised in keeping with the maxim that 'charity begins at home.' "[20] In fairness to the critics of the government of India, the patience that India displayed toward Pakistan was remarkable.

A new irritant was injected into Indo-Pakistan relations when Pakistan turned to the United States for military assistance. It had been a cardinal principle of Indian foreign policy to bring about an "area of peace," free from military entanglements. Referring to the Asian region, Nehru had declared: "We regard this area as a non-war area in Asia. Naturally we hoped that Pakistan which is similarly circumstanced would belong to that area also."[21] He said that "he did not think that any problem between India and Pakistan was incapable of solution, but they had to look at the thing in the context of possible military aid to Pakistan from America. Nehru stressed the need for growing friendship between India and Pakistan for the progress of both."[22] But Pakistan was playing the power-balancing strategies historically adopted by a state seeking to isolate its principal rival. And Pakistan's policy makers considered

[17] August 1, 1951.
[18] October 2, 1950.
[19] April 1, 1955.
[20] August 1, 1957.
[21] January 1, 1954.
[22] January 1, 1954.

India to be the major potential enemy. Obviously, Indian foreign policy had failed to achieve one of its major goals. The Western powers were not precluded from entering into alliance with small Asian countries, thereby neutralizing the independent line advocated by India.

The old fears of foreigners aligning themselves with Indian princes and eventually establishing an empire were, in part, revived by Pakistan's military pact with the United States. The Indian response to this bordered on the level of panic. Admitting to the seriousness of the developments, Nehru told a press conference: "The whole system of pacts and alliances of Europe has extended itself to the Middle East and has come through Pakistan to the doors of India. In other words, Europe now touches the borders of India, in the sense of conflicts, troubles, and alliances."[23]

The Congress party called out demonstrations against the military pact between Pakistan and the United States. There was almost complete unity among all political organizations in the conviction that this alliance was doomed to bring woe to India and eventually to all of Asia. Comment on Pakistan's alliance with the United States betrayed deep anxiety; nowhere does this come through more clearly than in the analysis made by Asoka Mehta. In his address before the national convention of the Praja Socialist party he noted how the Indo-Pakistan alliance exemplified "the eternal tragedy in Indian history when smaller states in their mutual fights invited a third power for help and instead of winning the fight against the enemy, they lost their independence."[24]

The Praja Socialist party leader, however, also warned against counter-alliances with Russia in order to contain Pakistani policies.

This was a bitter period for independent India, and in retrospect it might be said to mark the decline of Indian influence in Asian affairs. The emotional and political pressure exerted by Pakistan was now taking its toll. Nor did domestic developments aid the country during these critical times. In an impassioned speech Nehru strongly deplored the growing strains among the Sikhs and Hindus in the Punjab over linguistic issues. He exhorted a mass rally to "read newspapers in Pakistan. . . . Read how our enemies are gloating over happenings in the Punjab and Bombay. They think we are getting weak."[25]

Displaying anxiety over the continuing worsening of Indo-Pakistani relations, Prime Minister Nehru appealed to Chou En-lai, who was visiting India, to act as a messenger of good will to Pakistan. In the presence of the Communist leader, Nehru said "that it was neither desirable for India to reply to Pakistani threats nor keep silent all the

23 June 1, 1955.
24 January 1, 1954.
25 June 15, 1956.

time." He said that Chou, who would be flying to Karachi soon, should take "our message of good will and friendship for Pakistan."[26]

In a characteristically Hindu way, the comments of the antipolitical "successor" to the mantle of Mahatma Gandhi are a testimony to the continuing and all-pervasive importance of Pakistan for the Indians. In his address before the Sarvodaya Sammelan, Vinoba Bhave noted that India's rulers were incapable of planning for the villages. Contending that Indian plans were no plans at all, the saint in Indian politics "said that 'Indian planning' was a misnomer because the planners did not think independently. Their thinking was influenced by Pakistan's policies. Pakistan's policies, in turn, were influenced by some other nations. . . . It was therefore necessary that planning was freed from this stranglehold. Villagers themselves would have to plan for their villages. . . . Gram Rajya, based on planning by villagers, was the only way out."[27]

With the passage of years it became abundantly clear that Indian relations with Pakistan necessitated continued vigilance and military preparedness. It also was equally clear that both Indian security interests and internal development would continue to be influenced by a hostile neighbor in Pakistan.

[26] December 1, 1956.
[27] June 1, 1958.

CHAPTER 10 · COMING TO TERMS WITH THE WIDER CONTEXT: THE UNITED NATIONS, POLAR POWERS, AND CHINA

INDIA AND THE UNITED NATIONS

The position of India in the world has been difficult to define, not only today, but also in the last half century. For instance, even as India was governed through the India Office in London it was among the original signatories to the charter that established the League of Nations. While this peculiar status may be considered akin to the representation that the Ukraine has enjoyed in the United Nations, we might bear in mind that the government of India, while legally under British domination, formulated a foreign policy almost entirely on its own. The viceroys sent out by the King Emperor in concert with the elite corps of adminstrators—the Indian Civil Service (ICS)—conducted foreign relations with the adjoining states of India. It is certainly a fact that the British government of India was the agent of British imperialism in the East, but it is equally true that the policies of the government of India, under the British, were quasi-independent. The pattern was set as early as the days of Lord Curzon and faithfully executed by those who followed him. In this historical sense, therefore, the administrative elite of India should not have been entirely unprepared to deal with the external world. The difference, of course, lay in the fact that the achievement of independence in 1947 lent a new ideological perspective to policy making. An age of revolutionary change in power relations had dawned in Asia after World War II and, of necessity, the government of a free India had interests and perspectives that were wholly or in part divergent from those of dependent India. In the following pages we examine the nature of India's participation in the United Nations.

In the years since independence India's foreign policy has passed from the stage where idealism was dominant to a stage where a measure of realism has become an integral feature. While this realism undoubtedly is the result of operating in the world arena, the evolution of domestic politics has also helped account for it. The tenor of politics in 1947 was highly charged with patriotism and devotion to the national welfare. After a series of general elections, Indian politics increasingly resembled the model to be found in the older democracies. Patronage, brokerage, and political deals are the ascendant strategic styles in contemporary India and they make a decided break with the political style of early post-independence years. What we emphasize here is that the changes in political style within a nation are likely to reflect themselves in relationships with foreign nations. Where the symbol "trust" had been an integral part of the political style there now emerged the realization that "interests" were vital. One might choose to term this shift as the transition from a model of politics in which the demands of the conscience or even the "ego ideal" are increasingly replaced by those emanating from the ego: in other words, political sophistication assumes the place once occupied by political idealism.

The process has by no means been quite so smooth as the above description might lead one to believe. Political maturation, like the process of individual personality growth, involves the gradual, and often quite painful, transition from one set of values and practices to another. The painfulness to which we allude here arises from the fact that this transition occurs in such a manner that the older values and interpretations retain their emotional content and hence are able to influence responses. We have, therefore, the ingredients of internal conflict that can be resolved only by the assumption of power by newer generations with differing beliefs, faiths, and identities. Even then, we suggest, the conflict is never quite resolved, since enough of the older values have been internalized to generate feelings of doubt. Such a dynamic of political change is in no sense unique to the Indian case. It is to be anticipated in all societies that are no longer static.

In India, as in most emerging nations of Asia and Africa, the process of individuation has not quite run its gamut. Under such conditions the crises of identity and sense of personal worthiness are all the more acute, demanding of resolution, and suffused with intense emotional discomfort. In a society that has lived a fossilized life of tradition the abrupt changes in the rules of power distribution can be confusing and, we repeat, acutely deprivational. This is the more so when charges of double standards and hypocrisy are leveled by the invisible jury of the West whose prescriptions one attempts to follow—these prescriptions are, after all, essentially necessary to retain or regain the esteem that the leaders of the new societies crave for. In this context Indian pronouncements attain a meaningfulness that would otherwise be lost in any analysis of elite comment.

Early Indian reactions toward the United Nations do not find representation in our study. However, it is probable that initially India considered the United Nations in a highly favorable light which has since given way not to disenchantment but to a more differentiated awareness of the directions that the world organization may take. The changing composition of the member nations is fraught with possibilities that call for diplomatic exploitation for the benefit of national policy. There is, therefore, an element of wariness about Indian comments.

The lack of precision in Indian comments on the United Nations is, in part, owing to the vagueness in the role of this world body—there is, after all, a noticeable discrepancy between the stated aims of the United Nations and the limitations on power for the implementation of these aims. Moreover, the structure of the world organization has been such as to make it essentially the tool of the major powers who are capable of marshaling blocs of votes. Indian ambivalence is illustrated in the comments of V. K. Krishna Menon, who said that the hopes of the United Nations rested on "humanity's faith in its own destiny. This was not an attitude of escapism. It was a question of either survival or decay and the problem of mankind depended on the degree of progress maintained."[1] But there is sufficient realism present not to equate the United Nations with world government. Menon defined the United Nations as "a society of nations and not a union of governments. It was not a world government but it was a world of governments."[2]

Within this world of governments India's role was prescribed in terms of activity and not passivity. Indeed, it appears that India, while aware of the limitations of the United Nations, fully realized the opportunities provided by its framework for the advancement of national policy. The United Nations gained importance for India from the fact that India's power was not in being; it was largely potential.

Because of her emphasis upon internal development and the need to depend upon external assistance in this task, the Indian leadership has found itself in the position of being able to work vigorously for a lessening of international tensions and the prevention of the outbreak of con-

[1] *Times of India*, September 15, 1957. (The following notes, unless otherwise indicated, are from the same source.)

[2] September 15, 1957.

flict. Consequently, we find that at the United Nations the Indian delegation has been particularly active in promoting disarmament on a world scale. It was obviously in India's interest to seek to advance general disarmament in the expectation that security would lead to the release of capital to help develop her economy. Inaugurating a series of United Nations broadcasts, B. N. Rau, Indian delegate to the General Assembly, urged the nations of the world to "join forces in an economic offensive to root out hunger, poverty, ignorance, and disease. . . . If we must have total war, let us have total war, not against our fellow men, but against these, our worst common enemies!"[3]

At the United Nations, India has sought to function in an independent fashion—insofar as that is feasible under a system of bloc voting. Repeatedly the elite has tried to emphasize that India is not neutral but that rather, in the words of Krishna Menon, "We make our decisions in the United Nations and adopt our policies on the basis of conditions prevailing at a given time."[4] Regarding the methods used by India to seat the People's Republic of China in the United Nations, Krishna Menon declared: "Our business must be to persuade. I am not sure that that persuasion is not taking place."[5] Such statements often termed self-righteousness by outsiders are nonetheless the manner in which the Indian elite sees itself. But these remarks assume a quite different meaning when we place them alongside the assertions that were made in the one case where India was directly involved in a dispute before the United Nations—the conflict over Kashmir between India and Pakistan.

For India, Kashmir has involved not merely a matter of territory (although that consideration cannot be treated too lightly), but has raised the question of the secular basis upon which the Indian state was constituted.

The frustration experienced by India over the Kashmir issue in the United Nations led to increased cynicism regarding the functioning of the world organization. The blunt words of the former Prime Minister of Kashmir, Sheikh Abdullah, reflected a dominant Indian sentiment. He characterized the United Nations as "a tool of the world powers which failed to convict Pakistan of aggression in Kashmir and force them to evacuate. Of course, if such an order were given, the United Nations is powerless to enforce it."[6]

Neither Indian publicity abroad nor the efforts of the Indian delegations at the United Nations served to win support for the Indian

3 April 1, 1950.
4 September 15, 1957.
5 February 1, 1958.
6 May 1, 1950.

case on Kashmir. The majority opinion in India evidently came to acknowledge that it was a major blunder on India's part to take the issue of Kashmir before the United Nations. Defense Minister Krishna Menon reflected this frustration:

> India presented her case in respect to Kashmir ten years ago in all sincerity and hope that the United Nations would ask the aggressor to get out of that country. If India wanted to drive out the invaders from Kashmir she could have invaded Pakistan, but India did not want to pursue that policy. It had vainly put before the United Nations that there had been continued and continuous aggression in Kashmir.[7]

We have emphasized the notion that India felt aggrieved and distressed at the manner in which the Kashmir issue had been received at the United Nations. Having accepted the partition of the Indian subcontinent, implicitly on the basis of the two-nation theory, India valiantly attempted to create a secular society. Because she has the third-largest Muslim population in the world and because India is *not* a Hindu state (while Pakistan is officially an Islamic state), the Indian elite expected the world outside to commend and support the tremendous efforts required in the process of converting a traditional, religion-based society into a secular body politic. There is, regardless of the merits of the Kashmir case, an element of poignancy in the melancholy remarks of Nehru at a public meeting in Madras, when he charged the Security Council "with being blind to the facts relating to the Kashmir problem and of dealing with that human question in an extraordinarily casual way."[8]

All indications are that India will be cautious in again taking a dispute in which she is involved directly to the United Nations. As one observer so aptly put it: "India has lost its political virginity."

INDIA AND THE UNITED STATES

When we consider that the United States was one of the two major powers of the world at a time when India, in spite of her cherished hopes to remain outside the bloc alliances, was forced to rely heavily upon material assistance from the United States, it is striking to note the meager representation of comment on the United States in our investigation.

This paucity of elite attention is better understood in the context of India's official policy of non-alignment. References to the United

[7] September 15, 1957.
[8] February 1, 1957.

States as such were few, but the United States was included when references were made to bipolar powers, the two blocs, the world powers, and the West. Because India followed a policy of non-alignment at a time when she was economically beholden to the United States, and to a smaller measure to the Soviet Union, it behooved India to express foreign-policy positions generally and vaguely; and specifically only when circumstances arose which directly required an open and clear policy statement.

It is our impression that the Indian ruling elite, when it has been forced to criticize the United States, has chosen to be as ambiguous as possible; when, as has happened so often, a measure of gratitude has been due for aid rendered, Indian pronouncements have also been proper and lacking in a display of emotionalism. In both cases, it appears, the policy has been to exercise the utmost restraint. Evidently, genuinely independent and outspoken policy is not readily compatible with heavy dependence upon economic and technical assistance.

The most important political dispute with the United States reflected in Indian comment in our study concerned the extension of American military assistance to the South Asian region, and especially to Pakistan.

Prime Minister Nehru explained India's stand on this issue, prior to the signing of the United States–Pakistan military pact, in an address he delivered before the Indian National Trades Union Conference (INTUC): "One did not receive free military aid without certain consequences following. Obtaining the aid itself was a serious thing. It meant that the cold war came to Pakistan and, therefore, came to India's borders, and it meant that if a shooting war developed it also came right near to the borders of India. It affected not only India, but Burma, Afghanistan, and other countries in the Middle East as well as some in Southeast Asia."[9]

The United States was singled out for blame by almost all political parties; the United States was viewed as a successor to the European imperial powers. At the Praja Socialist party's National Convention, Asoka Mehta drew the lessons of the United States' action: "Pakistan, by seeking to gain strength at the feet of America, had displayed its weakness. It will become still weaker as its reliance on American arms and help grow. America, however powerful it may be," Mehta said, "would not add to its strength by perpetually carrying weak nations on its shoulders."[10]

Indian bitterness was that of the trapped, for India was not likely to counteract American moves by accepting Soviet arms aid. Appar-

[9] January 1, 1954.
[10] January 1, 1954.

ently, American policy planners had taken this into consideration; it was indeed extremely unlikely that were there some recognized possibility of driving India into the Soviet camp American policy would have risked association with Pakistan at the cost of totally alienating India. As a short-term proposition, it can be said that American action was well calculated. But were the long-term implications grasped at the time? The balance of power in South Asia had been upset and Indian policy would now seek to encircle Pakistan more effectively. Especially regarding the Kashmir conflict, a bargaining asset previously absent was now possessed by Pakistan. As Prime Minister Nehru made clear: "We were told by the American government that these arms are not to be used against India. I accept that. How the great American government could stop it, I wonder."[11] The general feeling in India was that the United States had deliberately plotted with Pakistan against India. Hostility, therefore, was directed at the United States in no uncertain terms; but it was the hostility of the aggrieved and powerless. American assurances, as we noted, did little to satisfy Indians; they saw that for Pakistan the major enemy had been, and remained, India. Anti-communism on a global scale was, and remained, only a theoretical issue, a justification with no bearing in reality.

Considering the impressive American presence, it is surprising that there were almost no exhortations to emulate the Americans and the United States, nor were there any statements that would indicate that India was closely linked to the United States. The ruling elite, it appears, had little emotional commitment to the United States and it was only of necessity that cooperation existed. There were differences not only in terms of foreign policy but in basic outlook. The Indian elite had derived its most lasting impressions of the United States via the British left wing and such evaluations had been largely unfavorable. But while British intellectuals, from whom the Indian elite took its cues, changed its American imagery after the 1930s, the Indian elite showed little resilience. Private opinions of the United States have been a mixture of contempt, fear, and envy; public statements, however, have been cautious, since American assistance is vital. The rising generation of Indian politicians, less dependent upon the British assessment, has been closer to independent judgment. However, the older elements of the elite continue to occupy positions of power, and until they give way to the next generation Indian attitudes toward the United States will remain what they are today—often misleading, usually envious, and nearly always suspicious.

[11] February 1, 1957.

INDIA AND THE SOVIET UNION

In quantitative terms, the Indian elite has manifestly paid very little direct attention not only to the United States, but to the Soviet Union as well. While it was not possible for India to ignore either of the two bipolar powers, it appears to have been part of the Indian style to refer to either in a general rather than a specific manner. Playing the precarious role of a nonaligned power in the contemporary world involved deliberate abstinence from verbal assaults coupled with a cautious celebration of "friendly relations" between India and America on the one hand and Russia on the other.

Cautious and jealous of her own independent role, India rarely communicated candidly the precise nature of this role to domestic audiences. An example of a rare exception to this pattern was a speech by Prime Minister Nehru before a public meeting in Patna. He noted that Communists at home wanted India to ally with Russia, and the Jan Sangh wanted an Indian alliance with America. "India was friendly with both America and Russia, but would not enter into an alliance with either of them. India would follow her own independent policy."[12]

When India gained her independence, those who constituted the first free government of India had almost no personal knowledge of the Soviet Union. During the freedom struggle, Prime Minister Nehru had made a brief visit to the Soviet Union. But he and his colleagues derived most of their information from secondary sources. The Soviet Union in its early phases had stood out as a heroic example of a nation that had pulled itself up by its bootstraps and was the only major country to renounce imperialist intentions. Almost everything about the Soviets appealed to the nationalist leaders, especially those who were modern and Westernized; but even traditionalists such as Lokmanya Tilak had expressed their admiration for Soviet society and values. Much of this legacy of favorable perspectives yielded before the realities that faced nationalist leadership upon the acquisition of power. Basically, however, there still still remained an admiration for the Soviet Union among most Indians involved in the political arena. Much of the negative feelings which existed about the Soviets were conveniently displaced upon the local Communist party which was branded, from time to time, as foreign-inspired and unpatriotic.

The declaration of an independent policy implied that India would start with a clean slate: she would extend her hand of friendship equally to the Soviet Union and the United States, as Nehru declared in his first major policy pronouncement upon assuming power. In time,

12 February 15, 1957.

the relations between the Soviet Union and India experienced great development in both scope and intensity. And, as Sino-Indian relations deteriorated, India moved closer to Moscow without involving herself in a fatal bear hug.

It is instructive that in our study more than three-fourths of Indian elite comment on the Soviet Union originated from Prime Minister Nehru. During the 1930s and 1940s Nehru was an admirer, albeit a reserved admirer, of the Soviet Union. In particular, Nehru was drawn favorably toward Soviet nationality policies, their eradication of illiteracy, and their public-health programs. Ultimately, Nehru felt, as Soviet society became industrialized and highly educated, the oppressive features would have to give way. In other words, Prime Minister Nehru never was anti-Soviet in his outlook; rather, he was an extremely wary admirer.

But given his evaluations of the self and nation, Nehru could not feel too close an affinity for the Soviet Union. Prime Minister Nehru described himself as possessing the sensibilities of an aristocrat; he also characterized Indian history and civilization as possessive of noble and unique elements. Both the United States and the Soviet Union would continue to fascinate him, but each in its differing manner would be too demanding and gross for one whose most formative years were spent in a Victorian environment, and for one who had found it necessary to make a voyage of discovery into the national past in order to connect himself meaningfully with the land of his birth.

This sense of establishing a personal identity was particularly important for Nehru and its value cannot be minimized. If, as Erik Erikson has suggested, a great leader can, through his private quest and resolution, establish an identity for a whole people who are in search of one, then Nehru came close to meeting the requirements. For, despite the attractiveness of various established systems, he sought to create a meaningful and distinct identity for himself and for India. For instance, regarding Russia's economic revolution in particular, the following remarks of Nehru illustrate both his attraction and repulsion. He said that "Russia was today a progressive nation, but her economic revolution just after the First World War had cost much blood. India would have her economic revolution peacefully and in a systematic way."[13]

Nehru's views of the Soviet Union were also noteworthy for the importance he gave to enlightenment values in a developing society. Making a connection between enlightenment and political control, Nehru stated that the education and progress which had followed the revolution had resulted in the masses demanding greater individual freedom and

[13] May 1, 1953.

more consumer goods. There had been conflicts between liberals and conservatives in Russia, he observed, but the liberals were now in control and their policies would lead to a lessening of tensions in international affairs.[14]

There is no failure to realize that the Soviet Union represented a major world force that had to be reckoned with, and that this force was not entirely evil or good. It was well understood in New Delhi that the Soviet Union was a world-revolutionary center from which ideological subversion projected tensions all over the globe. Asked if the dissolution of the Cominform could help in lessening tensions in the world, the Prime Minister, recalling his statement at Bandung, said that "the functioning of the Cominform constituted interference in the internal affairs of other countries and was, therefore, incompatible with the ten principles enunciated at Bandung."[15] There is little mistaking the vantage point from which New Delhi saw the Soviet Union. The position was independent—neither hysterically anti-Soviet nor intimidated, and certainly not pro-Soviet.

This independent outlook in foreign policy was also reflected by the opposition. At the Praja Socialist party's convention Asoka Mehta condemned Pakistan's military pact with the United States, warning that "any counteralliance with Russia, instead of getting any benefit, would only strangle ourselves."[16] We might also note the rather ambiguous position of Ajoy Ghosh, General Secretary, at a meeting of the Central Committee of the Communist party of India. Admitting that the Soviet Union's intervention in Hungary "was necessary for the security of the Communist world," he also termed this action "regrettable."[17]

THE BULGANIN–KHRUSHCHEV VISIT

In the last quarter of 1955 India was host to Bulganin and Khrushchev on their first major excursion into the world that lay outside the Communist orbit. The trip was significant in a symbolic sense for it could be interpreted as the beginning of a thaw in post-Stalin Russia. In another sense, the visit of the Soviet leaders to India was an indication of the emerging relevance of the position and sentiments of the developing nations. Of importance is the fact that India played a gracious host apparently without excessive fear of offending the anti-Communist bloc leaders. The visit of the Soviet leaders could be interpreted as a meaningful assertion of India's independent foreign policy.

[14] July 15, 1957.
[15] June 1, 1955.
[16] January 1, 1954.
[17] December 15, 1956.

At a mass rally in Calcutta, the center of Indian leftist politics, Prime Minister Nehru addressed the assembled crowds in the presence of the Soviet leaders. We see clearly that Nehru's remarks were designed to clarify the Indian position both to the audience and the visitors. The Prime Minister declared that he had often said that India's basic policy was not to join any camp or alliance, "yet we wish to cooperate with all in our quest for peace, security, and human betterment."[18]

The Prime Minister was fully aware that such an independent policy in a bipolar world was not to be pursued without the hazard of exposure to severe sanctions. To seek cordial ties with one meant that India would be suspect in the other's eyes. In a time of stress it was all the more necessary for the two major world powers either to view India as an opportunistic nation or a neutral nation leaning definitely one way. To presume to follow an independent policy under such trying circumstances—and with tremendous limitations of national power—appeared presumptuous. The concern thus generated was apparent to Nehru. He explicitly stated that India's friendship with the Soviet Union was not directed against any nation or people; and "it was not in a spirit of arrogance that India had chosen to follow an independent foreign policy. India could not do otherwise unless she was false to herself and to all she stood for."[19] With the Western bloc of nations in mind, the Prime Minister declared in the presence of Bulganin and Khrushchev that some of India's " 'friends' in other countries had become alarmed at the great welcome the Soviet guests had received in India. They could not help thinking in terms of rival camps and military alliances."[20] The note of irritation is unmistakable and we would venture to suggest here that the Prime Minister—if we indulge in mind reading—was annoyed at the temerity of some observers even to hint at the possibility of India's linking herself with any power bloc. Much too much of an investment in self-respect had gone into the making of an independent foreign policy for the Prime Minister lightly to accept any doubts as to his and India's posture of integrity.

In retrospect India's independent policies can be said to have yielded substantial dividends at home and abroad. But to assume that the policy planners were solely motivated by a calculus of playing one bloc against another is to miss much of the human element in the policy-making process. We doubt that Indian leadership was aware that its independent policies would appear to be so eminently successful. Rather, it is more likely that deep and essentially simple considerations of self-respect motivated the independent bent of Indian foreign policy. Other value

[18] December 1, 1955.
[19] December 1, 1955.
[20] December 1, 1955.

goals take on greater relative significance after a new identity and operating status have been fully vindicated; the initial impetus comes more likely from the humiliations imposed by alien powers and by the pride generated by rereading a past that seems infinitely glorious. So when Prime Minister Nehru celebrated India's being true to herself he was stating a value of enormous importance, and one which is not necessarily perceived by champions of a "materialistic" interpretation of history.

On the occasion of bidding farewell to the Soviet leaders we find the Prime Minister elucidating what he preferred to designate the "basic" Indian approach:

> We want to befriend every country so that our circle of friendship may grow and become wider, and cooperation and peace may thrive.
>
> What kind of friendship is that which envisages enmity with others? We should befriend all and stretch out our hand to all.
>
> For this reason our coming closer to this great country, the Soviet Union, is very important. But this does not mean that we have drifted away from another country. This is neither the position now nor will it be at any time in the future. We have always wanted and we will want cooperation among the countries of the world to increase and world peace to be strengthened.[21]

Admirable political rhetoric as this might be, we suggest that the sentiments underlying it were genuine. It was, in a sense, India's good fortune to be in a position where altruism on a world scale was in her national interest. Whether she can always be in such an enviable position is debatable. As her power potential becomes an actuality, the temptation to seek swift resolutions by armed intervention may prove irresistible. It is notorious that the meek and the powerless have no difficulty advocating morality to the strong, whether in primary or inter-state relations. At the same time the richness and complexity of motivation and culture are such that many value goals and many highly diverse interpretations of the self are always latent in any social context. Nehru tried to bridge the chasm that separated his own people from the peoples of the Soviet Union; he reminded the two Soviet leaders of the opportunities for empathy with India which they had shared on their travels. They had seen

> many old and new facets of India and saw the faces of innumerable Indian people. They also saw lakhs of pairs of eyes and got a glimpse into the hearts of lakhs of our people. After all this, what

[21] December 15, 1955.

more can I, an insignificant part of India, say on this occasion? So by seeing these millions of different faces of India, you [Soviet leaders] could have some idea of not only the olden times, but the wishes and desires of our people today.[22]

Here is an effort to convey to the outsider some of the manifold realities of present-day India. It is an exercise in appealing to the basic sense of decency in the powerful "other"—an article of faith in the Gandhian grammar of politics, and a technique which, as we have already noted, India has used on several occasions. Nehru sentimentally added that he wished his guests to "especially take with you one precious thing, India's message of love for your people."

Scarcely had the Soviet leaders departed, when the intensity of pressures and rumors began to manifest itself in New Delhi. The Minister for Commerce and Industry T. T. Krishnamachari, well known for his liberal views and his influential businesses, was forced to refer to the "tearing campaign" going on in some countries, sponsored by interested parties. He noted that India was being accused of "slowly attaching herself to one bloc. We are not, and it is not true."[23]

Indian appreciation of the liberalization tendencies within the Soviet Union took on a new dimension in the later years of our study. The aggressive nature of Communist Chinese policies meant that the Indian government had either to abandon its policy of independence in foreign affairs or to seek alternative courses. The result was that India sought to give up much of the "purity" of her independence by temporarily relying on a Moscow–Delhi axis in order to help restrain the Chinese tendencies toward expansion southward in Asia. Some military purchases were made in the Soviet Union especially, be it noted, in order better to patrol the Sino-Indian border areas. Faced by a belligerent Pakistan and a hostile China, India had to intensify her military mobilization. But drastic steps were also taken toward self-sufficiency in arms manufacture. Indeed, the establishment of an independent war machine has been a long-term goal of the Indian government. At the present, India is on the threshold. She has become the first Asian power to develop a supersonic jet and a locally manufactured rocket system. Consequently, too much cannot be read into the recent Indian moves toward the Soviet Union, for they may well turn out to be purely tactical while the original strategic design remains intact. The isolation of the Indian subcontinent was never a reality and the policy planners in New Delhi now seem to be sufficiently impressed by this fact. Projecting ourselves in the near future, we foresee no drastic revision in the independent

[22] December 15, 1955.
[23] January 1, 1956.

nature of Indian foreign policy even though India will seek limited collaboration with the Soviet Union—cautiously but steadily increasing.

INDIAN ATTITUDES TOWARD CHINA

On the surface, interstate relationships are often based upon finely cultivated myths—myths which have sometimes an uncanny way of being substituted for reality. Much of the emotional conflict that India has faced in her relationship with Communist China can be attributed to the assiduously cultivated myth of a historical record of close ties and friendship; the reality is simply that in the last thousand years few contacts have existed. In other words, declarations of friendship and historical ties, carried too far for too long a period in time, can lead to distortions of reality maps.

An example of the cultivated myth about China may be found in the following quotation from a speech by Mme. V. L. Pandit, leader of the Indian Cultural Delegation to Peking:

> We bring to this great country of China the greetings and good wishes of the government and people of another great country.
>
> My colleagues and I, who form the first official delegation from free India to New China, feel happy and proud that we should have been called upon to walk in the footsteps of those early pilgrims and pioneers, crossing the mountains and deserts of Central Asia or the perilous seas of Southeast Asia, traveling from India to China and China to India.
>
> We hope and pray that our visit may yield results as beneficent and enduring to our two countries and to humanity as those of our forefathers, who visited you in the dawn of history.[24]

There is, in retrospect, little reason to question the sincerity of these sentiments. The course of Sino-Indian relations over the last fifteen years abounds in instances where extreme consideration and many concessions were given by the government of India to the revolutionary regime of China. The speeches and statements of Pandit Nehru in the 1930s and 1940s vividly illustrated the tremendous amount of emotion that was invested in a future where India and China would collaborate for the welfare of Asia. Possibility of rivalry between the two major Asian states was either not fully grasped or deliberately suppressed. That these attitudes were carried over into the post-independence period by Prime Minister Nehru is now a matter of historical record.

The earliest reference to China in our study is the speech of Deputy

24 May 1, 1952.

Prime Minister Patel, then the right-wing rival in Nehru's cabinet, who criticized the Indian Communists for attempting to follow the Chinese example. The Indian Communists had hastily performed one of their self-intoxicating analyses and concluded that the government of India was equivalent to the KMT and that the Chinese model fitted their case. As has been stated elsewhere, the Indian government was able to crush the insurrectionary movements led by the Communists.

Domestic implications apart, however, on the international scene India was one of the first states to extend recognition to the Communist regime of China. It is interesting to note the element of respect for the former British masters evident in the justification for recognition of Communist China. S. Radhakrishnan, speaking as India's delegate to UNESCO, remarked that "the British have recognized the people's government of China out of their political wisdom. Can we not take an example from them, instead of sacrificing those who represent Chinese culture for the sake of the diminishing few in Formosa?"[25] More realistic and pertinent was the statement of Sir B. N. Rau, leader of the Indian delegation to the United Nations General Assembly meeting in Paris in 1951: "New China is a fact and, if the United Nations continues to ignore this fact, its deliberations become somewhat unreal."[26] This advocacy of the acceptance of Communist China in the comity of nations was to be pursued by the government of India, even when India's own territory was forcibly occupied by Communist Chinese armed forces.

We need to note, however, that very early in India's relationship with China conflict situations had arisen. The Indian government had been following a policy of appeasement in the expressed belief that the new, revolutionary leadership of China needed to be doubly reassured of the bona fides of the Indian government. The most dramatic illustration of Sino-Indian difficulties was the case of Tibet's occupation by Chinese forces at a time when the Tibetan delegation was in India, on its way to negotiate with the new rulers of China. In spite of repeated advice from India to settle the problem peacefully, the Chinese used armed force, thus snubbing India at a relatively early phase of the honeymoon. As is well known, India accepted the *fait accompli* and even turned over to the Chinese several of her own interests in Tibet. Prime Minister Nehru's speculations regarding possible Chinese motives are interesting to observe. "The current Chinese policy, Pandit Nehru suggested, was perhaps partly attributable to the fact that although Peking's policy might not be dictated by Moscow much of the information upon which this policy was based came through Soviet sources. For example, Moscow had re-

25 June 1, 1950.
26 November 15, 1951.

peatedly said that Anglo-American 'intrigues' in Tibet aimed at bringing that country into an anti-Communist bloc or sphere of influence. However unfounded these accusations might be, Pandit Nehru wondered whether they might not have influenced the Chinese decision to move into Tibet."[27]

These speculations aside, the Indian government chose to minimize the forcible annexation of Tibet. Nehru's rationalizing what he termed "the melancholy chapter of Tibet" led him to request members of the Indian Parliament "to view this relatively minor episode against the background of 'great historical transformations' which were shaping China and India into major world powers."[28] In other words, now that Tibet had been annexed to China much against India's wishes, he felt there was little point to remain fixated on this item of the agenda: rather, the correct course was to proceed with the cultivation of closer ties. That an event of such magnitude which involved Indian borders and interests was disposed of with such a cavalier attitude is significant to the understanding of the mentality of Prime Minister Nehru's foreign policy, especially as it pertained to Communist China.

A more intensive stage in Sino-Indian relations emerged after the Tibet invasion. Chinese good-will missions, exchanges of scholars, and cultural delegations were a common occurrence. And India's primary function appears to have been espousal of the cause of Communist China on every feasible occasion. The bases of Indian policy were enunciated by Prime Minister Nehru at a public meeting in Delhi in the presence of the Chinese Premier: "The influence of the two most populous countries in the world would be particularly great if their relations were based on friendship. That was why he was glad that the relations between India and China were harmonious and friendly."[29]

It is likely that the Prime Minister considered friendly relations with China not only beneficial for the Asian region, but also necessary from the standpoint of India's internal development. In practical terms, the main borders that India had to defend were those that adjoined West Pakistan; a military race with China would have called for accelerated defense moves all along the several thousands of miles of territory that constituted the Sino-Indian frontiers.

In pursuance of the policy of developing peaceful close relations with Communist China, India undertook to become the sponsor of the new regime. On the issue of Formosa, in Nehru's words: "India does not recognize the present regime in Formosa. There are two parties claiming

---

[27] November 1, 1950.

[28] October 1, 1954.

[29] December 1, 1956.

to be the rightful governments of Formosa and the matter must be considered on that basis."[30]

During the 1955 crisis, precipitated by moves to neutralize the Formosa Straits, India offered her good offices. In the Lok Sabha, the Prime Minister said that Chou En-lai's offer directly to negotiate with the United States was "a wholesome development which, if availed of by all concerned, could lead to an approach to peaceful settlement."[31] The Prime Minister also announced that V. K. Krishna Menon would go to Peking on Chou En-lai's invitation to continue discussions on Formosa, proposing "to avail ourselves of such opportunities as are open to us to help resolve this grave crisis."[32] In an obvious allusion to India's dispute with Pakistan over the status of Kashmir, Menon is reported to have said that just as China claimed Taiwan as part of her territory, India had faced a similar problem. But India had never used force in that situation, even to assert legal rights. Menon suggested that some people had termed such a policy "vegetarian," but he expressed confidence that it would procure favorable results.[33]

In addition to this persistent attempt by India to support Communist China on the crucial issue of Formosa, our study contains many references to the problem of the recognition of the Communist regime of China. Extensive comment emerged in a speech by Menon before the India-China Friendship Association: "Referring to the recognition of China, the Defense Minister said that India was one of the few countries to recognize the Republic of China early. She had never regretted this quick and prompt action. Some countries recognized China because of their friendship with India. . . . He expressed the hope that more nations would recognize China as it existed now. . . . If a person or nation shuts his or her eyes, that does not render the world dark, but he or she remains ignorant."[34]

Defense Minister Menon also expressed India's position on the admission of Communist China to the United Nations: "Only the wrong person sat on the chair. The admission of China is not a legal quibble, but it is of great importance. It is only a procedural matter."[35]

Indications that Sino-Indian relations might not be at their best were, however, already emerging in this same speech. While advocating recognition of Communist China, Menon noted: "We respect and at any rate

[30] February 15, 1955.
[31] May 1, 1955.
[32] May 1, 1955.
[33] February 1, 1958.
[34] February 1, 1958.
[35] February 1, 1958.

understand the prejudices and difficulties in some areas. It should not be construed as meaning that those prejudices were justified or that India was doing a favor to China."[36] Even more revealing is his discussion of the strategic factors involved in Sino-Indian relations:

> . . . the frontiers between the two countries, though it was the Himalayas, was not unsurpassable. They could come together in peace, realizing that the prosperity of one helped the prosperity of the other. China was not a problem today as some thought, but was a great country with the highest potential for ensuring peace. It would be futile to say that the two countries did not have problems as between two nations, but the two respected each other's interests and followed a policy of noninterference.[37]

It ought to be remembered that during this period India was already aware of the as yet minor Chinese incursions on her borders. The Chinese had issued maps showing large segments of Indian territory as Chinese. Repeated reminders from India to change the lines of the maps evoked no satisfactory reply from them. It is indeed a sad commentary on the policy planners in New Delhi that they failed to heed sufficiently the obvious seriousness of these matters, thereby demonstrating inability to appropriately project into the future. Only in 1960, when it was revealed to a bewildered Indian public that China was in actual control of thousands of square miles of Indian territory, did some of the complacency recede. It then became evident that national sovereignty had been treated in a rather cavalier fashion by Prime Minister Nehru and Defense Minister Menon, and for the first time sustained criticism was forthcoming in India on matters pertaining to relations with China in particular and foreign policy in general.

[36] February 1, 1958.
[37] February 1, 1958.

PART IV · THE
OUTER
     ARENA

UNITED
STATES

CHAPTER 11 · THE
ASPIRATION FOR
A PEACEFUL WORLD

At the end of World War II the American leaders, like the nation as a whole, assumed that they were undoubtedly entering a protracted period of peace. The expectation was that the Soviet Union and the United States would be working partners in the postwar arena, and that the new institution for world cooperation—the United Nations—would contribute mightily to the goal of universal security from the catastrophe of violent conflict. All this was reflected in the hasty demobilization of the American armed forces and the precipitate preoccupation of individual citizens with their return to normal peacetime life.

Yet this hope for peace was short-lived. Already toward the end of World War II it was becoming apparent that the Allied powers would clash over the constitution of governments in the wake of Nazi defeat. Whereas the Soviet Union would back the local communist cadres, the Americans and the British would seek to install relatively liberal or preferably conservative governments. Hidden from the public view, the seeds of eventual conflict were ever present. The monopoly over the atomic bomb provided the United States with a supreme confidence in its own strength.

The fundamental structure of world politics had not been changed despite the ravages of the most devastating struggle in the history of mankind. The elites of the globe were unwilling to commit themselves to an effective authoritative system of comprehensive public order. The new world covenant—the United Nations—presupposed the close and candid collaboration of Washington and Moscow in the Security Council, and left many fundamental questions unresolved. The top leaders of Moscow and Washington were separated by mutual suspicions which were exacerbated by ideological differences.

Prospects for peace were already regarded as dismal in 1950. It was becoming increasingly apparent that it was no longer possible for the United States to disengage from international political confrontation for even a brief moment in time. As the Soviet Union sought to spearhead communist movements over the globe the national security of the United States was perceived to be at stake. Not only was Europe a theater of internal conflict; colonies and former colonies were restless and agitated. By abstaining from engagement the United States could easily let large sections of the world slip, perhaps forever, into the Communist world.

By 1950 the importance of consolidating the non-Communist nation-states for the purpose of "containing" communism was a recurring theme of the principal spokesmen of the United States. This came about, not only in response to local incidents in various parts of the globe, but in reply to the propaganda offensive undertaken and executed through the Comintern against the United States. A world-wide agitation to put an end to the atomic weapon had been used to represent the United States as an aggressor nation and the chief threat to peace. One consequence of propaganda is to increase the self-consciousness of the target, and to evoke measures of defense and counteraction. When President Truman declared that no single nation alone could achieve peace, but that "together nations can build a strong defense against aggression, and combine the energy of free men everywhere in building a better future for all of us,"[1] it was abundantly evident that the United States had entered upon a long and difficult road in order to stem the Soviet advance. There were few assurances of success: unsettled world conditions provided a perfect opportunity for the Comintern to agitate, while the United States was largely dependent on diplomacy and similar organizational tools. There is a note of caution and much concern in the words of President Truman:

> The measures we are taking to bring peace to the world are necessarily imperfect. We are working to solve a problem larger and more difficult than we have ever faced. We shall inevitably experience setbacks, as well as successes, but we must continue to move forward, strongly and steadfastly, in cooperation and with other free countries. We have no other choice.[2]

The President attempted to dispel fears of American domination as alleged by Soviet propaganda: "Our program for peace is not directed against the people of any land. It is designed to bring to all people

[1] New York *Times*, May 15, 1950. (The following notes, unless otherwise indicated, are from the same source.)
[2] May 15, 1950.

the benefits of justice and freedom."[3] He underlined the fact that one of the avenues through which the United States was pledged to seek peace was the United Nations, and that America would stand by that commitment.[4]

The insecurity and uncertainty of the postwar world were reflected in Truman's remarks at a press conference upon the occasion of his descent from office. He declined to comment on a question about peace by saying he was neither "prophet nor columnist." But after the question was rephrased he suggested that "prospects were probably better than last year."[5]

General Eisenhower's assessment of the world's condition appears to have differed little from Truman's. In October 1952 he echoed a widespread feeling that "we have had a peace which is not a peace; a war which is not a war; an armistice which is not an armistice."[6] His prescription for a lasting peace included four points: "A strong America, a political leadership that earned respect, free allies throughout the world, and an active United Nations."[7]

In discussing the issue of peace the leaders of the United States made many rhetorically moving declarations. Both Truman and Eisenhower were united in giving expression to the desire and the demand for peace. They did not look upon peace as mere absence of violence; they had a positive conception of how peace could contribute to mankind. President Eisenhower phrased the point with great feeling when he voiced the hope that

> despite current difficulties with Communist governments and domestic division inflamed by "demagogues," the world would reach the point where "millions now under arms" could be "released to fruitful work" and scientists of all nations would concentrate on "the means to a plentiful life rather than the tools of sudden death."[8]

The Truman administration took the historic decision to confront Soviet expansionism, but it remained for the Eisenhower administration to coin the phrase of "positions of strength." This was the Dulles policy in words, although in actuality it is difficult to perceive how it departed from the policies of the previous administration. Hence, President Eisenhower was only repeating—not enunciating—a new policy when

---

[3] July 1, 1950.
[4] December 1, 1950.
[5] January 1, 1953.
[6] October 15, 1952.
[7] October 15, 1952.
[8] June 1, 1954.

he told a press conference in 1953 that "we must make it clear to both our friends and our enemies that we have but one intention in the world—peace—but we must speak from positions of strength to achieve this goal."[9]

The "positions of strength" formulation was later expanded to include Secretary of State Dulles's theory of "brinkmanship." This much-maligned theory held that there were occasions in international relations when calculated risks were necessary, and that the Eisenhower administration in particular would follow policies which at times might be construed as risking total war. What was essentially an explanation of diplomacy in action was stigmatized by many of the opposition as a callous and careless danger to world peace. Representative of such opposition was Adlai Stevenson, who declared: "I don't consider the art of diplomacy one in which we should repeatedly be led to the brink of war. The art of diplomacy, especially in this atomic age, must lead to peace, not war or the brink of war."[10] Vice President Nixon sought to salvage Dulles from the downpour of criticism. He explained "brinkmanship" and its relation to peace in the following manner: "The test of a foreign policy is its ability to keep the peace without surrendering any territory or any principle. And that great fact about the Eisenhower–Dulles foreign policy will stand out long after the tempest in a teapot over the expression [brink of war] is forgotten."[11]

The brinkmanship episode is instructive in many ways, particularly in the light that it shed on the task of the American elite in modernizing the nation's ideology as it refers to foreign policy. In a rather rare burst of pedagogical zeal the Secretary of State had talked about the requirements of effective strategy in the management of public policy toward other nations in a divided world. Dulles echoed a commonplace to students and practitioners of diplomacy when he said that diplomacy must be correlated in time with the other instruments of national policy, especially military strength. But by uttering the word "brink" he unfortunately employed an anxiety-arousing term that called up a swarm of fearful fantasies. Dulles's brief seminar on flexible strategy was shouted down by the class. The columns of the *Times* were full of hortatory ambiguities of the conventional kind, such as the deft symbol formation offered by Adlai Stevenson: "Leaders must lead where the issue is mankind's survival, and there can be no lasting world until a lasting peace is achieved."[12]

Such exhortations were the rule rather than the exception. Even John

9 October 1, 1953.
10 January 15, 1956.
11 January 15, 1956.
12 October 15, 1956.

Foster Dulles was well accustomed to voicing such ringing truisms, as he did when he declared, "The path toward peace is a broad path, open to all who wish to join in efforts to protect mankind from the dark consequences of another war."[13]

Such sermonizing is reminiscent of the Indian elite. The moral fervor and the appeal to righteousness are apparently as congenial to the American mind as they are to the Indian. In the American case the rhetoric of peace was not, as a rule, explicitly connected with ideological categories which would have drawn public attention to some of the most fundamental factors upon which peace—and the success of America's professed goals in foreign policy—depended. There were ample occasions for some of these fundamental conditions to have been articulated in the course of public statements by the elite. These opportunities were rarely grasped, especially in the early years of our survey. Consider, for instance, General Gruenther's statement in July 1953. He declared that, of course, Europeans were listening to the Soviet "peace offensive" because "that is what they want to hear . . . but they haven't swallowed it yet." But why did the Soviet peace appeal appear so seductive? Why was it not possible for American propaganda to have achieved the degree of receptivity which had been attributed to Soviet appeals? Such questions were seldom asked in elite discussions—at least in public.

[13] October 15, 1953.

ON THE SOVIET UNION
AND COMMUNISM

THE IMAGE OF THE SOVIET UNION

The principal stumbling block to the consolidation of a peaceful world—according to the perspectives of the American elite—was the Soviet Union. By 1950 the outlook of the public figures quoted in the New York *Times* had hardened, a process that had carried them from outspoken admiration of the Soviet Union during the anti-Nazi war to reproachful disenchantment. For a hard core of Americans, perhaps 15 percent, an anti-Soviet attitude had persisted even during the years of coalition. For a majority of American leaders an anti-Soviet outlook was a resumption of perspectives which had been conventional before 1941. By the early fifties the Soviet elite was perceived as treacherous, brutal, and ungrateful; hence, an appropriate object of rancor.

A sense of hurt, annoyance, and bitterness clearly permeates the comments revealed by our study. Closely allied to these sentiments were feelings of fear and anger. Governor Dewey struck an appropriate ideological note when he declared that "so long as Soviet Russia has slave labor and a totalitarian government, none of the free people in the world are safe."[1] He seemed to indicate that the conflict between the United States and the Soviet Union, which by now had involved most of the globe, could not be limited to specific and concrete situations resolvable through negotiation and concession. Rather, it was presented in terms of an irreconcilable conflict over goals and institu-

[1] New York *Times*, October 1, 1950. (The following notes, unless otherwise indicated, are from the same source.)

tions. Hence, traditional modes of interstate behavior were regarded as inapplicable to the Soviet Union. The Soviet Union waged unconventional political warfare, and relied on an international ideological apparatus which appeared to be remarkably successful, thus contributing to American frustrations.

Some sense of the scale of differences between ordinary interstate relations and the relations between the United States and the Soviet Union can be obtained by noting how President Truman characterized the Russians. Comparing them to the Barbary Coast pirates whom Jefferson had suppressed, he said that "now, as then, there is no room for piracy in a free world."[2] Such language suggested that the United States was quite likely to contemplate extreme measures to cope with the Soviet threat.

The American leadership searched for ways to penetrate the enigma of the Russians. The ideological orientation of the United States did not provide many intellectual tools for this purpose. Seemingly aware of this, Speaker Sam Rayburn remarked that "nobody can penetrate the workings of a dictator's mind nor pierce the stony heart of people who deny liberty and destroy democracy wherever they find it in the world."[3] American ideology did give credence to mechanisms popularized from psychology; and thus President Truman suggested that the real trouble with the Russians was "that they are still suffering from a complex of fear and inferiority where we are concerned."[4] In the same terms, it might have been said that the United States suffered from a superiority complex toward the Russians.

The degree of American hostility may be illustrated by noting some relatively extreme though not altogether untypical American reactions. Representative John E. Lyle, Jr., Democrat of Texas, in discussing the Japanese Peace Treaty saw fit to refer to the Soviet regime as "that gang of no-good Russian hoodlums."[5] Representative Pat Sutton, Democrat of Tennessee, utilizing the picturesque language of domestic American politics, suggested that "we should tell Russia to go straight to hell, and if they don't go there, we should send them."[6] Were such language used in referring to an allied state or to a nonaligned country, there is little doubt that the official elite would intervene with expressions of regret, attempting to explain that the public pronouncements of Congressional leaders do not necessarily reflect official policy. The fact that

[2] April 15, 1951.
[3] April 1, 1950.
[4] February 15, 1950.
[5] August 15, 1951.
[6] April 1, 1950.

such violent language was employed not only by Congressional leaders but also by the President of the United States should be sufficient to indicate the nature of American attitudes in the early fifties. Just as President Truman had compared the Russians to pirates, President Eisenhower sought to link the Soviet elite with the tyrants of history, without drawing distinctions among them. He spoke of the Russians' "uncontrolled ruthlessness of unbridled ambition," and, recalling the names of Genghis Khan, Napoleon, Mussolini, and Hitler, he warned "it is well to remember what happened to the dictators of the past."[7]

President Eisenhower evoked the image of an ordered and progressive world that could result for mankind were it not for the willfulness of the Soviet leadership: "Surely, even the men in the Kremlin must realize that before all mankind now lies a grand prospect of a far better life for everyone."[8] There is a ring of manifest destiny, of inevitableness in President Eisenhower's words:

> But so long as relatively few men—"only a handful in Russia
> itself"—must continue to thwart the will of hundreds of millions
> of people for knowledge and peace . . . the United States must be
> strong in weapons and in heart and mind against Communist
> tactics to exploit every difference of view among independent na-
> tions.[9]

There was a tendency for the American elite to portray the Soviet Union in terms that simultaneously evoked an image of a gangster empire and one of an astute nation armed with an almost magically successful ideology.

The accession to power by the Communists in China had created a feeling akin to panic in some American circles. It led Governor Dewey to speculate about a specter of Asiatic hordes, at the bidding of the Soviet Union, sweeping down into North America: "If Alaska should fall, it is difficult to be hopeful about our future. The enemy would then have air and land bases for the hordes of Asia on the North American continent."[10] This terrifying vision assumed that the new regime in China was, and would remain, a satellite of the Soviet Union.

Secretary of State Marshall lent credence to the fact that Governor Dewey's vision of a satellite China was perhaps also shared by official Washington, for Marshall agreed that "the Soviet Union had made what amounted to a 'conquest' of China."[11]

A different view of the might and the intentions of the Soviet Union

[7] May 15, 1954.
[8] June 1, 1954.
[9] June 1, 1954.
[10] August 1, 1950.
[11] May 15, 1951.

was provided by Senator Robert A. Taft, who advocated direct bombing of the Chinese mainland because he felt the Soviet Union was not willing to challenge the United States to an open conflict over this issue. Obviously ignoring the Sino-Soviet mutual defense treaty, Taft suggested that only where Russia was *directly* affected would she go to war, and that in the case of China and the satellites, Russia would not accept the American challenge. He asserted: "I think the Russians may bring on a third world war if they see something like invasion of Russia, but certainly the bombing of Manchurian bases or the use of Chiang's troops is nothing that threatens even remotely any invasion of Russian territory."[12]

Latent racism in the American ideological system had clearly hindered its capacity to distinguish the difference between races as biological entities and ethnic groups as bearers of distinctive cultures. The historical legacy of confusion was revealed when symbols of adverse reference to Soviet leadership were generalized to the people as a whole. The hordes of "Mongols" or "Asiatics"—like the "Huns" referred to incessantly in World War I—were often endowed with characteristics which were imputed to genes rather than to the processes of socialization.

It would be easy to exaggerate the prominence of racist allusions, however. Many of the negative references to the "Russian" people emphasized their "peasantness," which put the accent on the impact of social role rather than alleged biological predispositions. Millions of "Slavs" had come to the United States and merged uneventfully with the general population; and their presence and record provided a prophylaxis against the cruder forms of racist ideology in national politics. The "Asiatics," however, were less numerous, more conspicuous, and more vulnerable.

The principal theme of elite statements about the Soviet leadership was its deceitful malevolence against the freedom ideal and against the United States as the bulwark of a free world. In 1950, we find Governor Dewey stating that Americans should "get rid of the stupid idea that we can sit down and do business with Stalin while we are weak and he is strong."[13] And in 1952, Secretary of State Dean Acheson, referring to "bellicose" statements by Deputy Prime Minister Walter Ulbricht of East Germany, and Soviet threats against West Berlin, asserted that those actions "seem to us to be the other side of the peace and unity coin which is being put forward in such a determined way by the Soviet-Communist side."[14] Five years later the theme regarding Soviet deceit had still not receded. Henry Cabot Lodge listed as one of the

[12] May 1, 1951.
[13] December 15, 1950.
[14] May 15, 1952.

major accomplishments of the United Nations session "stripping away the sham and insincerity of the Soviet war scare that the United States was masterminding a threat to the security" of nations.[15]

There is little doubt that until 1953 the contempt for the Soviet Union and a belittling of her threatening tactics were accompanied by a self-satisfied assessment of American military capabilities. Despite occasional assertions of an alarmist character, the technological superiority of the United States was taken for granted. General Omar Bradley testified that "he did not believe that Russia would start a war 'in the near future,' unless she found the United States so weakened as to invite an attack."[16] The American elite seemed incapable of conceiving that an allegedly immoral, underdeveloped country such as the Soviet Union could ever develop military power comparable to that of the United States. Bernard Baruch, for instance, expressed confidence that Soviet aggression had thus far been prevented not only because the United States possessed the atomic bomb, but also because America produced "nearly as many airplanes, tanks, guns, and other war matériel as the rest of the world combined." Baruch could not imagine Russia being "a great land power, a great naval power, a great air power, a great atomic power, all at the same time. We know how difficult and expensive it is for this country to maintain our defense establishment, and Russia has infinitely less resources at her command."[17]

It was largely because of indulging in reassuring self-delusions of this type that the American elite experienced a rude shock when Russia entered the ranks of the hydrogen-bomb powers. As if there had been no prior intimation from intelligence sources of such a possibility, President Eisenhower reacted with the statement that "the knowledge that the Russians have the bomb is causing every official in the government more prayerful study than any other recent development."[18] He assured the American people that there would be an even more determined effort to learn what the intentions of the Soviet government and "associated countries" were. This appears to have been the beginning of a far more respectful American assessment of Soviet capabilities and potential.

There also began to develop, especially after the Stalin era, an unconcealed admiration for the diplomatic tactics of the Soviet Union. Not unexpectedly, American military leaders chided the civilian elite about the greater strength which they felt the Soviets possessed in the fields of diplomacy and propaganda. In this way, the unsatisfactory

15 December 15, 1957.
16 April 15, 1950.
17 April 1, 1950.
18 October 1, 1953.

components of the United States position were imputed to civilian authorities, who were most directly responsible for these instruments of national policy. Many well-established stereotypes aided and abetted such assertions. The idea that the wily foreigner can make a "sucker" out of American diplomats is widespread. Consider, for instance, Admiral Radford, chairman of the Joint Chiefs of Staff, who testified before the Senate that in political and diplomatic fields "we have to worry. . . . We should not be complacent. We have a great deal to do."[19] In his assessment, the admiral received support from congressmen, such as Senator Mike Mansfield, who summoned the country to develop greater flexibility in its diplomacy, especially with respect to the use of foreign aid as a weapon in the cold war. Mansfield went so far as to imply that America might take a lesson from the Soviets regarding diplomacy. As he noted, "one of the reasons for the success of Soviet diplomacy is that its leaders are able to move on extremely short notice and to achieve their ends because of flexibility."[20]

It was especially after Stalin's death that the American elite, suspiciously and hesitatingly, began to introduce some measure of flexibility in its attitudes and policies toward the Soviet Union. As a matter of party tactics the Eisenhower administration had an advantage in claiming that a lessening in the Soviet Union's aggressive proclivities could be attributed to its own policies. This would raise the prestige of the administration before the public and the Congress, and bolster the ego of the officials concerned. President Eisenhower claimed that it was the United States which had largely nullified the Soviet Union's "reliance upon force and threat of force."[21] And Secretary of State Dulles, noting that it was "encouraging" and an "immense relief" that Russia was lessening her stress on violence, hastened to add that this change was traceable not to "any spiritual conversion," but rather to "the free-world network of security treaties, sustained by the United States' foreign-aid programs and mobile striking power," all of which had made Russian violence unprofitable.[22]

The American elite refrained from pinpointing the nature of any potential or manifest shifts in Soviet policy. One explanation of this may be that American leaders were apprehensive about weakening their total position in dealing with the Soviet Union by encouraging a premature change in public expectations. There was always the very real possibility that the Soviet leadership might once again change and revert to Stalinist policies. As Eisenhower suggested, proof of the Soviet

[19] May 15, 1956.
[20] January 15, 1956.
[21] June 1, 1956.
[22] May 1, 1956.

Union's changes with respect to the use of force was the fact that it was now utilizing "different kinds of influence."[23] There is continuing evidence that the Soviet Union was approached as an adversary who could not be trusted and hence must always be viewed with the utmost suspicion, and often an explicitly "tough" attitude. Discussing a possible forthcoming meeting with Russian representatives, Dulles announced his approach:

> We welcome opportunities to settle specific disputes between us; to end the race in armament, and to reduce the risks of war. But let me also assure you of this. We do not look on the conference table as a place where we surrender our principles, but rather as a place for making our principles prevail. That is our resolve—a resolve which I am confident is backed by the Congress and by the American people.[24]

This determined attitude was not a temporary expedient but a relatively stabilized result of experiences in dealing with the Soviet Union. The apparent relaxation of Soviet forward policies was not regarded as sufficient to call for any changes in American attitudes. Secretary of State Dulles clearly pronounced his emphatic view that the Western alliance would be "neither intimidated nor lulled into a false sense of security by the smiling face Moscow recently had been presenting to the world."[25]

In spite of this extravagantly rigid attitude, however, by 1956 Secretary of State Dulles did publicly consider in detail the possibility of peaceful cooperation. The United States leadership was beginning to appear more relaxed in response to altered Soviet attitudes, and more willing than previously to lend constructive support to moves that promised to serve the cause of peace by agreement, long the preferred though often obscured objective of declared policy. The secretary's remarks were relatively flexible: "We believe that if conditions can be created so that neither the Soviet Union nor ourselves feel in danger of a crippling surprise attack then potential power can to some extent replace actual force in being, and that would open the way to some substantial limitation of armament."[26] Dulles also conceded that a disarmament agreement could serve not only American interests but also the national interests of the Soviet Union: the Russians would have more resources with which to aid underdeveloped countries, as well as raise their own people's standard of living.

It is significant that about this time the American elite began to

23 June 1, 1956.
24 December 1, 1953.
25 December 15, 1954.
26 March 1, 1956.

express its cognizance of the fact that under the new Soviet leaders there were hints of changes in domestic policies, including greater stress upon a consumer-oriented economy. The most authoritative comment on such changes came from President Eisenhower in June 1956. He suggested that the new leaders were "more concerned with development of consumer goods, more concerned with the status and the frame of mind of the people." He also informed the American people that it was now possible for a Russian laborer to change his job without official permission, and this fact could be interpreted to mean "progress."[27]

During the post-Stalin era, internal tensions which had been existing within the Soviet bloc made themselves manifest. The disclosure by Khrushchev of the ruthless measures adopted by Stalin also contributed mightily to the stresses within the Communist movement everywhere. Howard Fast's remarks capture the mood of disillusionment: "I was tried and convicted in 1946 under circumstances that made a mockery of our pretensions of justice here. But while that was happening, I was consoled by the belief that in the Soviet Union a person could receive justice. I can no longer believe this."[28]

He continued:

> I knew little about anti-Semitism in the Soviet Union before the Khrushchev speech. That little troubled me, but I repressed my doubts. Then the article appeared in the *Folksstimme* last spring telling what had actually happened. It was not an easy thing to live with. . . . It was incredible and unbelievable to me that Khrushchev did not end his speech with a promise of the reforms needed to guarantee that Stalin's crimes will not be repeated, reforms such as an end to capital punishment, trial by jury, and habeas corpus. Without these reforms one can make neither sense nor reason of the speech itself.[29]

The post-Stalinist leadership of the Soviet world occasionally succeeded in taking initiatives that discomfited many Americans, causing them to reflect on why they failed to discern the "mystery" of Russian propaganda successes. Senator Bourke Hickenlooper termed the Soviet Union's announcement that it had suspended nuclear testing as "just a propaganda move." But others, such as Liberal Democratic leader Senator Theodore Green, engaged in painful self-criticism, as well as unabashed wonder at the Soviet Union's unexpected talents: "The fact still remains that the announcement will be welcomed generally throughout the world. The fact still remains that we are once again thrown on

[27] June 1, 1956.

[28] February 1, 1957.

[29] February 1, 1957. The *Folksstimme* is a Yiddish-language Communist newspaper published in Poland.

the defensive. The fact still remains that our own policy has permitted the initiative for peace once again to pass to the Soviet Union."[30] Speaker Sam Rayburn similarly lamented what he considered the inability of his country to score propaganda triumphs: "On the talk of the Summit and the talk of stopping explosions of these bombs, Russia has beaten us on propaganda all around the world."[31]

In general, looking back over the changing images of the self and of the Soviet Union during the fifties, we note the "rootless" quality of those conceptions. The "good guy" versus the "bad guy" was the dominant antithesis; and there was little to call attention to the groups within the Soviet world, for instance, who were covertly or overtly acting upon one another to affect public policy. Evidently the ideology of yesterday proved sufficient to provide a stable way of describing, projecting, and interpreting change.

THE IMAGE OF COMMUNISM

References to the Soviet Russians were interlarded, naturally, with allusions to Communists and communism. The policy issues facing the United States were perceived in broader terms than a defense of the nation against a polar opposite in actual or potential strength. It was taken for granted that ideological issues were included and that these contradictions were of momentous importance for the future of American security and of all institutions of a free society.

The comments regarding world communism contained in our study emanated exclusively from top elite elements. Did this mean that communism as an international ideology was felt to be so serious or complicated that an elite newspaper did not feel justified in giving attention to comment by middle and lower-level sources? We pose this question because there is no dearth of comment by the middle and lower elites upon communism inside the United States.

General MacArthur saw communism as roaming the earth to crush human freedom.[32] Governor Dewey appeared to share this view. Although he confessed ignorance about the "timetable of world communism," he did profess to know that it "obviously included 'invasion by satellite nations from Bulgaria through Greece to the Mediterranean,' an invasion of Yugoslavia . . . as well as the conquest of Tibet, Indo-China, and ultimately all Asia."[33] At the same time, Governor Dewey declared: "The grand goal of communism, short of absolute world

[30] April 1, 1958.
[31] April 1, 1958.
[32] January 1, 1950.
[33] August 1, 1950.

domination, is winning the industrial capacity of Germany and Japan, which would free Russia from fear of American productive capacity."[34]

All significant figures are united in the perception that world communism is intent upon extinguishing the American identity. The world communist movement is presented as the enemy from which no quarter is to be expected or given. President Truman asserted that every sacred and worthy secular value is challenged and denied, "for the Communist policy feeds upon suspicion and hate and disunity. And the Communists are doing their best to break down the strength of the free nations of the world, in an effort to bring more people under the domination of their godless creed."[35]

The enemy, then, is aggressive, militant, determined, and has no scruples whatsoever. Besides this, the enemy is also disturbingly successful. These results are said to be achieved by appealing to the darker impulses of man, and by the ruthless use of conspiratorial methods to destroy individuals and nations. Such a movement of the godless implies that world politics is actually a temporal manifestation of the cosmic struggle between the forces of good and evil.

President Truman, addressing a rally of Boy Scouts, remarked in a melancholy fashion:

> The great tragedy of our times is that there are movements in the world that deny this fundamental ideal of human brotherhood. These movements have devoted themselves to preaching distrust between the nations. They have made a religion of hate. They have tried to turn the peoples of the earth against one another to create a gulf between different peoples that fellowship can not bridge.[36]

President Truman makes no reference to the fact that the Communist movement was ostensibly launched in order to bring about an era of human brotherhood. When the President suggested that the Communists were spreading distrust among the nations of the world, he made no reference to the fact that Communist ideology professed to bring about ultimate harmony among all nations. Such an *interpretation* applies a criterion of deeds rather than words, a method which is strikingly parallel to the Communist allegation that American democratic claims were sham, and that the United States was opposed to peace and unity, since it kept world tension alive.

There is little acknowledgment of the manifest content of the opponent's doctrine, but there are emphatic assertions about particular values and institutions. As we noted in dealing with America's self

[34] August 1, 1950.
[35] May 15, 1950.
[36] July 1, 1950.

image, religion and religiosity are highly treasured values of the American elite. It should thus not be surprising that President Truman indicted the Communist movement's treatment of youth in these terms:

> They are being taught to place the state above the obligations of family life, they are being brought to despise religion and to believe that God does not exist, they are being made into tools of power politics, and their masters will not hesitate to sacrifice their lives if that will advance the cause of Communist imperialism.[37]

And General Eisenhower observed: "What is our battle against communism if it is not a fight between anti-God and a belief in the Almighty? Communists know this. They have to eliminate God from their system. When God comes in, communism has to go."[38] We note in passing that General Eisenhower did not portray the Communist movement simply as antichrist, as might have been done not many years ago. By referring to the Communists as anti-God, he is adapting to the blurred lines between the various religious sects in the United States. The implication is that it doesn't matter which religion one professes so long as one professes.

Eisenhower also attacked the Communists as anti-democratic: "The theory of communism is that free men cannot govern themselves. It holds that we are too torn apart; we are too selfish; we are too paralyzed by strikes and lockouts and all kinds of economic strain."[39]

The striking fact about these images of world communism is that no allowance was made for the possibility that the elites of the Communist world might redefine their doctrine in ways that would reduce the gap between performance and verbal aspiration. No emphasis was given in these assertions to the possibility of a divided Communist camp, some of whose members might work closely with non-Communist states against Communist rivals. The preferred approach was dogmatic and hence final; it did not modernize the ideology of the nation by emphasizing an explicit strategy of hope that a versatile, determined, and persistent policy could modify the equilibrium of forces among Communists.

[37] July 1, 1950.
[38] September 15, 1952.
[39] June 15, 1952.

CHAPTER 13 · WEAPONS: ARMS ACCUMULATION AND ARMS REDUCTION

THE PROSPECT OF WORLD WAR III

The expectations of a peaceful epoch and of substantial progress toward permanent security were contradicted by another set of expectations which we have briefly reviewed—the image of the Soviet Union and of international communism. If conflicts were "inevitable," World War III was highly probable unless the elite of the United States was to capitulate to the enemy. And this, of course, was never discussed—it was out of the question. But if World War III was coming, the policy question was simplified. Should the United States precipitate World War III while it held an atomic advantage? It was almost impossible for this alternative to receive rational discussion in view of the mood of postwar America and the vigor of the traditional ideology which favored defensive, not offensive, war, and which had predisposed against initiating a world war in the name of "prevention."

Saber-rattling on the part of the military is missing from our study. Similarly, with a few exceptions, the civilian elite whose comments appeared newsworthy to the New York *Times* was restrained in its commentary on the possibility of World War III. The most drastic speculations were made by a member of the political elite and not by the generals. The speculations of Governor Dewey ran as follows:

> It is believed that the Soviet could easily conduct what is called "Operation Hot Springs"—that is, sending planes to bomb the great production plants and cities of the entire country, then having

their pilots bail out and spend the rest of the war comfortably as prisoners of war at Hot Springs. Needless to say, we could not make similar plans with any confidence that our pilots would be similarly treated.[1]

Such detailed fantasy strategy and hint of World War III and the consequent consideration of preventive strikes at the enemy are quite rare in American elite comment. Dewey went on to discuss his concern regarding the imminent possibility of America being a subject of surprise attack by the Soviet Union. As he noted: "We are living in times of the gravest national tension, when aggressive Soviet Communist imperialism may launch an attack on the free world at any point in any time. . . . In the event of World War III, every person everywhere in the world will be in the front lines."[2]

In contrast, General Marshall advised a state of readiness, not of all-out mobilization: "I would feel very much concerned if we plunge into an all-out wartime mobilization until we clearly have to do it."[3]

The United States enjoyed comparative military advantage over the Soviet Union for at least five years after the end of World War II. For some years the United States had a total monopoly over nuclear weapons. As we know, the United States did not utilize this superiority to score a military victory over the Communist bloc of states. This factor, in retrospect, has furnished convincing proof of the desire on the part of the American political leadership to contain the Communist world revolution by methods short of war. But the loss of superiority is a painful realization at any time, especially to the military. What this meant for the United States was tersely evaluated by General Curtis LeMay: "Five years ago the United States could have won a war with the Soviet Union without 'comparatively serious damage.' The United States could even now win a war, but 'we are not capable of winning it without this country receiving very serious damage.' "[4]

The expectation of war filtered through the comments of Assistant Secretary of Defense John A. Hannah. Referring to a new manpower plan, he declared that "the whole thing is geared to the day of active war with the Soviet Union. . . . Everyone up to the President agrees that we must have an effective reserve to meet the requirements of war with the Soviets. And that is the only war that counts."[5]

[1] New York *Times*, August 1, 1950. (The following notes, unless otherwise indicated, are from the same source.)

[2] April 15, 1951.

[3] December 15, 1950.

[4] May 1, 1956.

[5] August 1, 1954.

During 1952, the United States launched two powerful vessels which added great strength to its already formidable navy. It warned the enemy that these weapons would bring disaster to him in case he provoked the United States. On the other hand, the United States stressed its peaceful intentions, and the great reluctance with which it would utilize these weapons.

The first occasion was the launching of the *Nautilus* submarine. President Harry Truman remarked that the United States was left no choice but to employ the *Nautilus* as "an answer to the threat of aggression in the world." He said: "I pray that this ship, this first atomic submarine, will never have an enemy to fight. I hope she will be tied up someday as an historic relic of a threat of war long passed."[6] A month later, at the time of the laying of the keel of the U.S.S. *Forrestal*, Deputy Secretary of Defense William C. Foster cautioned that "those misguided leaders of enslaved peoples who may contemplate aggression weigh well the fact that not even in their innermost lairs can they escape the devastating force of this mighty weapon."[7] Foster's note of America's peaceful intentions followed: "It is our fervent hope that this carrier will prove an added deterrent to the outbreak of another world war. Though a man-of-war, we pray that it will be a factor of peace for all free men."[8]

The prospects of World War III were only occasionally referred to directly, and usually in the context of some specific policy question. The discussion among American leaders did display variations in tactical position. The conservative element tended to stress "toughness." The late Senator Robert A. Taft said:

> As far as preventing the war, the President in his speech says that we prevented World War III by moving against the first aggressor to break the peace since the Second World War. And then he says now we prevent World War III by not punishing the aggressor when the aggressor is bigger.[9]

This is representative of that section of the American elite which placed much store on dispatching the Marines wherever vital interests were at stake. Senator Taft's irritation at the decision by President Truman not to engage in hostilities inside China is reflective of the isolationist position which, when aroused, seeks quick military solutions. The leadership of the later fifties was increasingly sensitive to the cost of rash and

6 June 15, 1952.
7 July 15, 1952.
8 July 15, 1952.
9 May 1, 1951.

open conflict. More representative of latter-day Republican conservatism was President Eisenhower's observation that "the only possible tragedy greater than winning a war would be losing a war, and in all our calculations from now on, war should be excluded."[10]

Rather than a direct total war, limited engagements were envisioned in various regions of the world. Speaker Sam Rayburn expressed a fear—deeply pervasive but little remarked upon—that World War III might start inadvertently, "that somebody in Washington is going to try to do something sensational without judgment and bring us to the catastrophe of World War III."[11] But public comment did not dwell on the danger of "the great alert" because it seemed to serve no useful purpose. Scant references were made to the increasing mechanization of modern weapons, the use of remote-control devices, and possible error in human judgment.

Obviously, it was more advantageous in promoting specific programs to justify them as war-prevention measures, as did Averell Harriman in his capacity as the director of the Mutual Security Agency. Testifying before the Senate, he declared that if the United States pressed forward with its current policies through the Mutual Security Program, then "we can prevent World War III."[12]

Unmistakably, there existed a sense of constant tension as regarded the prospects of war and peace. Somewhat contradictory evaluations tended to cancel out, and there were fever charts at every stage. An example is Admiral Radford who noted in 1957 that "there was 'a decidedly lesser chance of a war that we may get into—a big or little war,' than was indicated when he became chairman."[13]

The leadership of the United States succeeded in adapting to the climate of perpetual tension without much panic or extremism. The elite recognized the worst that could happen, but it professed confidence that the worst could be avoided by sound policy. From time to time it was tactically expedient to vary the mixture of alarm and reassurance, depending upon the immediate policy proposals which were in controversy.

COLD WAR STRATEGIES

Among the adaptations required of American leadership was a comprehensive conception of cold war, including the strategies appropriate

[10] October 1, 1958.
[11] February 15, 1953.
[12] March 15, 1952.
[13] August 15, 1957.

to its distinctive features. The traditional ideology of the United States included a conception of minimum involvement with the contending powers of Europe. George Washington's Farewell Address came reverberating down the years, receiving a new lease on life whenever elite elements in the nation favored a policy of abstention from joint action with other nations in foreign affairs. An ideological bias was undoubtedly created in favor of "going it alone"; hence the advocates of any form of continuing coalition with foreign powers were confronted by a presumption against their policies.

The advocates of any policy of "alliance," or continuing cooperation on major matters of security, always found it necessary to distinguish between the overriding goals of American policy and the problem of choosing the strategic option best adapted to the maximization of national goals. "National defense" or "national security" were symbols of reference to the goals of the American commonwealth which no one acting in good faith could deny. It was necessary to show that a specific policy proposal to cooperate with an ally was true to the "spirit" of the policy of "no entangling alliance," a verbal device that distinguished between the value goals and the strategies of public policy. In this way it was often possible to create an intellectual and moral conflict in the personalities of individual elite members. Part of the personality was peremptorily in favor of "no entangling alliances," while another part was equally in favor of "national security." In the resulting campaign the conflicted individual might re-examine the present dimensions and future prospects of the international situation, and arrive at a conclusion which at first he had been loath to accept.

As the United States moved more actively into world politics toward the end of the nineteenth century, after the settlement of the Western states, a series of crisis situations called for ever more radical departures from the "no-alliance" policy. During the period of controversy prior to America's participation in World War II the "isolationist" symbol was given great prominence. When the United States joined the war, as Eisenhower noted in retrospect, "isolationism was dead."[14] At least it became necessary for the advocates of minimum involvement with foreign affairs to reverse the traditional tactic of political controversy in the United States and to declare that they were not isolationists.

A striking example of the new tactic was provided by former President Herbert Hoover who expounded the strategy of Fortress America. Herbert Hoover's proposal was no simple act of piety toward the tradition of "no entangling alliances." He insisted that the national

[14] November 1, 1952.

security of the United States—the value goal—was best protected against Soviet imperialism by developing the Western Hemisphere. The former President did not receive much support. His critics, such as Senator Douglas, for example, declared that to follow the course advocated by former President Herbert Hoover would mean that the United States would have to abandon its strategic bases of operation against the enemy. In his words, Hoover's theory implied that communism "would take over all of Asia and of Europe and then all of Africa and we would be left alone, with the exception, perhaps, of the northern part of South America. . . . Therefore when the ultimate struggle came, we would be alone with our backs to the wall."[15] The director of Mutual Security, Averell Harriman, spoke for the administration when he informed the Senate of the implications of former President Hoover's strategy:

> I don't believe this country can survive if the sources of vital war matériels are in the hands of unfriendly people who are determined to destroy us.
> We could not fight a war on the Fortress America theory. We would find ourselves eventually in the position of the Soviet satellites and have to send missions to Moscow to ask for matériels.[16]

The sense of urgency led other Republican spokesmen to advocate policies of alliances and encirclement of the adversary. In 1950, Governor Dewey emitted his dire warning: "The hour is very late—I do not know how late. Whether we still have a day or a year or two years, not a second should be lost. Our government, our people, the United Nations, and the spokesmen of the free world must rally now."[17]

How closely the two political parties were on the manner in which the cold war was to be waged becomes clear from a consideration of the statements made by Dean Acheson and Governor Dewey, delivered within a few weeks of each other. On the resolve to defend the interests of the United States there was, of course, no debate. Acheson observed that "we have power to retaliate against any aggressor who attacks us or our friends, and that power cannot be overlooked. We expect to make ourselves respected and deter aggression."[18] Dewey's position was expressed in remarks which bear a striking resemblance to those of Dean Acheson's. In Dewey's analysis, "the only thing that will stop attack is the sure knowledge that it will be met successfully with total defense and overwhelming counterattack."[19]

[15] January 15, 1951.
[16] March 15, 1952.
[17] December 15, 1950.
[18] January 1, 1951.
[19] April 15, 1951.

The evidence shows that the American elite was largely united in support of a policy of world-wide vigilance and precaution designed to check the expansion of the Soviet Union and of communism. The excerpts have faithfully indicated the stress laid upon the role of the military instrument in national policy. But the dynamic world situation could not be mastered by relying too exclusively on weapons. The Soviet elite was accustomed to the coordinated use of every policy instrument, and the active leaders of the United States became conscious of the advantages of perfecting a grand strategy in which the military instrument would be timed in harmony with diplomacy, economic measures, and propaganda. It was no novelty to use each instrumentality; the innovation resided in the application of the principle of contextuality. According to this principle the goals of national policy were to be optimized by discovering the best combination of strategies under all contingencies.

In a comparatively rare appraisal of national policy Secretary of State Dean Acheson described four sources of American strength: first, "the tremendous source of strength that our cause is right. We are on the side of freedom and on the side of the great spiritual values which have created our country." Second, "We have friends who believe in the same values that we believe." Third, both the United States and its friends possessed "the greatest industrial capacity in the world." And finally, the United States possessed not merely potential strength, but a "first-class" army, navy, and air force.[20]

In the following chapters we review the discussion of the four instruments of national policy which appeared in the New York *Times* during the fifties.

APPRAISALS OF THE MILITARY INSTRUMENT

We have commented upon the civilian-mindedness of Americans, which historically had been expressed in the willingness to improvise when war crises arose, and to return as rapidly as possible to civilian pursuits when active combat was terminated. This traditional predisposition reasserted itself immediately at the close of World War II; and it was with exasperation that Americans discovered the advisability of engaging in an arms race with the Russians. The comfortable assumption of nuclear superiority was challenged at this time, and the Korean War provided a dramatic test of the willingness of American leadership to go "all out." Pressure in all directions was on the increase, ranging from those who demanded the unfettered use of atomic weapons in

[20] January 1, 1951.

Korea to those who insisted that military instruments must be drastically underemphasized in a flexible, realistic policy.

An indication of the mood of Americans, as perceived by top elite members, was provided by President Eisenhower upon his return from Korea. He surmised that American forces there were unlike the World War II Army since they were not a "wisecracking force," and unlike their World War I predecessors since they were not a "singing army." The men were "doing a serious job without whining or complaining."[21] Violence and warfare had always been a romantic affair in American society and had never been approached with dread. If Eisenhower's analysis was accurate, it marked a trend toward matter-of-fact realism.

President Truman was responding to impatient critics when, with characteristic bluntness, he said: "I think the efforts that are being made to sell the American people on the idea that there is some cut-rate, bargain-counter route to national security are very dangerous."[22]

Secretary of State Acheson criticized these "salesmen" in a similar manner. He observed that there was "a tendency to feel that the more rapidly we appropriate billions and the more rapidly men are called into service, the safer we will be." He said: "I do not think the solution is so simple. We must not become involved by impatience or ignorance in an ill-considered overnight expansion which would smother well-considered methods and leave us in a dilemma of confused results, half-baked and fatally unbalanced."[23] Here, as in other sectors of life, we note a predisposition among Americans to approach issues in a problem-solving manner which calls for simple solutions which can be phrased in such concrete terms as inputs of men and matériel. Secretary Acheson's warning implied a more cautious, complex, and open view of the problems facing America in foreign affairs.

There seems to be abundant indication that discontent with America's defense posture was rife in the early 1950s. President Eisenhower's address to mayors on civil defense provided the opportunity to warn against the temptation to convert the United States into a garrison state. President Eisenhower declared that while there was a need to be ready, the nation could not be made into an "armed camp." He protested that "we are not going to transfer ourselves into militarists. We are not going to be in uniform, going around yelling "heil" anything. We are simply going to do our job, but do it intelligently."[24]

It is pertinent to observe that support for strong military policies was

21 December 15, 1952.
22 June 15, 1952.
23 January 1, 1951.
24 December 15, 1953.

no monopoly of the Republicans. For instance, Adlai Stevenson, representative of the liberal section of the Democratic party, could also be counted upon to criticize the military preparedness of the country. He charged that the Eisenhower administration was not spending enough either on defense or domestic programs. He accused the administration of "systematic withholding and misrepresentation of the truth about our situation."[25]

The debate on national-defense expenditures was full of confused estimates and recommendations. Averell Harriman, for example, told the Senate: "We can stand this budget and if we continue to go forward vigorously we can have a free world. I think we have the Kremlin off balance and are on the way."[26]

Not many months afterward Henry H. Fowler, director of Defense Mobilization, seemed to suggest that the Russians had recovered their balance. He reported that "we still have a long way to go before we will have the military strength in being, the industrial readiness, and the assurance of continuing technical superiority that our national interest demands."[27]

It is noteworthy that civilian and military figures made the same kind of confused or contradictory assertions. This is doubtless a strong indirect indication that civilian-military lines were far less important than other factors in influencing estimates of the situation. In general, all public figures tended to share an unrealistic overevaluation of the American capabilities in relation to the Russian; and public figures of all camps—partisan, civilian-military—tended to overact or to keep a level head when conspicuous new developments cast doubt on conventional complacency.

A few reminders of the range of difference may be given: Soviet achievements were either minimized or ignored. There was, for example, the "myth of Vannevar Bush" that totalitarian powers can never match democracies in scientific achievements. Even more important, perhaps, was the persistence of the image of the uncouth, Slav, peasant population of the Soviet Union. Hence, when the Soviets launched their first satellite, there was a distinct note of consternation in America. One could very well say, with perhaps some basis in fact, that the Soviets had been able to make way in nuclear weapons by espionage. Yet, here was a technical feat that had not yet been accomplished by the United States. As Senator Stuart Symington, the leading authority on defense matters in the United States Senate, noted about this launching, it "proves that

[25] February 1, 1958.
[26] March 15, 1952.
[27] January 1, 1953.

they are well ahead of us. . . . There had better be a speed up if the United States is to remain a free nation."[28] Senator Symington also estimated that the Soviet Union was now "two or three years ahead," and although they did not yet have an operational intercontinental ballistic missile, "within two to three years they will have one capable of attacking all the United States."[29]

It was a matter of relief and reassurance when the United States swiftly followed the Soviet satellite launching with one of its own. But an unfamiliar note was sounded in connection with the new knowledge of man's habitat and of the technology of space exploration. Nuclear privacy had been and in fact remained an object of monopoly; given the new facts of world life, a policy of sharing seemed to commend itself.

The Secretary of the Army W. M. Brucker declared on the occasion:

> The entire free world has been anxiously looking to the United States for this accomplishment. I speak for the entire United States Army when I say that we are extremely proud to have had the opportunity to make another historical contribution to the scientific progress of our country and the world during this International Geophysical Year.[30]

In a similar manner, Defense Secretary Neil H. McElroy, regarding the launching of the first United States satellite, pronounced that "the data the satellite will gather will be made available to all nations and will enrich the scientific knowledge of all the world."[31]

Differences which were linked with interservice rivalry and with the views of contending scientists, engineers, and suppliers were abundant; and in the relatively open forum of the American polity these differences often rise to the surface.

The clearest statement of dissent with official policy was indicated by General Matthew Ridgway in a letter addressed to Defense Secretary Wilson. It was General Ridgway's contention that "present United States military forces cannot support fully American diplomacy." He declared: "The commitments which the United States has pledged created a positive requirement for an immediately available joint military force of hard-hitting character in which the versatility of the whole is emphasized and the preponderance of any part is de-emphasized."[32] General Ridgway was alluding, of course, to the traditional interservice rivalry

28 October 15, 1957.
29 October 15, 1957.
30 February 1, 1958.
31 February 1, 1958.
32 July 15, 1955.

within the American defense establishment. So intense and insidious could this rivalry become that one might not be entirely wrong in reading between the lines when Admiral Radford, chairman of the Joint Chiefs of Staff, told the Senate: "I do not think the Communist nations have superior air power. I see no reason why they should get into that position. I believe we will be able to stay ahead."[33] A statement such as this one is likely to be read by the United States Air Force as a plea by a Navy officer for limiting the appropriations for the air arm of the services.

Perhaps the most striking fact about the public discussion of military policy among American leaders is the substantial degree of unanimity on the wisdom of thinking globally, of confronting the enemy challenge everywhere, and of enlisting the capabilities of allies in the common task. However "isolationist" American policy may once have been, the postwar world gave scope to a world-inclusive view of the arena in which American security was at stake. Within these broad limits controversy continued over questions of weapon balance and the appropriate assignment of responsibilities.

The most notable statement of strategic policy during the fifties was sloganized quickly as "positions of strength" and "massive retaliation."

In a formal manner, Secretary of State Dulles stated in a speech in January 1955 that the National Security Council had reached what he called a basic decision on security matters. This decision, Dulles stated, was "to depend primarily upon a great capacity to retaliate, instantly, by means and at places of our choosing."[34] Vice President Nixon, utilizing a colorful phrase to explain the circumstances which led to the doctrine of massive retaliation, referred to the "new look" of the Eisenhower administration, which would not let the "Communists nibble us to death all over the world in little wars."[35]

The fundamental point is that American leaders were substantially of one mind throughout the period about the necessity of firmness in meeting Soviet aggression. Of course massive retaliation did not mean that the United States would totally abandon fighting small wars. It sought to create bases abroad to make its striking capability more mobile, more destructive to any potential enemy. As early as 1950, Dean Acheson, addressing a joint gathering of the House and the Senate, had stated:

> The President has authorized me to say that he supports Secretary [of Defense] Johnson and me in our view that we must make this principle [of balanced collective force] work.

[33] May 15, 1956.
[34] January 15, 1955.
[35] March 15, 1954.

> For we can see no other way to accomplish the job of defense
> and at the same time get ahead with the constructive task of build-
> ing a successful functioning economy in the free world.[36]

The principle of collective defense was faithfully followed from the
beginning of the cold war. Similarly, there was continual concern with
the relationship between defense and the national economy. A lucid statement to this effect was provided by Frank Pace, Jr., Secretary of the
Army in the Truman administration. He declared:

> Year by year our national production is expanding. The heavy
> armament burden we have to carry can be absorbed without cutting
> too drastically into our national standard of living. The aid we
> extend our allies under the Mutual Security Program is only a
> fraction of our annual increase in production.
> There are those who urge that we restrict this enormously
> creative talent of ours. I suggest that they should read Christ's
> Parable of the Talents to learn the fate of the man—or nation—
> which buries its talents. There could be no quicker way to national
> decline.[37]

This statement alluded to critics of the United States government's assistance to its West European allies. Yet, it is significant to note that these
critics do not find so prominent a place in our study as the secretary of
the army assigned to them. We suggest that such critics were either in a
very small minority or, more likely, their communications were discounted as unworthy of prominent display in an elite newspaper such
as the New York *Times*. For instance, no statements originated from
the Progressive party nor from the then still active Communist party of
the United States. In a similar manner, pacifist organizations are totally
missing. From this we infer that presentation of elite communications in
the United States and in India as well is often highly selective and
deliberately excludes certain counter-elite elements from the focus of
attention.

We note that throughout the discussion of defense strategy it was more
or less implicit that the total strategy involved allied states in Europe
and on other continents. This, more often than not, involved the sta-
tioning of American troops at bases overseas. The official American
position on these bases abroad was cogently stated by Henry Cabot
Lodge in the United Nations. He made a fine and indeed remarkable
distinction—remarkable in its plausibility—that "United States bases
overseas were not 'foreign' but 'mutual defense' bases, since they were
established only by the free consent of other nations."[38] There are a

36 June 1, 1950.
37 March 15, 1952.
38 December 1, 1955.

sufficient number of cases where the United States had established these bases overseas with treaties with independent governments to lend credence to the statement by Lodge. Similarly, the United States had been responsive to pressure to vacate bases when the host nation preferred it. Sensitivity to public opinion with regard to these foreign bases was displayed by as important a military figure as General Nathan Twining, who noted that "the United States forces abroad 'were never meant to be there indefinitely.' "[39]

It is instructive to note that there emerged throughout the discussion a strong faith in America's peaceful intentions. The feeling was that it was not a cold war of America's own seeking, that it had been imposed upon this country by nations which were inherently belligerent. Consequently, the American approach had to be one which sought to build up a formidable strength—the only factor, it was assumed, that the potential enemy respected. Senator Knowland's statement in its briefness and simplicity neatly summed up the general American philosophy on defense affairs. He stated that a strong air force and guided-missile program were "our greatest guarantee of peace." The Germans had begun World War II, he added, and the Communists struck in Korea, because they thought "we were too weak to strike back."[40]

THE DISARMAMENT AND ARMS CONTROL PROBLEM

Throughout the period of this study the leadership of the United States continued to be involved in pressures for and against disarmament or arms reduction, and in favor of or opposed to specific proposals in this field. In view of the predispositions throughout the American body politic—and the world—arms reduction and disarmament were bound to receive vast popular support. The leaders of the United States were themselves committed to peace, but they were also committed to other values, such as freedom. Hence the continuing challenge was to emphasize the costs as well as the benefits of specific policies put forward in the name of a goal that was almost universally acceptable.

No serious disagreement existed on such fundamental expectations as that modern weapons might have disastrous consequences for mankind. Soviet and American leaders presumably differed in the intensity with which they perceived the threat; hence they could be expected to differ among themselves in the degree of vigor with which they promoted policies designed to put an end to the common danger. These individual variations were often on public view in the United States. In the Soviet

[39] August 15, 1957.
[40] May 15, 1957.

Union, on the other hand, the policy of secrecy prevented the disclosure of personal and factional diversity.

In the early postwar years every candid and expressive observer of the world arena could see that the short-run political benefits of drastic arms reduction would accrue to the Soviet Union, unless arrangements were made for effective means of preventing an aggressive upset of the existing balance of power between the Soviet-headed coalition and the United States-headed combine of states. If the reduction were selective, applying to nuclear weapons only, the conventional weapons available to the Soviet Union would enable it to bring greatly heightened pressure against all its neighbors. The "power vacuum" left by weakened United States capability would presumably be filled by Russian-dominated expansion. The assets (base values) at the disposal of the United States would lose much of their deterrent affect upon Soviet decision makers.

It was equally evident that proposals to allow outside powers to penetrate the secrets of the Soviet Union for inspection purposes would be perceived as dangerous to the power elite of the Soviet Union. If they were much weaker than their external image claimed, they would be suddenly vulnerable to pressures abroad. Any elite faction that would acquiesce in curtailing Soviet power would be exceedingly vulnerable at home as well as abroad. Correspondingly, the American leadership, if it consented to drastic arms reduction without realistic guarantees of access to the knowledge required to assess Russian conformity, would be exceedingly exposed to attack by rival politicians at home.

In such a context the prediction could have been made that negotiations once entered into would go on for some time, and also that the arms problem would become more and more complicated.

One tends to sympathize with Adlai Stevenson when he suggested, in 1958, that the United Nations assist in ending the disarmament deadlock. He suggested that the United Nations secretary-general select a group of private citizens from all parts of the world to evaluate the present disarmament recommendations so as "to clear the air of all the bunk and phony proposals. This committee would be composed of private citizens, top men of affairs and science, chosen by the secretary-general from anywhere and everywhere and acceptable to the nuclear powers. It would work in private. It would render an advisory report."[41]

The American position remained quite stable and cautious. In the words of Benjamin V. Cohen, United States delegate at the United Nations, "no responsible government can agree to cut its own defenses without knowing where such cuts will leave it in relation to the armed forces of other countries."[42]

[41] February 1, 1958.
[42] March 15, 1952.

At the same time, the importance of achieving effective agreement was often reiterated. Secretary of State Dulles, in his appearance before the Senate Foreign Relations Committee, spelled out the assessment made by the United States. "He noted that with nuclear weapons in the arsenals of both the East and the West a situation of 'mutual deterrence' was developing. But it would be reckless to assume that this is a permanently reliable preventive of war. Events could happen which could lead, perhaps by successive stages, to the use of these awesome weapons."[43]

As early as 1951 we note President Truman expressing his attitude toward disarmament in a letter to congressmen: "Continuing emphasis on disarmament is a necessary and vital part of our foreign policy. We must always be seeking for new approaches to this problem, and we must take advantage of every opportunity that presents itself to work toward genuine disarmament proposals."[44]

And President Eisenhower, noting the positive aspects of disarmament, argued that "if the whole world could understand how the great atomic discovery would benefit mankind he believed that world opinion would be marshalled to get rid of the horrible cloud that threatens destruction."[45] More practically, there was ample awareness of the drain upon national resources entailed by the arms race.

General Matthew Ridgway struck a balance between prophecy and contingency forecasting in a letter to Defense Secretary Charles Wilson:

> In the nuclear arms race, the day of nuclear plenty draws nearer; the cost of fabrication drops; and hence the day when even smaller powers may likewise possess such weapons is already foreseeable. Common appreciation of the consequences of unlimited nuclear war may well result in general unwillingness to employ these weapons, in recognition of the mutual disaster which would follow, wherein the peoples, property, and institutions of much of the world would vanish.[46]

No one must assume that emphasis upon the importance of the disarmament issue was "good politics" during the years under review. Just before the "bomb balance" shifted toward parity between the top polar powers Senator Brian McMahon declared:

> I am fully conscious that many people will say that here is a man obsessed with a single idea. I am fully conscious that they will say here is a man who ignores many things of interest to our public. I

43 March 1, 1956.
44 March 15, 1954.
45 July 15, 1956.
46 July 15, 1955.

concede this. I will gladly sacrifice whatever political advantage I
might gain through discussing such issues if I can help awaken the
American people to the one issue that supremely matters.[47]

The source of the public's de-emphasis upon the arms problem is not
puzzling. Given the accepted perspectives on the realities of the world
arena, frequent allusions did no more than contribute to anxiety. No
one saw that any more could be feasibly attempted than was already in
the works.

Toward the end of our period there were indications of changing
perspectives on the vexing problems involved. Possible Soviet eagerness
to reduce armaments could not be attributed to moral considerations—
at least from the viewpoint of the American elite. Senator Walter F.
George, chairman of the Senate Foreign Relations Committee, acknowledged that such a move could not be dismissed as " 'wholly insincere,'
even though the Soviet's ultimate objectives may remain unchanged."[48]
But, more commonly, any Soviet move toward agreement was construed
as a shrewd and perhaps realistic concession to intense pressures. On
the one hand, as we noted earlier, the elite explained that these pressures originated outside of Russia, resulting from policies pursued by
the United States. On the other hand, as Dulles noted, the Soviet Union
might also have been expressing willingness to agree on disarmament
because its own people were " 'in a state of very considerable dissatisfaction' with their low standard of living": a degree of disarmament
could release funds to be diverted for raising living standards.[49] In
addition, the Soviet Union was presented as seeking political advantage
in the eyes of the underdeveloped world by exhibiting itself as the
champion of disarmament and thus standing for a peaceful utilization
of resources.

The American public was not subjected to a continuous and meaningful debate pertaining to the central issues involved in disarmament.
Nothing akin to the great debate inside the British Labor party took
place in United States political circles. But toward the later fifties indications existed of public willingness to tolerate more discussions on the
prevention of nuclear war. Most of the concrete warnings about the
hazards of nuclear war which reached the New York *Times* emanated
from scientists and scholars rather than politicians. Dedicated to the
task of private negotiation and public enlightenment, Dr. Isidor Rabi,
a Columbia University physicist, noted that the launching of the Soviet
satellites had left the American public alarmed, and that this was a

[47] June 15, 1952.
[48] May 15, 1956.
[49] March 1, 1956.

good sign. "We have every reason to be alarmed. Attempts to calm us down are no good. We must take immediate thought as to what we shall do."[50] Dr. Rabi spelled this out in greater detail:

> It is no secret that a large fraction of the American population lives near the seaboards. Even now, if they have done as well as we have done in rocket development (and the evidence is that they have done better), a major part of our population—our whole seaboard—is exposed. In contrast, Russian population is not concentrated near seacoasts.
>
> Here we reach rock-bottom fundamentals—our logistic and geological situation. What has been the shield and defense of this country—polar wastelands to the north, our oceans—make us vulnerable and easy to approach. The Russians do not have to be sophisticated technically to have a severe advantage in an exchange of nuclear weapons. . . . There is no question that we are facing the severest problem that civilized humanity has had to face at any time.
>
> We have to solve our problem of living together on this planet or we won't live. By we, I mean the major part of the globe, the United States, Russia, and other nations. The end of our national existence is in sight unless we solve this problem.[51]

During the years of seeming "atomic stalemate" research workers in and out of government were preparing themselves to play a more conspicuous and influential role in determining the future of the world. In more recent times a harvest of new tactical proposals have come into the open. The principal accent has been laid upon the need of integrating diplomatic issues in the realm of arms control with all other instruments of policy.

[50] January 1, 1958.
[51] January 1, 1958.

CHAPTER 14 · DEALS, DOLLARS, AND IDEAS: OTHER INSTRUMENTS OF POLICY

AGREEMENT AND DISAGREEMENT: THE DIPLOMATIC INSTRUMENT

The diplomatic instrument specializes in the use of negotiation as a means of advancing national objectives. Hence it is concerned with agreement or disagreement, and with developing (or blocking) new channels of continuing official contact among governments. It is not unusual for the political elite as a whole to entertain serious reservations on the skill with which the diplomatic instrument is used by their own foreign offices. The United States is no exception to this lack of confidence in the nation's diplomacy.

PERSPECTIVES ON THE UNITED NATIONS

When the United Nations was established at San Francisco at the end of World War II, hundreds of national civic associations gave their enthusiastic support to the new institution. No other development could dramatize more vividly the evolution which had occurred in the arena of world politics from the days of almost exclusive reliance on bilateral contact as the established mode of elite-to-elite communication.

Although the volume of general comment on the United Nations is not great, the tenure of articulate opinion was largely favorable. Over the time span covered in our study there is an unmistakable trend toward considering the United Nations less and less as a dependable adjunct of

American foreign policy. At least in the early 1950s, the United States controlled enough votes to negate Soviet influence in the General Assembly. Hence the Soviet Union utilized the veto power almost as a matter of course, while the United States had no need to exercise its veto. These were the years of automatic majorities lined up behind the United States.

Despite the seemingly automatic majorities obtained by the United States, an undercurrent of dissent continued. The most conspicuous anti-United Nations elements were "ultrapatriotic" groups who often construed American participation in international organization as acknowledgment of alien authority. Donald R. Wilson, a past national commander of the American Legion, told the convention that the Legionnaires should exercise caution so that their children, their rights, their citizenship, and their flag were not

> given away by the United Nations chowder, marching, and conversation club.
>
> Let's make sure that our future generations don't have to die under a sickly blue flag with a world bled white in the middle.
>
> The Stars and Stripes are good enough to live and die under when the time comes.[1]

President Eisenhower endorsed the United Nations in no uncertain terms in a letter to the president of the American Association for the United Nations. President Eisenhower stated that it was because the United Nations was dedicated to the "preservation of mankind from the scourges of war," it was an organization through which the United States could exercise leadership. He wrote that was why he had chosen it before which to deliver the United States proposal for peaceful uses of atomic energy.[2]

It would be an error to infer from these comments that the United States depended upon the United Nations as the major channel of diplomacy. As the underdeveloped nations increased their weight in the United Nations, the United States had to exert itself to muster a majority. While this was the case in the General Assembly, in the Security Council, of course, there was the Soviet veto. Lincoln White, State Department spokesman, made the following rather candid statement:

> We, of course, wish to work through the United Nations to the maximum degree possible in efforts to prevent an outbreak of hostilities in the Middle East. That is our guiding principle.

[1] New York *Times*, September 1, 1953. (The following notes, unless otherwise indicated, are from the same source.)

[2] March 1, 1954.

> Should, however, the United Nations be paralyzed as it has been
> in the past by the Soviet veto, there would be no alternative but
> to work outside the United Nations in our continuing efforts to
> assure a just peace in the area.[3]

The realization that the United Nations might not be able to offer
the same opportunities for American foreign policy that it had presented in the years immediately after World War II dawned upon many
American leaders especially at the time of the Hungarian revolt. We
find the deputy United States representative to the United Nations,
Wadsworth, telling the American Bar Association that "the Soviet
slaughter in Hungary, in complete defiance of the United Nations,
was agonizing proof how little the United Nations can do, peacefully,
to restrain a country which has very great power and no morals."[4]
Evaluating the role of the United Nations, he declared that while the
United Nations had " 'no power to compel, it has enormous power to
persuade,' and a consequent influence on governments and world
opinion." He felt that its impact was "profound" on the Communist
movement in countries outside the Soviet orbit. He interpreted the
United Nations' response to the Hungarian revolt as the lighting of
"fires of condemnation" which would be "plaguing the Soviet rulers
today and will continue to plague them for years to come."[5]
What the United Nations meant to the United States is indicated by
the listing of the "four major accomplishments" at the end of the 1957
session by Henry Cabot Lodge. We note that there is more to the
functions of the United Nations than simple propaganda value. Lodge's
list of these accomplishments included:

> 1. Stripping away the sham and insincerity of the Soviet war
> scare that the United States was masterminding a threat to the
> security of Syria. This cleared the air considerably in that part of
> the world.
> 2. Approval of the new proposal by the United States for ex-
> tending economic aid under the auspices of the United Nations.
> This provides a new way to strengthen underdeveloped countries
> against subversion from abroad. It could greatly improve prospects
> for solving big political problems. It created and will create good
> will for the United States.
> 3. Reduction in the share of the United Nations assessment
> which the United States pays. . . .
> 4. Overwhelming endorsement of our disarmament program.[6]

[3] February 15, 1956.
[4] July 15, 1957.
[5] July 15, 1957.
[6] December 15, 1957.

Although all "four major accomplishments" were especially note-worthy to Lodge because they had been "done in the midst of the sputnik blitz," none of them would appear to be of crucial importance to the United States.

FORGING A GRAND ALLIANCE

As a means of consolidating national security, American leaders fashioned a system of alliances less inclusive than the United Nations. The principal coalition was NATO, the North Atlantic Treaty Organization, which brought North America and Western Europe into a continuing program of collective action aimed against Soviet dynamism.

Undertakings of this kind were bound to rearouse residual hostilities to "foreign entanglements" and to alleged losses of "sovereignty." Another source of embarrassment was the apparent contradiction between an alliance on behalf of "free nations" and the inclusion of some non-democratic states among its members. Elite speeches adopted various tactics to support the formation of NATO and similar coalitions. The principal tactic appears to have been to emphasize the security necessities generated by the present structure of the world arena. However, many speakers invoked various features of America's ideology in the hope of sustaining a sentiment of continuity in national policy. Adlai Stevenson, for instance, harked back to "the dawn of the American Revolution" when "great men who had defined the ideals of our country had seen 'America as the Old World's savior.' "[7] Stevenson waxed lyrical over the new ties: "We of the NATO countries and the other free nations are bonded together, once and for all, in sickness or health, till—or rather—lest atomic death us do part."[8]

Visions of sacred and secular destiny were rather closely related to considerations that were eminently practical. They might be stated in the words of General Omar Bradley, who held that "whether we recognize it or not, the American people have decided to hold and save Western Europe for the free world."[9] Or, more bluntly, in the question which Senator McFarland, Democrat of Arizona, posed: "Is it cheaper to arm European boys or put all of our own young manhood in uniform?"[10] In a similar vein, General Gruenther remarked that NATO was "in no sense 'a community chest,' for contributions to our own

[7] October 15, 1952.
[8] February 15, 1953.
[9] April 15, 1950.
[10] September 1, 1951.

survival."[11] General Omar Bradley met one argument bluntly. Admitting that "a small bit of sovereignty" may be relinquished in collective defense arrangements, he continued: "When I think that national pride and sovereignty are often paid with the life and blood of soldiers, I feel that we must accept the more difficult alternative which comes with this joining of hands in collective defense."[12]

W. Averell Harriman, in an appearance before the Senate Foreign Relations Committee, made reference to the vast sums that the Soviet Union spent on its satellites, and proceeded to suggest that "we are facing a world-wide struggle, and it is very much in our interest to help our allies build up their military strength."[13] When he was criticized for describing America's mutual-security aid, amounting to $7 billion, as a "very small sum," he responded that the sum was "relatively small in relation to the importance of building up the strength of our allies and the cost of any known alternative program."[14]

From the Republican side, Governor Dewey was a stanch advocate of a military alliance system. He proposed that the United States should "make friends with everybody who has the will to fight and the combat divisions to put into the field."[15]

The task of alliance building was no simple one. Even the most experienced American statesmen would give occasional utterance to an unfortunate phrase that wounded the self-respect of actual or potential allies. Usually these slips were criticized by domestic critics, who assisted in this way in broadening the American view of the world. No less a figure than General Eisenhower made occasional slips of this kind. On one such occasion, Oscar R. Ewing, President Truman's federal security administrator, declared that Eisenhower's charges to the effect that "the French government is dominated by atheists . . . is not only tactless but dangerous. . . . Schuman is a noted Catholic lay leader. He originated and nurtured the present plan for a united Europe. He has weathered a number of French Cabinet changes and now gets hit below the belt by Eisenhower."[16]

Similarly, Eisenhower's reference to Asians fighting Asians in 1952, a remark easily capable of being misunderstood, received Adlai Stevenson's attention. He charged that Eisenhower had displayed "alarming disdain for the sensitivity of our allies both in Europe and Asia. We entered the fight to resist aggression and in this there can be no color

[11] June 1, 1956.
[12] April 15, 1950.
[13] March 15, 1952.
[14] March 15, 1952.
[15] December 15, 1950.
[16] July 15, 1952.

line. The slogan 'let Asians fight Asians' is the resurgent voice of isolationism."[17]

Alliance building in troubled Europe was difficult, especially when a country was lacking in stability. The temptation to interfere in internal affairs was not always resisted. The American Ambassador John E. Peurifoy openly stepped into the domestic politics of Greece and warned that the retention of the proportional election system, "with its inevitable consequences of continuing instability, would have a disasterous effect upon the efficient use of American aid in Greece."[18] Ambassador Peurifoy was reported to have issued an authoritative statement warning that "the United States could not favor the existence in Greece of a system that fostered small parties, resulting in a patched-up and ephemeral coalition cabinet after an election."[19]

The role of the United States differed greatly from ally to ally. In the case of weak states, such as Greece, the United States exercised semi-tutelage; with allies such as Great Britain, direct interference in domestic policies was not possible. Although it would be an error to suggest that the relationship of the United States with junior members of the alliance was identical with that of the Soviet Union with its Eastern European states, it would also be wide of the mark to accept at face value pious rhetoric to the effect that the Western alliance, led by the United States, was an alliance of equal states.

The helplessness of many states greatly embarrassed the United States and gave rise to some impatient demands by American leaders to impose uniformity. Prominent political figures warned against this propensity to interfere with others. Senator Connolly, for example, in responding to a move to put Congress on record in favor of European federation, stated that Western Europe would resent it "if we try to tell them what form of government they should have."[20]

At appropriation time many Congressional elements combined to demand that conditions be laid down for NATO allies. Spirited leadership by respected figures was necessary to warn against these proposals. General Clay vigorously argued on more than one occasion that he knew "damned well" that only by refraining from laying down conditions could you "get men to fight."[21] He held:

> If each nation puts down the conditions under which it will deal with the others, then you might as well wipe out the North Atlantic Treaty and the whole idea of collective security.

[17] November 1, 1952.
[18] March 15, 1952.
[19] March 15, 1952.
[20] September 1, 1951.
[21] March 1, 1951.

> The minute that a single nation in Europe started handing down
> its own conditions, our own people would revolt. You just can't
> deal that way with free nations.[22]

The political elite of the United States, though willing to abstain
from "throwing its weight around" in many arenas, was always aware
of the demand to retain its ultimate right of decision. Former Secretary
of Defense Louis Johnson spoke of the impatience that Americans feel
when they find themselves isolated from those very states whom the
United States has helped so generously:

> The element of getting along with people . . . calls at times for
> the United States to speak as but one nation of many associated in
> that group.
> There come other times when the sovereignty of the United
> States and the death of its sons make it imperative that we stand
> on certain fundamental principles. . . .[23]

Interwoven with the policy of encouraging NATO was the objective
of encouraging Europe to form an enduring structure of continental
unity. The military contingency which appears to have given the initial
impulse for the creation of NATO eventually led to considerations that
called for the establishment of a community of nations based upon
certain ideological premises, counterpoised against the Soviet system of
states. Reflecting upon the increase in NATO strength, Secretary Acheson declared: "All of these things were undertaken not merely for their
military sake—important as that is—but because they are part of the
still larger idea of helping to bring about real unity to the European
community within the framework of the Atlantic community."[24]

In this connection American leaders were much disappointed at the
failure of the French government to cooperate in the projected European
Defense Community. Conveying his frustration over this, Secretary of
State Dulles accused the French of displaying nationalism "abetted
by communism . . . so as to endanger the whole of Europe."[24]

The trajectory of American policy had obviously come a long way
since the early days of the republic. The political leaders of an ex-colony
whose independent identity had been achieved by violent secession
from Europe in the eighteenth century were now aiding and abetting
the powers of Western Europe to go as far as possible toward a United
States of Europe. Obviously, policies of alliance were intertwined with
programs of world-wide defense and consolidation of zones of relative
freedom throughout the globe. The ideological inheritance of the Ameri-

[22] March 1, 1951.
[23] June 15, 1951.
[24] September 1, 1954.

can people had far from exhausted its political impact upon the goals and structures of public order at home and abroad. A sensitive and articulate speaker would occasionally give utterance to a revised version of "manifest destiny." Listen to Adlai Stevenson declaring that the Americans were "ordained guardians" of the faith of their fathers:

> Let us lift up our hearts, then—glad of our strength, proud of the task it imposes. So far from being half-defeated, half-divided, half-bankrupt, while we are true to ourselves we can never be defeated; while we accept the honorable burden of leadership we can never be divided. And in the name of that burden, we shall find the means and the determination to spend in money and in labor and in hard thought whatever is needed to save ourselves and the world.[25]

THE ECONOMIC INSTRUMENT:
AID AND TRADE

The importance of economic measures in the field of national policy has been evident to American leaders and to the electorate for many generations. The Boston Tea Party furnished a dramatic episode in the interdependence of economics and politics. However, many established policies were not adapted to the advancement of American interests in the post-World War II arena. One tradition was that in time of peace the outflow of American investment should proceed through private not governmental channels. Economic assistance for noneconomic and other nonpolitical ends was also assumed to be suitable to unofficial institutions. The outflow of funds for missionary activities, for instance, rested on private volition. For decades the policy of restricting foreign imports on behalf of "infant industries" and the "American standard of living" outweighed the strength of appeals in favor of "free trade." By 1950 the United States was well launched on "Marshall Plans" and "Foreign-Aid Programs" which syphoned billions of dollars abroad through government channels. It was not uncommon for public leaders to give powerful support to "healthy competition" from "foreign imports."

Recognizing the latent strength of opposition to these policies, the most responsible elements of the American elite gave heavy emphasis to the importance of these programs for national security. This was important in the middle fifties when a reviving Europe and a "more friendly face" in Moscow tended to weaken the sense of urgency and benefit from these programs. As Adlai Stevenson explained, "A bold, sustained economic-aid program . . . is as imperative and urgent as

[25] October 15, 1952.

'missiles and nuclear weapons—and much less expensive.' "[26] President Eisenhower's remarks illustrate the importance and the difficulties inherent in the foreign-aid program. He said it was his job to represent "all of the people" and therefore, because foreign aid had no lobbies or special pressure groups, it was his job to speak out for it.[27] He even suggested calling a special session of the Congress if the latter failed to sanction sufficient funds. Some senators termed this move a "threat," but the President insisted he never made threats of any kind.[28] During the course of this crisis in 1957, when drastic cuts in the Eisenhower administration's requests for foreign-aid funds appeared imminent, Senator Hubert Humphrey forcefully came to the defense of the President. He said the President, if he "really goes to work on it," could head off the proposed Congressional cuts. He then proceeded to underscore "the importance of President Eisenhower really staking his personal reputation and his personal political strength upon promoting and backing an effective foreign-aid program."[29]

Such steps as the threat to call a special session of the Congress and the appeal by a leader of the opposition party to the President to directly appeal to the people are indicative of the degree of importance attached by members of the elite to the aid programs. There is little doubt that the issue of foreign aid has formed an extremely significant part of the over-all foreign policy of the United States.

The earliest and the bluntest statement of the objectives of the foreign-aid program in our study was in reference to the Point-Four program. Speaker of the House Sam Rayburn maintained that because America needed friends to "hold the line until we can get there" in case of conflict, the "paltry" Point-Four funds needed to be increased, "otherwise, the next war will have to be fought in the Western Hemisphere. I don't want that and you don't want that. We need friends and we will need them when they have the strength to go with their courage."[30] We need to emphasize here that Speaker Rayburn was pleading for more funds for a program which was supposed to be concerned solely with nonmilitary assistance. Yet, as we note, his justification for increased funds rested entirely upon military contingencies. Equally candid were the remarks of President Eisenhower in this regard. He chose to call foreign-aid funds "the cheapest money we spend as long as we are talking about getting security for the United States. If we did not have this working effectively I just would hate to guess what would be the sums I would have to ask in the defense appropriations next year."[31] And upon the passing of the Foreign-Aid Bill in 1956, Senator Green frankly announced that "what we have done here is to attempt to make crystal clear what has always been a fact: That the actual result of this program primarily is the defense of the United States."[32] Far from representing isolated interpretations, this point was reiterated continuously and consistently. Secretary of the Army Frank Pace, Jr., pithily characterized the Marshall Plan and Point Four as the two "key arches in our post-World War II foreign policy." Charles E. Wilson, Eisenhower administration defense secretary, in his appearance before the Senate in 1956, declared that "any substantial reduction in foreign-aid program would create 'serious risk' to this country and the free world. Such an action by the Congress would force 'a complete re-evaluation of our own international position and of our own military budgets.' "[33] And Secretary of State John Foster Dulles, designating foreign aid as a form of "national insurance," declared that any reduction in it would "gravely endanger the security of the United States."[34] Dulles repeatedly denied the charge that the foreign-aid program was a "give-away" program.[35]

From the intensity with which the program was defended and the cuts which were made in the Congress, we are led to infer that a strong opposition must have existed. Yet it is surprising how little of this criticism reached the front pages of the elite press. One obvious exception was Senator Wherry, a Republican senator from Nebraska, who chose to describe the Marshall Plan and the Point-four Program as "throwing money down a rathole."[36] Another exception was the extensive coverage of the views of Senator Bridges.

From the perspective of Senator Bridges, foreign aid should have been limited to countries which were explicitly aligned with the United States. The official view, on the other hand, was that economic aid should not only reward and strengthen allies, but build eventual support for the free world among noncommitted powers. Senator Bridges felt that while foreign aid was "essential for world security in the 'evil shadow of Red imperialism,' " he was of the firm conviction that extension of aid ought to be predicated upon political conditions. By exercising a certain sense of discrimination and judgment, the United States should select as recipients of its aid only those countries "willing

[31] August 15, 1957.
[32] June 15, 1956.
[33] May 15, 1956.
[34] May 1, 1956.
[35] July 1, 1956.
[36] August 15, 1950.

to be willing partners in this great program," those who are "our true allies and friends—people we are confident will stand with us in any emergency." To Senator Bridges, and the segment of the elite he represented, the use of foreign aid as a subtle weapon of attraction in the cold war appears to have been incomprehensible. He felt that any consistent display of independence in foreign policy ought to be sufficient grounds for terminating United States aid to the offending country. In particular, "aid should not be given to potential enemies or so-called neutral nations that play 90 percent of the time with the Soviet bloc. By that reference I mean Yugoslavia and Tito and countries like India."[37]

Despite opposing rumbles, however, there was a consistent feeling in high echelons that the foreign-aid program was beneficial to the national interest of the United States. The United States was committed to the thesis of international "equality" of states and to "self-government," and could not blatantly use economic instruments as coercive bludgeons. Nonetheless, the administering of the foreign-aid program gave to the United States an influential voice in the policy making of recipient states. One of the aspects of the program which especially facilitated the extension of this influence was the fact that appropriations were made on an annual basis. In fact, this was undoubtedly a strong reason why Senator Knowland professed a belief "that it would be far better for the administration to come up and make its presentation each year than to seek a ten-year commitment in advance."[38] Once a recipient nation had come to depend on foreign aid, and had incorporated such expectations in its developmental plans, it made itself susceptible to policy influences from the aid-granting nation. Sometimes United States influence has been openly exercised in attempts to influence the internal policies of recipient states (as in Greece in 1952).

Many influential Americans were aware of the anti-American animosities that could develop under such conditions among recipients of aid. Foreign elites who accepted assistance from the United States were in an advantageous position so long as their fellow countrymen acknowledged that such foreign assistance was useful. But nationalist and anti-imperialistic sentiments were potent political factors, and they could prove disastrous to future careers if a leader appeared as nothing more than a compliant tool of American policy. Great tact was needed to demonstrate respect for the integrity of other peoples and trusted leaders. When Mrs. Eleanor Roosevelt spoke of the "human approach" she obviously had such considerations as these in mind. "She told of

[37] July 15, 1956.
[38] January 15, 1956.

meeting a Point-Four administrator in India and said she asked him if there were anything she should tell the State Department for him. He told her that what they needed most were skilled technicians but that no technician was any good to India without a heart. 'I think this is the wisest thing that could be said to any government.' "[39]

Such human factors involved in the extension of American resources and technical assistance to tradition-based societies did not receive much discussion in quoted statements. We occasionally encounter the rudiments of this approach, such as Senator Mike Mansfield's designating of the Point-Four Technical Assistance Program as a "people-to-people" program.[40] But beyond remarks of this nature we do not perceive any attention directed toward sociological or anthropological aspects of the foreign-aid program. The absence of such comment is surprising inasmuch as Americans, as a people, generally demonstrate particular sensitivity to their own problems of interpersonal relationships. One might assume that this sensitivity would extend into the intercultural sphere. In the case of foreign-aid programs, however, we have little evidence of this.

In some ways the most remarkable shift in American views was in the area of foreign trade, and particularly regarding the encouragement of imports, which were seen as essential to a revived and expanding free-world economy. The defense of the Swiss watch industry by an American president had few, if any, precedents. President Truman noted that an increased duty on Swiss watches or any restrictive measure against imports into his country must be clearly justified "if we wish to avoid a serious loss of confidence in our leadership, in the world."[41] He stated that the "escape clause" was not intended to leave the domestic industry "free to ignore the changing pattern of domestic demand or to provide an escape from normal, healthy competition."[42]

The representatives of affected industries were often disturbed that the government gave an overly sympathetic ear to foreigners. The 1950s were largely dominated by the primacy of political considerations in the use of economic instruments. The "logical approach" suggested by John D. Biggers, president of Libby-Owens-Ford Glass Company, was not likely to appear logical to the policy planners of even a supposedly friendly Republican administration. Biggers's credo was:

> I believe in the soundness of a tariff sufficiently high to protect this standard of living. General reductions or eliminations of tariff cannot be made without unwarranted injury to the American

[39] February 15, 1953.
[40] January 16, 1956.
[41] August 15, 1952.
[42] August 15, 1952.

economy. The logical approach would be to negotiate country by country and product by product.[43]

The most extensive plea for drastic shifts in the traditionally protectionist policies of the United States came from President Eisenhower:

> I believe the reasons for the United States membership in the proposed organization [Organization for Trade Cooperation] are overwhelming. We would thus demonstrate to the free world our active interest in the promotion of trade among the free nations. We would demonstrate our desire to deal with matters of trade in the same cooperative way as we do with military matters in such regional pacts as the North Atlantic Treaty Organization and with financial matters in the International Monetary Fund and in the International Bank for Reconstruction and Development. We would thus cooperate further with the free world in the struggle against Communist domination to the greater security and the greater prosperity of all.[44]

President Eisenhower listed the manner in which participation would directly help the United States:

> Such action would serve the enlightened self-interest of the United States. As a member of this organization we could work more effectively for the removal of discriminatory restrictions against our exports. We could help establish conditions favorable to convertibility of currencies. We could further the expansion of markets abroad for the products of our mines, our farms, and our factories. We could assist in the development of conditions conductive to international flow of investment capital so urgently needed to expand production throughout the free world, especially in its underdeveloped areas.[45]

President Eisenhower warned the Congress that if it did not authorize American participation in the Organization for Trade Cooperation serious consequences would follow for the country. American absence, the President declared,

> would constitute a serious setback to the momentum which has been generated for the expansion of world trade.
> It would strike a severe blow at the development of cooperative arrangements in defense of the free world. It could lead to the imposition of new trade restrictions on the part of other countries, which would result in a contraction of world trade and constitute a

[43] March 1, 1953.
[44] April 15, 1955.
[45] April 15, 1955.

sharp setback to United States exports. It could result in regional realignments of nations. Such developments, needless to say, would play directly into the hands of the Communists.[46]

When the Congress continued to be reluctant to approve American participation, President Eisenhower termed the delay "almost ridiculous."

American trade policy was so completely subordinated to the objectives of national security that commercial intercourse with Communist areas was strictly opposed. A long list was drawn up of strategic materials which were not supposed to get into Communist hands. Secretary of Defense Charles E. Wilson, commenting on East-West trade, declared that his department was convinced "that any goods, or any services, reaching or serving these areas increase the capabilities of the Communist forces in Asia not only to continue, but even to intensify and extend, the present areas of aggression."[47]

Emphasis on the desirability of a trade embargo between Communist nations and the West was particularly strong after the entry of Chinese "volunteers" into open conflict with United States forces in Korea. Some members of the American leadership expressed a gnawing bitterness against friendly states which persisted in trading with Communist China. A passionate indictment was delivered on free trade with Communist China by Senator Knowland:

> Many of the articles now to be shipped to Communist China must be considered strategic by any rule of reason. Locomotives, machine tools, trucks, perhaps entire rubber plants, may someday in the not-too-distant future strengthen Communist China to the point where it can feel it dares to take the risk of taking over the crown colony of Hong Kong.
>
> This is a calculated risk for which Her Majesty's ministers must alone bear the responsibility. When they weaken their forces in Europe, as was recently done, we might question the wisdom of it; but as good and stout allies, we understand some of the economic reasons behind that action.
>
> But it is far more difficult to understand an action which can only strengthen our common enemies both in Asia and in Europe, for, up to the present time, Communist China has not agreed to a peace treaty with Korea; it has violated the armistice agreements in Korea; it still holds American citizens in prison.[48]

Senator Knowland's sentiments might have been shared by large segments of the American public. But by and large the policies of the

[46] April 15, 1955.
[47] April 1, 1953.
[48] June 1, 1957.

government were closer to the views of Senator John Sparkman who noted: "I think we have to be realistic. It's easy for us to resent trade with Red China, but our economy doesn't depend so much on it. The economics of other countries, notably Britain and Japan, do. I think we can be more realistic so far as their trade goes."[49] The United States was realistic enough never to endorse such trade relations but neither did it see fit to impose pressure for total severance of the trade. As long as strategic materials were kept from entering the Communist bloc (and by and large they were not shipped) the United States preferred not to pay undue attention to this delicate problem.

THE PROPAGANDA INSTRUMENT:
THE VOICE OF AMERICA

The United States entered the post-World War II period with no established expectation that official propaganda would figure conspicuously among the instruments of national policy. Hence the assumption among many if not most members of the political elite was that the broadcasting and related activities which had been developed during the crisis of war would be suspended. Although sharply reduced in available funds, the "Voice of America" was saved largely through the energetic initiatives taken by influential publishers, advertising men, public-relations specialists, and others who were convinced of the worth of a big-scale propaganda effort.

It is clear from the comments about propaganda which were made during the fifties that American leaders were still rather confused about the proper role of planned communication as an instrument of the foreign policy of popular governments. Democratic politicians are exceedingly alert to the possible abuses of power that may result from official propaganda. Although the party in power was entirely justified in everybody's view in providing information about American policy, and this included the dissemination of favorable news about the President and other top figures, there was fear that the "buildup" of the party in office would weaken the opposition. Coupled with these partisan apprehensions are scruples about the encouragement of "lies." In many minds the propagandist is not only a special pleader, an advocate, but an expert in deceit. Unlike the lawyer, who works under the scrutiny and control of a judge, the propagandist is believed to have a free hand in the poisoning of minds. These suspicions rest in part on lack of knowledge about the propagandist and lack of agreement about the proper synchronization of the propaganda instrument with military, diplomatic, and economic measures.

[49] June 1, 1957.

Our excerpts show that the American leadership had achieved very little clarity about propaganda. The simplest way to get appropriations was to point to the Russians, who were unmistakably engaged in large-scale propaganda, and to argue that national security demanded that we do the same thing. Opponents of the United States Information Service found that it was more damaging to attack the agency for "wasting the taxpayer's money" than to join issue on its goal.

The connection between propaganda and foreign policy was reiterated in many speeches which denounced Soviet propaganda while lamenting the alleged failure of the United States to project a satisfactory image abroad. It is impossible to examine these statements without recognizing the confused and ambivalent perspectives which were characteristic of the prevailing approach to the evaluation of propaganda. Why was it so congenial to assert that "the battle for the minds and hearts of men" was being lost? We suggest that American leaders were relatively reluctant to assess the realities of the world situation and to recognize that many fundamental factors were working to the advantage of the Communists. If some of the speeches are taken literally, they present world politics as a competition among image makers in which the most deceitful rival wins.

Sometimes the role of propaganda was exalted as a tool of revolution. During his campaign in 1952 Senator Taft was reported as urging "that the United States should reorganize its propaganda efforts in foreign countries instead of relying entirely on the Voice of America and should try to reorganize the free forces behind the Iron Curtain."[50] We take it that Senator Taft wanted to intensify American propaganda activities abroad; evidently he was in favor of more than one medium of propaganda, and assumed that the prime target would be the Soviet bloc of states. The function of propaganda was conceived as offensive; it involved the fomenting of rebellion even in states with which the United States maintained diplomatic relations. Domestically, the call to liberate Eastern European states was likely to produce votes among ethnic groups who originated in this area; it identified the caller as a tough-minded, patriotic figure who was by no stretch of imagination "soft" on communism.

Representative Rooney declared that he had made intensive studies of the operations of the United States Information Agency in its overseas operations. As a result the congressman felt "I cannot in good conscience say that I feel the American taxpayers have been getting the value they should for their money."[51] Among the reasons that the congressman

50 July 1, 1952.
51 April 15, 1957.

from Brooklyn gave for his opposition to the United States Information
Agency was that it

> had increased its employees last year despite the fact that Congress
> had cut its funds; that it had "used tax money to try and shape
> opinion in this country," and that it had improperly tried to in-
> fluence "our British friends" by such methods as free subscriptions
> to American newspapers for the 644 members of Parliament.[52]

Congressman Rooney stated that: "the agency's efforts in the Hungarian
crisis were 'almost a complete failure' because the United States was
'unable to convince a majority of the United Nations that "enforcement measures" should be taken against Soviet Russia for its brutal
and immoral aggression in Hungary.' "[53]

The agency was criticized for distributing information to Members of
Parliament, and also for failing to persuade successfully America's allies
and other powers to join with the United States in actions against
Soviet Russia. Contradictions of this kind were characteristic of the
persisting confusion.

It was necessary for President Eisenhower to give his strong personal
support to the United States Information Agency. In a letter to Congressman Rooney, he referred to the functioning of the United States
Information Agency in these terms: "He described the agency's budget
as of 'critical importance' because imperatively, in key areas of the
world, America's voice of truth must become more clearly heard. There
is a pressing need for expansion of our information functions in the
Near East, Africa, and the Far East . . . at the time of the Hungarian
uprising our informational efforts demonstrated great value. The capacity of the agency to react to future crises should be at the least
maintained. My considered judgment is that they need to be substantially increased."[54]

President Eisenhower characterized the positive role of the propaganda instrument in typically moralistic and proselytizing terms: "The
United States Information Agency was a vital part of the national effort
to wage peace by counteracting false propaganda spread by the Communists. 'We tell the truth about freedom and the rights of man and
seek to win adherents to these concepts.' "[55]

[52] April 15, 1957.
[53] April 15, 1957.
[54] April 15, 1957.
[55] May 15, 1957.

PROBLEMS OF SPECIAL DIFFICULTY: CHINA, KOREA, AND OTHER AREAS

During the fifties the leaders of the American nation were faced by a series of problems of special difficulty in many parts of the world lying between the United States and the Soviet Union. The excerpts that follow will provide many indications of the reinterpretations which enabled political leaders to maintain a sense of continuity in change.

CHINA

The seizure of power by the Communists in China and the flight of the Kuomintang leaders to Formosa were among the most startling deprivations to which American foreign policy had ever been exposed. In order to grasp the significance of this event for Americans it is essential to recall the extraordinarily broad involvement of many levels of society in all parts of the country with China. New England had cultivated close commercial relations with China for many generations. The Pacific Coast was deeply engaged. New York investment interests were involved in shipping, public works, real estate, oil, and other economic ventures. However, the ties that bound hundreds of thousands of Americans to China were the missionary and educational operations which had reached into the small towns and provided an outlet for thousands of young men and women from all parts of the United States. For decades young Chinese had been able to obtain educational advantages in the United States as a result of the agreement to use Boxer indemnity funds for this purpose. Most recently the United States had spent billions of dollars attempting to bolster the Kuomintang government headed by Chiang Kai-shek.

Given these predispositions among American leaders and led, it becomes more intelligible to read that "we've lost China to the Communists." To a less involved outsider this might appear to be a rather peculiar response. China, after all, was an independent power. While it is valid for the British to say that they "lost" India, which they had ruled, it is less obvious why Americans felt with such intensity that they had "lost" China; a country they had never ruled.

The problem of recognition of the Communist regime of China was complicated by the removal of the Nationalist regime to Formosa. Yet, it is not very likely that American policy was guided solely by the interests of the defeated government now residing in Taipei. So highly charged were American elite emotions on the question of China that an otherwise liberal American, Senator Estes Kefauver, demanded that "we should classify the China Communists as outlaws, and cease to do business with them."[1] Such sentiments of ostracism were widely shared among the American leaders. Indeed, to suggest sentiments contrary to these was considered as being "soft on communism" or an appeaser. Senator Knowland from California, a prominent China expert of the Republican party, commented on United States' China policy: "Our policy of appeasement of the Communists . . . was almost immediately followed by this new unfriendly act of the Chinese Communists. This is always the result of paying international blackmail. Appeasement is but surrender on the installment plan."[2]

In other words, China's new regime was seen as outside the pale of the law. Red Chinese leaders were perceived in the same way that local gangsters from the criminal fringe of society are looked upon by law-abiding and well-established citizens. The spokesmen of the United States elite gave little indication that the Chinese Communist government represented a potent historical force that must be reckoned with regardless of personal sentiment, or even of views on the timing of diplomatic recognition.

Ambassador Ernest M. Gross, testifying before a Senate subcommittee, declared in October 1951: "I foresee no conditions under which I would approve the recognition by the United States of Communist China."[3]

The shock of the "loss" was so great that deep psychological mechanisms were stirred into action. An available scapegoat had to be found against whom impotent rage could be discharged. It goes without saying

[1] New York *Times*, January 15, 1950. (The following notes, unless otherwise indicated, are from the same source.)

[2] January 15, 1950.

[3] October 15, 1951.

that Republican party leaders would assert that the Democrats were the most eligible targets. Senator Styles Bridges declared: "It should be clear to the American people that if our responsible officials cannot change our policy it is time to change our officials."[4] And Senator Knowland suggested that "it is now time that the men responsible for that policy submit their resignations to the President so that the nation may have a new and nondefeatist team in whom the Congress and the nation could have confidence."[5]

But the intensity of response was such that a more sinister explanation was called for. Evidently the sequence of reaction among many Americans was this: We have suffered a severe deprivation in terms of national power, prestige, and other significant values; I did not expect such a complete rout; evidently I, and others, have been betrayed by subversive Americans who have been instigated by Communists. The man who pointed to the scapegoat with repetitive fervor and effect was Senator Joseph McCarthy whose role we have described above.

Dissenting voices were rarely raised; and if they were loud enough to get a hearing, the emotional quality of the replies was unmistakable. In 1951, Justice Douglas commented on the recognition issue is these terms: "Recognition will require straightforward and courageous thinking by all Americans, but it is the only logical course."[6] Reaction to such unorthodox opinions was swift and emphatic. Senator Everett Dirksen, Republican of Illinois, declared that Justice Douglas's call for recognition of Red China was not merely a matter of a private citizen, but that the Justice could not be "divorced from the party in power."[7] Senator Connally, a Democrat, not only condemned the viewpoint of Justice Douglas, but attacked him personally: "I think he ought to stay home instead of roaming all around the world and Asia making fool statements. We're really at war—in a sense—with Red China now."[8]

The arguments presented by top American officials on the recognition issue were singularly confused. President Eisenhower, in an address before editors, attempted to clarify the official policy: "Recognition of a nation was interpreted differently in various countries. He said he thought that in this country, since Woodrow Wilson's time, recognition had implied a tacit approval. The other interpretation was that recognition meant merely acceptance of the fact that in some important sector of the world there was a de-facto ruler."[9] These remarks betrayed lack

[4] January 15, 1950.
[5] January 15, 1950.
[6] September 1, 1951.
[7] September 1, 1951.
[8] September 1, 1951.
[9] May 15, 1953.

of conviction as to precisely what traditional American policy had been. Indeed, it is a commonplace that the speed with which recognition is accorded to new regimes is often interpreted as a sign of approval or disapproval. To suggest that the recognition of the Soviet Union, of the East European satellites, or of several Latin-American dictatorships implied moral approval on the part of the United States would hardly be convincing.

Democrats such as Mrs. Eleanor Roosevelt, testifying before a Senate subcommittee on the question of Communist China's admission to the United Nations, recalled how the United States had objected to Russia's use of the veto to block the admission "of any state" to the United Nations; she said she would "deplore our having to do what we disapprove of in other governments."[10] But only many years later did Senator Fulbright outrightly term the "Eisenhower administration's policy of adamant rejection of Chinese Communist regime 'sterile.' "[11]

On the China issue it could be said that a genuine debate did not occur, at least at the level of the New York *Times*. Proceeding from nonrecognition to containment to actual subversion of Communist China: this appears to have developed as an opportunistic rather than a planned middle- and long-range pattern of policy.

Complicating the recognition issue was not only the over-all strategy of the cold war but the direct military confrontation of American and Chinese troops in Korea. The capture and the intensive indoctrination—often termed "brainwashing"—of American soldiers by the Chinese contributed to intensifying general hostility against the new Chinese regime, highlighting the diabolic image of Communist Chinese. Never before, it was declared, had such a large proportion of American troops surrendered and lent themselves to denunciations of their own country.

Our investigation reflects special concern with prisoners of war taken by the Chinese during the Korean conflict. One suggestion, proposed by Senator Knowland, called for a blockade against China until the prisoners of war were released. Like Knowland, Representative Thomas A. Dodd, Democrat of Connecticut, declared in a letter to the President that "if after a reasonable period of time these Americans have not been released, then I suggest that the United States and its allies in the free world should set up a naval blockade of the China coast."[12] During the period December 1954 to January 1955 it appears that serious advocacy of such a blockade was fairly common. Agitation was strong enough to call forth responses from the President, Secretary of State, and prominent

[10] October 15, 1951.
[11] June 1, 1957.
[12] December 1, 1954.

congressmen. Secretary of State John Foster Dulles, alluding to American policy regarding the proposals to blockade Red China, said that the United States would "react and react vigorously, but without allowing ourselves to be provoked into action which would be a violation of our international obligations and which would impair the alliance of the free nations."[13] Senator Walter George argued that rather than facilitating release of the prisoners, a blockade would more likely "invite war and retaliation on our own people" and lead to the "speedy death" of the very prisoners America wished to liberate.[14]

There is some indication that there was a less belligerent attitude in the administration than outside it. Quite likely it was the constant criticism and the condemnation of Communist China that contributed to a state of affairs in which the administration felt that it could not attempt alternative policies. Compared to the shrillness of comment by Congressional figures, there is an air of restraint about the comments of United States representative at the United Nations Henry Cabot Lodge. Referring to the Security Council's invitation to Communist China to help in the termination of hostilities in the islands off the Chinese mainland, Lodge declared: "We believe that in any effort to end an armed conflict to which the Chinese Communist regime is a party it is useful for this regime to be present. This was our attitude in 1953 concerning the Korean political conference. It is also the case here now."[15]

When one remembers the common and widely held American aversion to "being pushed around" and how easily any unpleasant situation is transformed into "being pushed around" then one understands the violent potentialities inherent in the increasing hostility toward Communist China by the Americans.

President Truman's interposition of the Seventh Fleet between the Chinese mainland and Formosa so as to neutralize both sides in the Chinese civil war was designated by General MacArthur a "fundamental error which has contaminated the entire Far East situation."[16] When President Eisenhower reversed this policy, thereby ending the "freezing" role of the Seventh Fleet and opening the way to potential attack on the mainland by Nationalists on Formosa, he was widely acclaimed. Fleet Admiral William D. Leahy, a former chief of naval operations, welcomed the ending of the "freezing" role of the Seventh Fleet as a move toward the utilization of the Chinese Nationalists. This, Admiral

13 December 1, 1954.
14 December 1, 1954.
15 February 1, 1955.
16 February 1, 1953.

Leahy felt, was "a bright idea . . . to help us to settle the problem on the China coast."[17] General MacArthur even more jubilantly praised the Eisenhower policy as one which "should be supported by all loyal Americans irrespective of party. It certainly is time for a change."[18] He hailed the Eisenhower administration's decision as a measure that would "correct one of the strangest anomalies known to military history."[19] No correspondingly high military figure expressed dissent with the measure.

The political elite also, especially the Republicans, rallied to support the Eisenhower decision. Senator Homer E. Ferguson, Republican from Michigan, and a member of the Senate Foreign Relations Committee, spoke about keeping the Chinese Nationalists "frozen" on Formosa as having been a "bad policy."[20] And Senator H. Alexander Smith, Republican from New Jersey, described the decision to end the "freezing" as "one of the most effective steps we could take in the direction of settlement of the Korean issue."[21]

When we turn to those who registered opposition to the Eisenhower policy of ending the "freezing" role of the Seventh Fleet, we note that the division between the supporters and opponents is almost entirely along partisan lines. Senator J. William Fulbright, Democrat from Arkansas, declared that if the American military authorities approved of the Eisenhower plan then he "wouldn't quarrel with the plan. . . . But what do we do if the Reds try to invade Formosa?"[22] Senator Albert Gore, Democrat from Tennessee, reflecting upon this move by the Eisenhower administration, similarly limited himself to addressing questions which, however, implied that he had serious doubts as to the wisdom of the policy. Senator Gore asked: "Is this to be unilateral action and if so how will it affect our relations with other members of the United Nations, particularly India, Britain, and Australia? What further military action would this portend?"[23]

The only openly blunt criticism came from Senator Wayne Morse, then an independent from Oregon. He thought that if the "freezing" role of the Seventh Fleet was ended then this move by the administration might go down in history as "a sly tactic for encouraging incidents that may start World War III."[24]

The paucity of such remarks leads us to infer that in spite of the

[17] February 1, 1953.
[18] February 1, 1953.
[19] February 1, 1953.
[20] February 1, 1953.
[21] February 1, 1953.
[22] February 1, 1953.
[23] February 1, 1953.
[24] February 1, 1953.

fears that American official policy *might* lead to a global conflict, there was very little in the way of open and direct opposition to these policies. The stronger the measures adopted against Communist China, the more support the administration could expect from a large segment of the Congress as well as the military. But despite the nearly unanimous expression of negative evaluations of Communist China, it is worthy of note that American leadership was split. The "liberal" elements were unable to carry the debate fully into the open because of the atmosphere of suspicion that contaminated so many of their leaders and experts. Although the public debate over China was muffled, we have found some indication that a fairly sizable and important part of the elite were prepared to consider and accept drastic revisions of the nonrecognition policy.

KOREA

Intertwined with the bipolar conflict involving the Soviet Union and the acute tension with mainland China, the Korean conflict provided an extraordinarily difficult testing ground for American leadership. As it turned out, the Korean operation was a limited war which threatened at any moment to become generalized if the Americans were willing to gamble that the Russian leadership would refrain from precipitating World War III. The voices of moderation finally won; the gamble was not made. We can interpret this as a tribute to the realism and basic self-restraint of United States leadership. The decision, nevertheless, will be criticized by scholars who agree with the late Senator Taft that the Russians would not have regarded their interests as sufficiently involved to "push the button" for all-out atomic war. Americans are not famous for patience in the face of frustration. But the Korean case suggests that the image of American leadership as lacking in tenacity is mistaken.

In the early stages of the decision to support South Korea with armed might there were some who desired a situation whereby the war might be carried onto the Chinese mainland. There is no denying that the presence of Chinese "volunteers" contributed to an acceleration of the fears and frustrations, and the solution appeared to some to be that of resolving the conflict once and for all. A telling indictment of the Truman administration was made by Senator Robert Taft when he declared:

> As far as preventing the war, the President in his speech says that we prevented World War III by moving in against the first aggressor to break the peace since the Second World War. And

then, he says, now we prevent World War III by not punishing
the aggressor when the aggressor is bigger.[25]

The conservative wing of American leadership continued to face
foreign involvements with reluctance. At the same time when they
conceived American interests to be at stake they seemed disposed to act
with some lack of restraint in favor of a "hard line." But the preference
for unilateral solutions in the arena of foreign policy went hand in
hand with an inclination to win as quickly as possible by the vigorous
use of as much coercion as seemed required. As Representative Charles
A. Eaton from New Jersey, an ordained Baptist minister, said of the
original decision to dispatch troops to Korea: "We've got a rattlesnake
by the tail and the sooner we pound its damn head in the better."[26]

The American decision to intervene in Korea was justified as follows:
If aggression were allowed to go unchecked in Korea, then the aggressors
would be encouraged to initiate a host of similar conflict situations.
Hence, the United States as the leader of the free states must take the
initiative in halting the aggression. In this task, the United States must
be supported by all peace-loving states of the United Nations.

The conflict in Korea, we must remember, was not solely an American
concern. It was, officially, a police action carried out under the auspices
of the United Nations, albeit largely under American direction and
with American arms. Hence, initially, the United States had to rally
behind it the support of a majority of member states. In speaking of the
United States aid to South Korea, Warren Austin, the United States
delegate at the United Nations, declared that the world was "responding
to the bugle call of the great principles of nonaggression, personal freedom, and security from violence and lawlessness." He declared that those
who supported the resolution on Korean intervention would "surround
themselves with glory . . . [for their] unhesitating, voluntary, and spontaneous action."[27] Austin hinted at this time at the ambiguity in American aims when he suggested that the United Nations must destroy the
war-making potential of the North Korean state:

> The opportunities for new acts of aggression, of course, should
> be removed. Faithful adherence to the United Nations' objective
> of restoring international peace and security in the area counsels
> the taking of appropriate steps to eliminate the power and the
> ability of the North Korean aggression (sic) to launch future
> attacks.[28]

25 May 1, 1951.
26 July 1, 1950.
27 July 1, 1950.
28 October 1, 1950.

As later developments were to show, and as the United Nations mandate clearly indicated, the police action was authorized merely to expel the North Korean forces from South Korea. Yet, at least in the early stages of the American intervention in Korea, there would appear to have been some temptation to exceed the mandate of the United Nations. The American commander of the United Nations forces in Korea, General MacArthur, expressed sentiments similar to Austin's in a message broadcast to North Korea asking for surrender: "The early and total defeat and complete destruction of your armed forces and war-making potential is now inevitable."[29] As the situation later developed, the lack of precision in the United Nations mandate was to contribute to much confusion, culminating in the exercise of presidential powers in the dismissal of General MacArthur from his commander's post.

President Truman lucidly outlined the reasons that prompted the United States to come to the assistance of South Korea. It would appear that Korea was interpreted as a possible Munich, the Soviet bloc of states as embodying the tendencies of the Nazi regime. President Truman warned: "If the United Nations yields to the forces of aggression, no nation will be safe or secure. If aggression is successful in Korea, we can expect it to spread through Asia and Europe to this hemisphere. We are fighting for our own national security and survival."[30] As the conflict in Korea continued to drag along, the resultant impatience led President Truman to note that "if we got out of Korea, the Communist leaders would strike somewhere else. They would strike at Japan, or the Middle East, or in Europe. And sooner or later they would go on to strike at South America and at our own country."[31]

While there might be the preference and the inclination to treat the Soviet Union and its allied states as a rattlesnake whose head should be pounded in, there was at all times a very lively and intelligent appraisal of the relative strengths of the Soviet bloc and the American bloc. This, as might be expected, was especially true of the military elites. Admiral Sherman, for instance, in his testimony before the Senate, suggested that "Moscow if it wished could call off the invaders in Korea but that the United States was not strong enough to put the necessary diplomatic pressure on the Kremlin for that purpose." He said it would be as much of a strain on Russia to "provide sufficient force to wage a decent fight" in all the areas that a world war would set aflame, as it would be for the United States.[32]

[29] October 1, 1950.
[30] December 1, 1950.
[31] April 14, 1951.
[32] June 1, 1951.

The differing appraisal of the military and the civilian authorities was dramatized during the Korean conflict. General MacArthur's recommendation to bomb the Chinese "volunteers" bases across the Yalu River is presumed to have been the major reason for the conflict. Whereas the Truman administration had decided that because of political reasons the Korean conflict had to be prevented from becoming a direct confrontation of the American and Soviet blocs, General MacArthur, for reasons which from the military point of view appear to be sound, advocated a bombardment of the enemy's bases and supply lines. Yet, it is interesting to note that both President Truman and General MacArthur, in their public pronouncements, stated that their intentions and recommendations were made with the idea of retaining the localized scope of the Korean conflict. General MacArthur, however, declared that by refusing to act upon his recommendations the Truman administration was following a policy that would alter the localized character of the conflict. In his reasoning, the Truman policy of refraining from bombing across the Yalu River was such that "it laid the basis for altering the localized character of the Korean conflict and set the stage for further involvements just as appeasement and indecisiveness have always done."[33]

The analysis of General MacArthur was shared by large segments of the American elite, especially the Republicans. These commentators were ready to strike across the Yalu River, to utilize Chinese Nationalist forces in the Korean conflict, and to welcome the "unleashing" of the Chiang Kai-shek forces onto the Chinese mainland. In other words, the Korean intervention was conceived almost wholly in American terms, to the total neglect of the fact that the "police action" in Korea was being carried out under the United Nations flag, in association with member states of that world organization. Between those who sought to forge a genuine alliance of states and those who sought to convert allied states into satellites in fact, not in name, there appears to have been a grave and continuing chasm. In grossly oversimplified terms we might suggest that this was a cleavage between the liberal and conservative elites within the United States.

We suggest that this is a gross oversimplification because those elements who wished to strike hard at the international Communist movement were liable, at times, to turn almost sulkingly toward total withdrawal. Out of the domestic American political scene emerged certain charges and countercharges that betrayed an uneasy awareness of what appears to have been the close relationship between the war machine and the level of prosperity. These charges were leveled against the

[33] February 1, 1953.

Democratic administration during the 1952 campaign. In our consideration of Adlai Stevenson's response to these charges as they pertained, in particular, to the Korean conflict, we note that the theme of war and prosperity emerged with clarity. Accompanying it was the isolationist impulse. The situation was further confounded when we recall that the Republican party's standard-bearer was the one who gave the call for disengagement in Korea, although Republican party members were the most militant when the operation began.

Adlai Stevenson, responding to these charges of prosperity being a result of participation in the Korean conflict, noted with apparent anguish: "Must this inspiring record now be ridiculed for campaign purposes? Must our credit for using the capitalist system wisely and humanly be undermining Europe—and by General Eisenhower of all men? Must our proud all-American achievement be pictured as a Democratic party plot?"[34]

Candidate Eisenhower, on the other hand, offered to go to Korea to end the conflict there, an offer predicated on being elected to the presidency by the American people. His appeal to the people on this issue was simple, resting almost wholly upon his personal capabilities. There is no evidence that he indicated possessing a political or military formula that was in any manner different from that being followed by the administration. As he himself stated, "I have no magic military wand to bring that war to an end. But I know that on the spot I can learn something that will be helpful to the American people."[35]

What Eisenhower did offer was emotional comfort, not a political and military solution. It was in Texas that he asked for only "one birthday present above all others," namely: "I would like to ask every God-fearing, loyal American of every faith or party, to offer tonight a prayer for peace in Korea. In my heart, as in yours, it cannot come too soon."[36] In stating his plans and intentions in a manner best calculated to attract the American public's notice to his military expertise, Eisenhower tailored his image very precisely for the culture he was addressing himself to. The American public lays great faith in expertise, and it also looks upon most problems as being capable of solution provided that the best minds get involved.

For appealing to the public on such a basis President Truman brought Eisenhower to task. He charged that Eisenhower had been in Korea in 1946, and that later he had recommended the withdrawal of troops from that country. President Truman called this recommendation "wrong." He noted that "there was no reason to suppose that he

[34] October 15, 1952.
[35] November 1, 1952.
[36] October 15, 1952.

would be right in 1953."[37] He asserted that Eisenhower "can't bring our troops home any sooner than the other good generals working on the Korean problem."[38] And in reaction to the Eisenhower offer to go to Korea President Truman is reported to have "scorned the proposal as a vote-getting idea worked up by a 'ghost writer.' "[39]

The journey to Korea by President Eisenhower did take place shortly after the elections. In a statement issued after the return from the Korean journey, we note the vagueness of intentions, evaluation, and recommendations and the lack of any specifics in the Eisenhower pronouncement:

> This journey marks not the end but the beginning of a new effort to conclude honorably this phase of the global struggle. This is not the moment to state more than the resolve. For we face an enemy whom we cannot hope to impress by words, however eloquent, but only by deeds—executed under circumstances of our own choosing.[40]

In other words, the trip accomplished nothing of the near miracle that candidate Eisenhower had promised. While the enemy no doubt was not impressed by eloquent words, the American public was. Years later, Korea, free of overt conflict, still was considered an American liability. The entanglement was still present, contrary to Eisenhower's hopes and promises during the electioneering.

The American leadership exhibited great fortitude and suppleness in dealing with the Korean challenge. The dominant elements affecting these decisions, although chafing at the limitations of a local war, were realistic enough to play it safe and to abstain from acute risk of a global nuclear war. It is, however, of interest to observe that no postmortems appear in our sample of elite opinion. There is no searching after the reasons that could account for the swift collapse of South Korea or the firm and well-executed strategy of the Chinese "volunteers." Similarly, although the Korean "police action" was carried out under the auspices of the United Nations, there is little appreciation of the aid (albeit limited) offered by member states of the United Nations.

THE IRON CURTAIN

The rigidity of postwar relations between the United States and Russia can be traced in part to the domination of Eastern European states by the Soviet Union. This domination partially resulted from the

[37] November 1, 1952.
[38] November 1, 1952.
[39] November 1, 1952.
[40] December 15, 1952.

heroic image of the Communist underground which was created in those countries during the period of German occupation. However, in no case did the Communist party succeed in gaining power without significant overt and covert assistance from the Soviet Union.

It is well to bear in mind that traditionally Russia sought to exercise control of Eastern Europe. The history of Polish-Russian relations is an example of the centuries of long struggle for power. When both Eastern European states and Russia have been weak, the vacuum has been filled by other powers, especially the continental powers of France and Germany, although Turkey, too, exercised domination in parts of this region.

With perhaps the sole exception of Czechoslovakia, the Eastern European states did not have functioning democratic systems. The borders of most of these states were sorely disputed after the dissolution of the Austro-Hungarian Empire. Similarly, it is necessary to bear in mind that again, with the possible exception of Czechoslovakia under Benes and Masaryk, Eastern European countries were dominated by Britain, France, or Germany. The real Soviet domination, however, was of a far different order of magnitude, since it was total and included the regulation of all external contacts. The effective sealing off of Eastern Europe by the Soviet Union eventually gave rise to the expression "Iron Curtain" put forward by Winston Churchill in his famous speech at Fulton, Missouri. Closely linked to official reactions in the United States against the Iron Curtain was the fact that millions of American citizens originally came from this region.

American antagonism had become firmly fixed by 1952. At that time the United States paid Hungary the sum of $120,000 for the release of four American fliers shot down by that country. The intensity of feeling may be gauged in part by the response of Senator Connally to the ransom deal. He termed it as "blackmail" by "a gang of ruffians."[41] Each party, by 1952, included the "liberation" of Eastern European states in its official platform. And they vied with each other in claiming expertise in the politics of liberation. Note, for instance, Adlai Stevenson's approach. He depicted the Eisenhower administration as incapable of capitalizing on the developments behind the Iron Curtain, which he claimed were rocking the Kremlin control in that region. Stevenson claimed that "only a humane and liberal government in Washington can communicate with these worker movements abroad."[42] Stevenson's understanding of the role of empathy in successful communication with diverse groups and governments is indeed a laudable political insight. However, we note in passing that this was perhaps the only example in

41 February 15, 1952.
42 November 1, 1956.

our entire study where reference was made to Communist states as being essentially (at least partly in theory, partly in actual practice) class based. Such an analytical approach was extremely rare in American elite comment as it pertained to communism.

The liberal or left elite in the United States was emotionally disposed to welcome any sign of liberalization in the Soviet area. For instance, Howard Fast, resigning from the Communist party, commented with perhaps exaggerated enthusiasm upon such tendencies within Poland: "Poland has been an inspiration. Poland has been a living proof of the dream of many people that socialism and democracy can exist together."[43]

Comment issuing from the highest echelons of the elite scarcely reflected enthusiasm or even tolerance: indeed, it was straightforwardly belligerent. Illustrative of the dominant view prevailing within the administration were the remarks of Deputy Secretary of Defense William C. Foster on the occasion of laying the keel of the U.S.S. Forrestal. Since the day on which he was to lay the keel was Bastille Day, he reminded his audience that this was

> a memorable milestone in the historic struggle of man for free-
> dom . . . a day of hope for those who may lie in bondage behind
> Iron Curtains everywhere.
> The laying of the keel on this historic date should serve to re-
> mind the citizens of the free world that not only do we proclaim
> the ideals of freedom but we are gathering strength so as to defend
> them.[44]

It may be noted that high-ranking American officials are not easily prone to issue such revolutionary statements. Normal activity having been suspended between the United States and the Eastern European states, American officials arranged to communicate directly with these peoples. Such tactics are reminiscent of ideologically committed and revolutionary states. Yet such appeals were projected at all levels, a spectacular example being the message broadcast over the Voice of America and Radio Free Europe by President Eisenhower:

> I hope there will be ways and means to forward my New Year's
> greetings to all those young people behind the Iron Curtain whose
> good wishes for 1953 are extremely touching.
> I want to assure them that they are not forgotten. I know how
> many of them fought bravely against Nazi tyranny and that they
> tried to build up representative governments after the war.
> So long as the spirit of freedom lives in the youth, the future is
> one of promise.[45]

43 February 1, 1957.
44 July 15, 1952.
45 January 1, 1953.

It is not generally the style in democracies such as the United States to address such appeals directly to the citizens of countries with whom diplomatic relations exist. Such appeals are, of course, the stuff out of which political warfare is waged during periods of belligerency. The contrast can be illustrated if we imagine the President of the United States addressing a speech of liberation to the peoples living in Portuguese colonies.

It is also of value to observe the style of the remarks of Henry Cabot Lodge in the United Nations General Assembly:

> The American people cannot accept with indifference or apathy the situation which the Soviets have created in central Europe. We will not reconcile ourselves to the relentless Soviet assault on human dignity and freedom.
>
> So long as independence remains unachieved, so long as the Soviet Union continues to intervene in the affairs of these countries, we cannot and we will not remain silent and unprotesting.[46]

The humane convictions that appear to underline this appeal before the United Nations by the American representative cannot but leave the impression that a quiet determination persisted in American goals. The harsh language of "liberation" is absent, but certainly the intentions toward that end emerged clearly enough. Henry Cabot Lodge's further remarks best illustrated this.

> It is natural that we should be concerned about the people of Eastern Europe and concerned about the fate of its people. We desire to see them free and independent, able to pursue their own lives and pursue their own destinies, I mean independent of Soviet control, independent of American control, independent of any control.
>
> We will do what we can, always in conformity with the principles of the United Nations, to show these hapless victims that they are not forgotten, that they are not lost.
>
> We will continue to supply these people with the truth about our world and the truth about their world. At every opportunity we will assure them that, no matter what they hear from their masters of today, the old ties of kinship and friendship have not been broken and that this is but a long night and that the end of that long night is the dawn.[47]

It is difficult to see how more solidarity with Eastern European peoples could be expressed. Lodge's remarks can be interpreted to espouse the liberation of these nations. Yet, American elite comment

[46] March 1, 1957.
[47] March 1, 1957.

and style were rarely of this restrained though firm order. To the revolutionary and polemical Soviet appeals there was a tendency to retort in almost identical style albeit the language of the "hard sell."

The explicit comments which appeared in the New York *Times* gave little indication of the guilt and shame which had been felt by many American leaders who believed that national security required them in the years prior to the Soviet takeover to keep alive a degree of optimism among anti-Soviet elements in a country. Being official representatives, they could not concede in advance that the United States would stay out of the fight if the Russians should move. The friends of America were cruelly disenchanted by this deception.

FORMER ENEMY POWERS: GERMANY AND JAPAN

The most significant fact about the references made in the fifties to Germany and Japan was that American policy had brought about rapprochement with both former enemies. American elite comment included remarkably few reminders of the bitter sentiments which had divided the United States, Germany, and Japan from one another a few brief years before. A rare exception was elicited by a Japanese source. In a letter to the chairman of the City Council of Hiroshima, former President Harry S. Truman took the occasion to explain the reasons for the attack by atomic bombs:

> The need for such a fateful decision, of course, never would have arisen had we not been shot in the back by Japan at Pearl Harbor in December 1941.
> And in spite of that shot in the back, this country of ours, the United States of America, has been willing to help in every way the restoration of Japan as a great and prosperous nation.[48]

The policy of nonrecall was supplemented on the positive side by references to the cold war situation. This, of course, was the factor that made the postwar realignment possible. In April 1950 we find Bernard Baruch declaring that sooner or later "we must expect a show-down over Germany because that country 'cannot be expected to remain divided indefinitely.' "[49]

What had been a device to control a defeated Germany had rapidly deteriorated into a power confrontation between the allies themselves. At this period the Communist parties of Italy and France were formidable forces which were close to winning power by way of the ballot box.

[48] March 15, 1958.
[49] April 1, 1950.

The important role played by the Communists in the underground in wartime Europe at a time when the liberal elements of many European countries had either remained silent or allied themselves with the Fascists and Nazis—this fact possibly accounts for some of the genuine popularity of the Communist parties in many countries. Communism had emerged as a triumphant ideology and appeared to many as the wave, and perhaps the salvation, of the future.

During the late forties the United States responded in an unprecedented manner by mobilizing its economic resources for the rehabilitation of the devastated economies of the European continent. Given sufficient time, it was reasoned, the strength of the Communist parties in Western Europe could be nibbled away by growing prosperity and by the rise of new associations and organizations. Into any such grand design Germany had to occupy a place of importance; and this was recognized by the United States. Indeed, such an alliance between Germany and the Western allies was not a novel policy suggestion. Ever since the Soviets grasped power in Russia there had existed influential segments of the elites in all the major European countries and the United States who had advocated openly, or secretly desired, an alliance to crush the Communist state in Russia. Hitler had hoped for some such alignment and Winston Churchill had long envisioned the possibility of a Soviet-Allied Powers conflict.

The Soviet Union's radical and aggressive policies hastened the abandonment of the program of denazification. Aggressive Soviet policies, especially in regard to the status of Berlin, rapidly called forth a counter-response from the United States. In no uncertain terms we note Dean Acheson declaring at a news conference: "I think that it is well understood by you and by everybody, including the Soviet government, that we are determined to maintain our position in Berlin and to assist and protect the interests of Berlin in the Western zone."[50]

As for reunification, Ambassador James B. Conant declared at a Bonn press conference that "the entire apparatus of dictatorship must disappear in East Germany before we can make a start on any practical measures leading to Germany's reunification."[51]

It was abundantly clear that the Soviet Union would not willingly allow East Germany to slip from its control. It was also clear, from past experience, that the dictatorship established under Soviet auspices was not willingly dissolved. Hence, the United States adopted a policy of strength, at last drawing a line beyond which Soviet domination would not be permitted to pass. Upon this there appears to have been an agreement among the leadership of the Republican and Democratic

[50] May 15, 1952.
[51] July 1, 1953.

parties. Adlai Stevenson phrased it simply: "If we maintain our position, the Communists must give way as they did on the Berlin airlift."[52]

American policy toward the new Germany was brought home in no uncertain terms by Secretary of State Dulles five years later when he declared:

> We do not accept any arrangement which is based upon the present partition of Germany, and let me add this: that in anything which touched directly or indirectly upon Germany and its prospects for reunification we would act only in the closest concert with Chancellor Adenauer.[53]

The cold war basis of reorientation toward Japan was indicated in a New Year's message from General MacArthur who declared to the Japanese people, then under his tutelage, that "so long as predatory international banditry [communism] is permitted to roam the earth to crush human freedom under its avarice and violence, the high concept to which you are pledged will be slow in finding universal acceptance."[54]

We assume that General MacArthur's reference to the "high concept" to which the Japanese people were pledged referred to that clause in their constitution that forbade rearming or preparing for war. This clause, we must remember, was suggested and imposed by the Allied occupation forces upon Japan; yet barely five years after the promulgation of the constitution there had arisen the necessity to reconsider, and abandon, the notion of a Japan dedicated forever to remain peaceful.

The complete shift in allies and enemies is well illustrated in John Foster Dulles's remarks on the Japanese Peace Treaty: "The Soviet Union has no legal power to veto. It has no moral due-bills, for its vast takings in Manchuria, Port Arthur, Darien, Sakhalin, and the Kuriles repay it a thousandfold for its six days of nominal belligerency."[55]

Mr. Dulles's legalistic language and references to "due bills" were an indication that the World War II era had been superseded by an altogether different period in history. Indeed, the shift is clearly demonstrated in Dean Acheson's remarks upon the Japanese Peace Treaty. His interpretation was that the treaty indicated the sincere desire of the United States and Allied nations to foster international peace and harmony. In Acheson's words: "It surely needs no emphasis of mine to point out the importance of taking every opportunity to repair the fabric of world peace."[56]

[52] November 1, 1952.
[53] May 15, 1957.
[54] January 1, 1950.
[55] April 1, 1951.
[56] September 1, 1951.

Acheson insisted upon making the issue of the Japanese Peace Treaty one by which the intentions of nations would be judged: "Actions at this conference will demonstrate clearly which nations really want peace and which nations merely talk peace while acting in ways that prevent peace."[57] It will be remembered that the Chinese People's Republic had not been invited to the Japanese Peace Treaty Conference. When it is taken into account that China, more than any other nation, bore the brunt of Japanese aggression, the remarks of Acheson lose some of their sanctity. When India refused to consider the absence of China from the conference as appropriate and therefore refused to be a signatory to the Japanese Peace Treaty, we note the anger and annoyance of Representative John E. Lyle, Jr., Democrat from Texas, who said that he was tired of "these damn fool statements" by Prime Minister Nehru on the Japanese Peace Treaty.[58]

OLD ALLIES AND NEW NATIONS

The postwar world presented the United States with no more awkward problem than arose in connection with the adjustment of relations with old allies who found themselves targets of anti-imperialist attack by new nations struggling for independence. The American tradition was conceived as anti-imperialist and pro-independence. Since many new candidates for statehood were certain to remain weak for some time, and the need of containing Soviet expansion was deemed to be urgent, the task was to steer a course that would not alienate and weaken all concerned. In no part of the globe were problems more acute than in the Middle East. Partly because of the political importance of the Jewish vote in the United States the governing elite was committed to back Israel. However, the Arab states were of vast importance, not only for their oil, but as a consequence of their strategic location as an intermediate zone between the Soviet Union and Africa.

From the United States standpoint the Suez crisis of November 1956 was one of the least welcome issues that could have arisen. The combined attack of Anglo-French and Israeli forces could have led to a military solution of the canal question. At this juncture active support of the attacking forces by the United States might have overthrown the Nasser regime. However, there is little doubt that Soviet intervention was a distinct possibility in case the United States took sides with its traditional allies. Moreover, here was a situation in which former imperial powers were engaged in gunboat diplomacy. Con-

[57] September 1, 1951.
[58] August 15, 1951.

siderations of the sentiments of the newly emerging states undoubtedly entered into the policy considerations of the Republican administration as regards the Suez issue.

The policy of the United States had finally been forced to a stage where it had to reckon with its long-range interests in the Middle East, and the United States, stand met with almost undivided acclaim in the emerging states of Asia and Africa. The high moral tenor of President Eisenhower's remarks was synchronized with concrete acts in a specific situation. Eisenhower declared: "We do not accept the use of force as a wise or proper instrument for the settlement of international disputes . . . we are forced to doubt even if resort to war will for long serve the permanent interests of the attacking nations."[59] In appropriately moral language, President Eisenhower declared that "there could be no peace without law and there can be no law if we were to invoke one code of international conduct for those who oppose us and another for our friends."[60]

Fully realizing the humiliation that would be suffered by the retreat of France and Britain, President Eisenhower declared in phrases reminiscent of the nonaligned elites that the United States wanted to be friends with everybody. On the sensitive issue of Arab–Israeli hostility, Eisenhower stated the American position thus: "We believe this: that our efforts to be friends with both sides in the Arab–Israeli war is the best thing we can do for both sides in order to bring about friendship finally, and relations between them, because it is perfectly clear that in the long run they need each other."[61]

For once, at least, the United States succeeded in separating itself from the stigma of association with imperialist allies.

Secretary of State Dulles left little doubt as regards the firmness with which the United States intended to act in the Middle East. In plain words this was a show of strength to match Soviet policies in the region. Dulles declared:

> The view here is that Egypt and Syria have a perfect right to reject any economic or military aid from the United States, but that they do not have the right to speak for the other states in the area that might be attacked by the Soviet Union or a nation friendly to the Soviet Union. . . . Egypt and Syria could not expect to veto United States aid to Iran, Iraq, or Saudi Arabia if those nations were under Communist attack and called on Washington for help.[62]

[59] November 1, 1956.
[60] November 1, 1956.
[61] November 1, 1956.
[62] January 1, 1957.

In plain words, it appears that the United States did not wish to respect the Egyptian versions of a "Monroe Doctrine" and that the republican, militant nationalism of Cairo was to be curbed in case it sought to extend itself into the neighboring Arab kingdoms. The references to "Communist attack" and attack by "a nation friendly to the Soviet Union" gave the United States tremendous latitude to intervene in the Middle East. The strategy was revealed by Dulles himself when he explained:

> It is hoped here, however, that the proposed United States economic program of aid for the Middle East and the United States declaration that it is prepared to fight, if necessary, against Communist aggression in the area will encourage the natural anti-Communist tendencies of the Moslem nations and thus deal with the Communist subversion problem indirectly.[63]

It is of interest that Dulles made use of one of the most common and dubious stereotypes of politics when he alluded to the "natural anti-Communist tendencies of the Moslem nations." We note that one of the largest Muslim states in the world—Indonesia—had the largest Communist party in the Afro-Asian region. Similarly, the Communist party (the Tudeh party as it was called) of Iran had strength and appeal among a people which was Muslim.

In making his policy pronouncement as regards American intervention in the Middle East, we note that toward the end of his statement Secretary of State Dulles qualified American intervention in this region: "If the Soviet Union attacked Iran or if a Communist-dominated Syrian government attacked Iraq, the United States would act in the light of the circumstances at the time and only if requested to do so by Iran or Iraq."[64] Two weeks later Secretary of State Dulles told the Senate that "There had been 'a cataclysmic change' in the Middle East 'in the last few weeks.' He called it one that 'totally altered the situation in a sense, initially at least, very much in favor of international communism.' "[65] This threat of possible international aggression in the Middle East was described by Dulles as "the most serious threat we have faced over the past ten years."[66]

This, then, was the American assessment of the situation in the Middle East, and the background for the proclamation of the Eisenhower Middle East Doctrine. It was described by Assistant Secretary of State Robert C. Hill, in his letter to the Senate, as a doctrine designed

[63] January 1, 1957.
[64] January 1, 1957.
[65] January 15, 1957.
[66] January 15, 1957.

as "a shield against destruction of the nations of the region by sub-version from within."[67]

Lodge explained the Eisenhower administration policy to the United Nations in the following manner:

> His policy is an anti-aggression policy. It is a policy which is aimed at peace. It is a policy which can only be carried out with the consent of the affected countries.
>
> It is a policy which is aimed at preserving national sovereignty and independence of small states and preventing outside inter-ference in their affairs. It is a policy which aims to prevent the same thing happening to the sovereign countries in the Middle East which happened to Lithuania, Estonia, Latvia, Czechoslovakia, Poland, Hungary, Bulgaria, and Albania, not to mention North Korea and North Vietnam. It is undoubtedly for that reason that the Soviet Union does not like it.[68]

The "tough" diplomatic line of Dulles was appropriately criticized by Senator Fulbright upon the occasion of the United States decision to withdraw from the offer to build the Aswan Dam in Egypt. Senator Fulbright pointed to the flaw in Secretary of State Dulles's policy: "I believe the Secretary of State confused Egyptian nationalism and neutral-ism on the one hand with communism on the other. . . . [Dulles] did not recognize that Egyptian nationalism was a powerful force which could . . . be directed toward political freedom instead of com-munism."[69] In the course of the same speech, Senator Fulbright made allusion to the rift within the State Department over the appreciation and evaluation of nationalism and neutralism. He noted that "although 'able State Department career officials' felt 'that Nasser had some ap-preciation of the dangers of dealing too closely with the Soviet Union, Mr. Dulles seemed to believe that Nasser had become a Soviet puppet.' "[70]

This analysis of Dulles as well as his general conception of neutralism or nonalignment as something inherently evil and approaching com-munism clearly expressed the view of a large section of the American leadership. The approach of Senator Fulbright was close to the view of the nonaligned countries.

[67] March 1, 1957.
[68] February 15, 1957.
[69] August 15, 1957.
[70] August 15, 1957.

PART V · CONCLUSION

CHAPTER 16 · POLITICAL IDEOLOGIES IN ACTION

It is impossible to follow the language of top leaders in two such great nation-states without acquiring a heightened sense of the formidable role of public attention and also of political generalization in the political life of large-scale bodies politic. Whatever reaches the focus of attention is a precondition of collective confusion, agreement, or action. Unless the stream of communication is helpful in clarifying goals, summarizing trends, explaining conditions, projecting futures, and evaluating public policies, a nation is likely to drift into disorganization and eventual anarchy. Because of the necessary interpenetration of particular terms and generalized conceptions, the participants in a communication process are engaged in perceiving and adapting an inclusive map of the total situation in which they live. If the map is lucid and realistic, the results are likely to prove favorable to the value position of the body politic.

With the aid of numerical tabulations the present chapter will provide a concise overview of some characteristic features of reported elite utterance in India and the United States during years that followed Indian independence. Information in the various tables confirms the broad impression that the effective power officials of India and the United States were willing to play the guiding role that their positions implied. Prime Minister Nehru accounted for 55 percent of all statements by Indian leaders that were quoted in our sample (Tables 2 and 3).[1] Combined with President Prasad the figure is 63 percent. The preeminence of Nehru is indicated when we examine the attention accorded to American presidents. President Eisenhower made 23 percent of the

[1] Tables referred to in this chapter are in Appendix A.

statements attributed to American leaders in the New York *Times* (Table 4). The combined figure for Presidents Eisenhower and Truman was 34 percent of the United States total (the two most-quoted persons).

The relative ascendancy of a few top figures in India is reflected in the fact that nine Indian spokesmen who constituted less than 11 percent of the quoted Indian leaders originated 81 percent of all the statements made. In the United States sample fifteen spokesmen (10.5 percent of the Americans quoted) accounted for 68 percent of United States statements.

Presumably the prominent role of Prime Minister Nehru had contradictory consequences for Indian policy. On the one hand, Nehru was able to obtain the degree of attention that he wanted in order to carry on the tutorial tasks that he felt called on to perform. Quite likely a negative consequence was that vigorous young successors were not brought into public view.

An analysis of spokesmen reported in the New York *Times* and the *Times of India* is particularly revealing when we classify it according to professional background or political role. The relative prominence of the military reveals a remarkable contrast. The American military are the source of 5 percent of all quoted statements (Table 2). The Indian military account for less than 1 percent of the material summarized in the *Times of India*. Actually a single professional soldier makes the grade in India—a retiring commander in chief. The figures reflect the political predispositions of both countries. Whereas in the United States military commanders are frequently interviewed and are at liberty to express themselves within limits imposed by security considerations, the Indian tradition subordinates the public role of military to civilian authority, and keeps the officer in the background on matters of public policy.

It is questionable whether the degree of subordination imposed on the military in India is suitable to the requirements of a popular government in a period of chronic mobilization. The situation in India may be modified as a result of the shock administered to the nation by the Chinese Communists in 1962. If military components of public life are not given candid and competent attention, there is danger of further shocks that might topple the prevailing system of public order.

Diplomats played about the same modest part in the New York *Times* and the *Times of India*. Despite the far-flung commitments of the United States, diplomats were somewhat less visible than in India. About the same number were quoted in both countries (8 percent of all leaders).

Although a few groups, such as academic intellectuals, obtained relatively more exposure in the New York *Times*, the spokesmen of pluralistic associations did not obtain great prominence in either newspaper. Table 2 indicates that "labor," "business," designated spokesmen for other pressure groups, and "intellectuals" account for less than 7 percent of the sources quoted in the New York *Times*. In the *Times of India* the corresponding figures are between 4 and 5 percent.

The relative role of the executive, legislative, and judicial branches of national government is indicated by the results. The Cabinet (and high officials) of the United States provided more spokesmen than in India (about 19 percent versus 10 percent). Senators and representatives account for more than a third of the quoted sources in the United States (24 percent in India). The authority of the Prime Minister obviously cast other members of the Indian legislature in the shade. Despite the deference given the judicial branch, the judiciary was not conspicuous among the day-to-day interpreters of top-policy questions.

It was not foreseen by the framers of the Indian constitution that the states would take the role that they have played in independent India. States have been much stronger than anticipated, as suggested by the fact that 18 percent of the leaders quoted in the *Times of India* were identified as state figures.

The emphasis in India on party organization is registered to some degree in the use of party labeled sources (about 7 percent as against 1 percent). In the United States the party label was more often submerged by the official identity of the speaker.

If we turn from the "who" of communication sources and examine "what" was said, several results are directly relevant to the hypotheses formulated in the first chapter. It was proposed that elite attention is affected by value indulgent or value deprivational changes in the environment of elite members (individually and collectively). The probable role of an elite press, considered in this context, is to perform a *self-surveillance* function in reference to members of the established elite of a nation; also to report on the *disloyal opposition* at home, as well as *hostile, friendly, or uncommitted elites abroad.*

Table 5 indicates that front-page speakers reported by the New York *Times* were about 50 to 50 in their concern with inner or outer affairs. The figure in India was closer to 60 to 40, with the emphasis on internal matters. The nearest active threat (or obstacle) in the world arena, as expected, rates high in the share of attention received. Pakistan and Kashmir account for two-fifths of the comment in the *Times of India* (Table 7a). The Portuguese colonies register about 12 percent. During the same period the United States was involved in no clash with neighboring powers. However, awareness of the opposing polar power is indicated by the degree of United States preoccupation with the Soviet Union (23.5 percent).

India and the United States are oriented toward contrasting sources of indulgence and deprivation in world politics. One percent of the

American comment dealt with India; Indian references to the United States were only 4 percent of the total volume of Indian comment. For the Indian elite other Asian nations were overwhelmingly important, and accounted for more than 71 percent of the total. The United States was about half as much interested in the same countries (35 percent). Even this degree of overlap is deceptive. United States comment was narrowly concentrated on Korea (more than 18 percent); Korea rarely figured in the *Times of India*. United States commentators gave no attention whatever to Pakistan, Kashmir, and the Portuguese colonies in our sample; the Indian spokesmen, on the other hand, allocated 52 percent of their attention to these territories. Indian sources gave about a third as much space to the Soviet Union as the American; but China received twice the attention (13 percent). The United States was rather heavily concerned with the Middle East (8 per cent); Indian references were scant.

Britain and the Commonwealth continued to hold a fraction of India's interest (about 4 percent), which was approximated by the United States. The commentators of both papers shared two blank spots, all of South America and Africa south of the Sahara. (Not until the Cuban revolution did the American elite develop a more regular concern for Latin America.)

Various ideological factors exert influence on the pattern of reference in the *Times of India* and the New York *Times*. Nehru and his colleagues were determined to play a decisive role in world politics as mediators between the Soviet and American blocs; they hoped to consolidate an effective "third force." They were unwilling to alienate the Soviet bloc by adopting the "free-world" label for the coalition led by the United States. About 10 percent of American sources referred to the free world as a matter of course; Indians ignored the symbol (Table 7a). It is of interest that the "West" enters into the political vocabulary of both with similar connotations.

Whatever the subject matter of reference in the quoted utterances of elite speakers, we find that a degree of generalization was involved. Table 6a summarizes the general statements related to "political orientation" made when internal policies were under discussion.

Included were references to the self image of the nation and to identifying symbols of the whole; allusions to history, national goals and values, and basic political doctrine. About 43 percent of the statements by Indian speakers had something to contribute to these categories. About 31 percent of the Americans made corresponding assertions. For persons who assume that Americans are "non-ideological" these results may be somewhat surprising, since the total for the Americans is roughly three quarters of the Indian figure.

A function of ideology is to make articulate the overriding value goals of the body politic; and it is of interest that the speakers quoted in both papers are about equally preoccupied with goals (India 7 percent; United States 6 percent. Table 6b). The category of "doctrine" gives the United States an edge, principally as a result of the prominence given to the discussion of "subversive communism" (the United States 10 percent; India 6 percent. Table 6b). A newly independent nation will presumably be exhorted by its leaders to cultivate unity; this hypothesis is sustained by the data (15 percent. Table 6b). But unity is a theme in every body politic when internal or external threats are perceived by any considerable component of the elite (we note that the figure in the United States was about half the Indian, or 8 percent).

Attention was called earlier to the fact that the social structure of India perpetuates a formidable array of local and cultural identities, and that the sentiment of national unity so characteristic of industrialized states is relatively tenuous. The poverty of symbols of reference to the whole community is reflected in the figure for "national symbols" (less than 1 percent in India; 3.5 percent in the United States).

Both India and the United States were preoccupied with elaborating their self images; and it is of interest to examine the value categories that were applied. Indian elite members gave more stress than the Americans to affection, rectitude, well-being, or wealth; American references were usually in terms of enlightenment, power, respect, or skill. The results tend to confirm the impression that the world political role of the United States brought with it an acute sense of power (28 percent United States; 21 percent Indian). As expected, the Indians emphasize ethical and religious values in projecting the national self. The same category also figures prominently in American statements. (Indian 20 percent; United States 16 percent.) Respect and enlightenment receive about the same degree of emphasis. Indian stress on well-being and wealth is presumably to be attributed to the importance ascribed to bringing the benefits of modern science and technology to the nation. It is not surprising to discover that the new status of the Indian nation evoked relatively frequent expressions of loyalty (affection).

Taken in their entirety, the results indicate that the top political elites of India and the United States are members of the same universal civilization and that they share the same relatively secular and democratic perspectives. We must, however, keep in mind the tremendous gap between Nehru (and his associates) and the village-bound outlook of most Indians. It is not unlikely that the future will see a strong tendency to revive traditional religious and magical myths at the national level.

The treatment of controversial issues provides further insight into the role of basic perspectives in guiding debate. Economic discussion in India seemed to deal rather more with generalities than the corresponding comments reported in the United States. The concern for inclusive national goals is reflected in the references to "planning" and "general" economic topics (Table 6a: about 6 percent in India; 1 percent in the United States). References to political institutions seem rather more specific than in India (12 percent in the United States; 6 percent in India).

Many issues grew out of the contrasting problems and relatively distinctive approaches cultivated in the two countries. Under the rubric "social problems" are put the challenges to the Indian government that resulted from the arrival of refugees from Pakistan and from the acute friction among religious communities. The traditional insistence by Americans on civil rights is important enough to be noted separately (3 percent). In India, on the contrary, the conception of individual rights against the state is out of keeping with the traditions of an authoritarian, though gradually democratizing, culture. The accent on individuality in the United States is indicated by the attention given to "personalities" (about 20 percent in the United States; 5 percent in India).

It is when we reflect on the role of ideology as an instrument of solving public problems that the full complexity of its function comes into view. If on the one hand, ideologies provide a stabilizing approach to reality, it is obvious that they were far from inflexible in either India or the United States. The political generalizations of India appear to have undergone more change in the period of our survey than the American; and this, certainly, is to be expected, for the elites of the newly independent Indian nation were faced by a wider range of novel problems than those that engaged the attention of the top leadership of the United States. *The key symbols, slogans, and statements of any body politic—we suggest—vary directly with the variety and significance of the problems with which the nation is concerned.* These perceptions, of course, are partly conditioned by the frame of reference provided by the ideology, since a problem is a discrepancy between valued goals or strategies and the current or anticipated state of affairs. If value realizations are substantial, one set of problems at least is satisfactorily disposed of, and furnishes value indulgences for all who are identified with the fate of the nation. Among those who are most intensely identified with the status of the body politic we must, save in exceptional circumstances, number the members of the power elite.

Although by 1950 some of the novelty had worn off it is apparent to any reader of public communications that the vast majority of Indian leaders welcomed the improved power position of the national self with excitement and enthusiasm. New sources of self-respect were immediately available as the new Indian state received the usual recognitions given to an independent state.

It would show little comprehension of the human personality to dismiss as formalistic or trivial the new stream of respect indulgences enjoyed by all who identified themselves with the new India. An entire superstructure of alien origin disappeared from the social scene, leaving Indians free of the duty of self-abnegation in regard to foreigners. Partly as a result of their all-pervasive character such alterations of respect position tend to lose visibility; they are simply taken for granted. The fish presumably does not return thanks for the water that surrounds it, and free peoples are likely to lose awareness of the ambiance of respect in which they live. This is especially true of young people, who have no significant recollection of the humiliations of the colonial period; and the unending procession of young people continually crowds the elder generation off stage.

When we commented above that the power elite is usually, though not invariably, identified with the status of their body politic, we had some exceptions in mind. A thin but influential stratum of educated Indians had been partially incorporated into the British version of Western civilization and, as pointed out earlier, often carried this identification to the extreme of accepting a low estimate of fellow Indians. Having come to terms with a way of life that gave them a vested and sentimental interest in the British raj, they were vulnerable in the new India to ambitious fellow countrymen who sought to share their advantages. To some extent the dawn of independence signified a new era of competition and possible deprivation.

No seer would have been needed to prophesy that the realities of political independence would fail to fulfill all of the sanguine expectations generated in the course of revolutionary agitation. So long as the British exercised authority and control they were the obvious scapegoats for every alleged failure of government to serve the needs and aspirations of the Indian populace. Politicians of the Congress party could vie with one another in indicting the raj for its shortcomings; such exercises of skill in denunciation were rewarded in power terms by preferment within the independence movement, and by hearty applause and other tokens of respect from fellow Indians. During the later stages, in particular, economic opportunities were made available, not only within the agitational corps, but in an ever-widening circle of Indian enterprises. With independence comes power (and other assets); but with power also came vulnerability to power deprivations resulting, not from lack of agitational proficiency, but from whatever dissatisfactions were imputed to the new government.

We can now make explicit the face-saving function that can be performed by a skillfully manipulated ideological system. For years the symbolic scapegoat for any Indian failure was the raj which provided a built-in explanation for national limitations.

To the extent that the explanation retained credibility, the newly established elite could forestall either a powerful loyal opposition or a successful counter-ideological movement.

The "colonialist," "imperialist" explanation had the advantage of plausibility. After all, there was ample evidence that the British raj had indeed exercised the ancient strategy of "divide and rule" and played the religious, linguistic, tribal, territorial, and other components of Indian society against one another. But the explanation was not wholly convincing. Other factors—rooted in Indian society long before the advent of the British—were obviously involved. Responsibility for the orgies of violence connected with the partition could not all be laid at the door of Britain. As time passed it became less and less acceptable to assert that every act of official inefficiency, corruption, or petty tyranny was part of the long shadow of colonialism. Indians were often too gifted in inefficiency, corruptness, or tyranny to fail to bear some onus for the result.

The colonialist alibi was also vulnerable to the sense of responsible realism on the part of Prime Minister Nehru and his principal associates. Nehru was perfectly willing to employ the colonialist theme and within limits to benefit from the alibi effect. But he was unwilling to let it go at that. Nehru was too aware of his role in history to fail to try to adapt the ideology of independent India to reality. To some extent his role was deliberately paternal and tutorial; hence the Prime Minister did not fail to acknowledge that some of the shortcomings of India were to be explained as failures of Indian culture to mold responsible participants in the political process. Nehru did not fail to increase the palatability of these negative self-appraisals by paying enthusiastic tribute to the positive image of the nation. For he had ample experience to draw upon in acknowledging the ego damage that came to every Indian during the period of subordination to outside powers, and to perceive that a positive self image was necessary if the members of the new nation were to adapt with dignity and competence to their changed status. At the deeper level Nehru was doubtless ambivalent about some aspects of his own image; but this, if true, seems to have prepared him to empathize with many millions of his fellow countrymen, and to introduce elements of reality testing simultaneously with the confirmation of an elevated view of their common Indian identity.

The Prime Minister also made limited use of another potential alibi

that was closely associated with the colonialist theme. Nehru had long
flirted with Marxism, and reiterated the Marxist emphasis on the ex-
ploitative tendencies of capitalism, especially among the "imperialists."
There is ample evidence that the Prime Minister was genuinely afraid
of imperialist-capitalistic exploitation, and feared that foreign investors
would overwhelm the poor though independent Indian state. Evidently
Nehru was surprised at the unwillingness of "imperialists" to invest.
Pressed by the desperate need of economic development, Nehru modified his conventional Marxist vocabulary and cultivated foreign aid on
the relatively generous terms offered by the United States. Ideology bent
to meet new expectations in regard to reality.

As with active and responsible political leaders Nehru was not primarily concerned with explanation, but with policy goals and strategies.
The most drastic revisions that occurred in the political ideology of the
top leadership of India were related to foreign policy. In the perspective
of future historians the first few years of India's life as an independent
state may seem to be one of the most tragic chapters in human aspiration. Nehru and his principal colleagues had been nurtured in the
perspective of Gandhian politics. They had witnessed the phenomenal
impact of mass withdrawals of support from nominal heads of government. As joint leaders of the non-cooperation movement they had ample
evidence of the world-wide repercussions of the Gandhian approach,
since men of good will everywhere had seized on the doctrines of Gandhi
as offering new hope for mankind. Little wonder that, with fiery
imagination, Indian leaders began to dream of a world revolutionary
mission for independent India. Might not the new nation provide a
model of civilized and humane conduct for the governments and peoples
of the globe?

We have quoted many excerpts from the utterances of Indian leaders
who gave voice to this aspiration. In the realm of active policy such an
image of India's mission played a significant part. We have traced it in
the initial stages of the dispute with Pakistan, and during the years of
forbearance in Kashmir. The vision was unmistakable in the moralizing
discourses by Indian spokesmen at the United Nations and in the re-
sponsiveness of the Indian elite to Soviet pronouncements in the name
of peace. Some of the enduring devotion to an all-Asian ideal stemmed
from the same source.

Whatever the dimensions of the original dream, it was unable to
endure the brutal stabs of reality. The United Nations did not come to
the aid of India in the dispute with Pakistan. Nonviolence did not
subdue tiny Goa; rather, Goa gave way before an active exercise of force.
Obstinate confidence in the influence of moral suasion crumbled before
Chinese troops. And the Indian state did not do away with professional

policemen or transform the military into a "nonviolent army." Nor could Indian leaders disassociate themselves from the long tradition of violence in Indian politics, not excluding the independence movement itself. The world revolutionary vision of a fraternal and pacific commonwealth of peoples grew dim in the glaring light of incongruities at home and abroad.

If the political evolution of the United States was less full of adventure, there was also much less disenchantment. The absorption of Americans in their own affairs had the remarkable effect of preventing the nation from pressing its power advantage at the end of World War II. The nation experienced no frenzied outburst of imperial sentiment. American armies did not try to conquer the impoverished, disorganized, and exhausted globe. There was, in fact, a period of such rapid withdrawal of American forces abroad that Communist forces were given a new lease on life in many countries. With obvious reluctance the United States presently began to recognize the tragic reality of the arms race, the diplomatic race, the economic race, and the ideological race with Soviet communism.

So reluctant was the American dragon that its measures were often slow and initially ineffective, with the result that American opinion was dangerously divided against itself. What possible explanation could there be for the seeming weakness of American policy, such as the slow, bleeding war in Korea? What explanation, indeed, save sedition? Such, at least, was the claim of the militant nationalist Americans who sought to put an end to the Roosevelt–Truman era by rallying around the dynamic public image of Senator McCarthy.

The McCarthy episode did not last many years; and in the end the repudiation of McCarthy's brand of truculent extremism was emphatic. The man was thoroughly discredited before death removed him from the stage. The self-regulating tendencies of the American commonwealth brought the ship of state back on a less adventurous and divisive course. Americans had enough confidence in one another to reject as grotesque the insinuation that the nation's leaders were secret agents of a foreign power. After more than a century and a half of independence, American ideology was interwoven with a tough network of governmental structures, political parties, pressure groups, and other private associations whose occasions of cooperation were too frequent to be disrupted by a wildly ruthless and ambitious faction.

The nation has subsequently shown its determination to apply the commitment to human dignity with full seriousness, and to root out the incongruous institutions of racial inequality that survive from the past. Most Americans are prepared to admit that the humiliating spectacle of racial inequity is a continuing source of national weakness; and that the world position of the nation does not permit the United States to remain "half free and half fraud." The internal costs of transition are now being paid in every American community. In the end the American commonwealth will undoubtedly emerge the stronger for the ordeal of living up to its proclaimed faith in man.

It is neither plausible nor essential to claim that the absence of imperial policy and the rejuvenation of concern for human rights were solely determined by the ideological propensities of the American people and their leaders. If ideologies survive from one generation to another, and if they are given more perfectionist manifestations in behavior, it signifies the presence of an institutional environment that provides and is expected to provide net value advantages to those who measure up to the norms of the ideological system.

We emphasize in this context the interpenetration of symbolic systems and social situations. The point is that ideologies are not to be confused with recitations, whether of the ringing affirmations of the Declaration of Independence, or, in India, of the sayings of Gandhi or Nehru. True enough there are rewards of respect, rectitude, and other value expressions for the act of quotation; and these situations, whether in home, school, or elsewhere, are not to be overlooked as a stable pattern of institutional practice. However, the permeative effect of ideology is to be found in the innovation, diffusion, and restriction of patterns anywhere in the whole social process that are inspired by the doctrines, formulas, and miranda of the political myth. As a rule only detailed inquiry is able to locate the spontaneous or deliberate innovations, or trace their subsequent pathways. In a rapidly developing nation, however, these changes are often conspicuous, as indeed they are in contemporary India. As this survey reminds us, the dynamic role of an ideological frame of reference is never to be underrated, even after generations of failure to narrow the discrepancy between word and deed. To say the least, the repetition of doctrinal norms smoothes the way for the invention and acceptance of "perfectionist" interpretations in concrete circumstances. The "cost" of such redefinitions is less than where the general framework is missing or rejected.

We have underlined thus far the statements in the flow of political discourse that deal explicitly with problems of public or private action. Equally significant are the silences, or the subdued passages in the stream of public communication. No outsider would realize from our report that one of the fundamental transformations of Indian society is making relatively rapid progress, a transformation that is in many ways far more revolutionary and anxiety laden than the racial readjustment in the United States. The proclaimed goals of Indian government and society are in harmony with the Universal Declaration of Human Rights, envisioning a national and world commonwealth of value realization. The dignity of the individual in a mobile society is taken with ever-increasing earnestness. But the struggle is seldom referred to in the public prints despite the ever-present tensions generated by the proclaimed doctrines and formulas that condemn or outlaw the deeply entrenched institutions of caste.

Such silences by the apex elite are of great interest to the student of comparative politics. Presumably these singular omissions are to be explained by the intensity of the anxieties that would be generated by repetition, and by the general assumption that nothing is to be accomplished by publicity. Such profound modifications of social practice are taking place everywhere in varying degree; and the process is now piecemeal but genuine. "Little arenas" are springing up throughout Indian society in which specific issues are joined. We are at a phase in a vast social movement when progress (in changing the mores) is sufficient to prevent an eruption in the national arena. The innovating ideology is being taken too seriously to be the theme of everyday talk.

Any attempt to appraise the impact of an ideological system must distinguish between its double role as a source of *criteria* of judgment and of the *procedures* to be employed in making judgments. The criteria clarify the goal values of national action, and hence indicate relevant trends, conditions, projections, and alternatives. Procedures emphasize the importance of an agenda of problem solving that includes the deliberate consideration of each dimension—goal, trend, condition, projection, alternative. Usually this is expressed as a set of demands to discuss issues of policy in private or public forums of deliberation. The ideology of the United States is particularly rich in detail relating to methods of decision making—including the role of judges and the judiciary in dealing with controversies over the application of established prescriptions. Procedural patterns cover such relatively minute points as the assumption of a conversational, fraternal style by political leaders. We noted how the authoritarian tradition in India permits the leader to "talk down" to his constituents—a style, we suspect, that will disappear as Indian citizens become more confident of their role in public affairs.

The study of India and the United States has provided a basis for more specific suggestions regarding the role of ideology than we have thus far formulated. We have commented on the relative magnitude of change in India's ideological system; and we suspect that this can be generalized to furnish at least a provisional model for the transformations characteristic of (a) a newly independent ex-colonial nation-state and (b) a nation-state that is concerned with modernization, giving priority to economic growth. By examining the United States, attention has been directed to the role of political communication (especially ideological) in the life of a highly industrialized superpower. Although India lacks the techno-scientific assets to play a superpower role at present, her human and physical resource potentials are sufficient to allow her leaders to dream of such a role, if they will.

We have called attention to several somewhat distinctive features of the Indian body politic. As a newly independent nation-state, for example: (a) The colonial state relinquished power without being the target of military revolt; (b) on the contrary, independence was largely perceived as the result of massive noncooperation, with little supplementation by the use of violence; (c) trained political, administrative, military, and other elite elements were available to carry on immediately; (d) the latent disunity of the two chief communal subcultures—Hindu and Muslim—found expression in the creation of two states rather than one (a result that was attended by mass violence on a tremendous scale); (e) the ideology of the elite that led the independence movement was relatively cosmopolitan, even when it deliberately mobilized the traditional predispositions of India's civilizations; and (f) the new elite accepted the importance of modernization; and the most potent element was strongly committed to the necessity of achieving an industrial, urban basis of economic strength while holding peasant discontent in check.

After the separation of India and Pakistan the elite of India began a process of redefinition of the nation's myth that can be regarded as characteristic of newly independent, modernizing bodies politic, save for the influence of localized factors. A model of this process is provided here.

From (Phase I)	*Toward* (Phase II)
1. The new identity: self-glorifying references Power position noted and celebrated High respect to independence movement and its heroes.	Self-acceptance
2. Demands on self Positively evaluate ego as part of national self ("feel Indian") Subordinate lesser loyalties to national loyalty Pursue common national interest	Realism

From (Phase I)	*Toward* (Phase II)
Strive for wider role in world	
Overcome economic and other disadvantages	
Justify in terms of national contributions, past and potential; and of assets (traits and so on)	

3. Expectations in regard to self — Realism

    Long-range achievements will be great

    Immediate limitations (blame projected)

4. Demands, expectations in reference to others — Reciprocity (equal bargaining)

    Recognize our new status and importance

    Assist us in overcoming temporary disadvantages (without "strings")

The model predicts that the direction of change—thanks to the continuing discipline of value realization, both indulgent and deprivational—will be toward accepting the self with less exaggerated distortion of the image as perceived; toward greater realism in setting goals and appraising capabilities; and toward the strategy of reciprocity rather than special treatment as a way of dealing with the world community. Our analysis of the Indian case suggests that the greater the initial distortions the greater the subsequent readjustments will be. The "pro-self by self" exaggerations during the early years are obvious compensating substitutions for the anxiety-producing features of the image of the collective self. The success of the nonviolence strategy in obtaining independence, when extended to the world arena, proved to be utterly inappropriate. Fortunately for India these limitations were exposed at relatively small cost, thanks to the self-restraint of China in view of the world balance of power. Having scored little success in foreign affairs, the question of most urgent importance for India's future is whether national policy will be sufficiently rewarding to enough components of the body politic to sustain a continuing demand for unity. And this depends in no small measure on the skill with which the leaders of the nation provide a "communications experience" that tends to keep loyalty, belief, and faith alive during the difficult years of transition.

It will be recalled that in comparing public political communication in such different bodies politic as India and the United States we were motivated primarily by the desire to examine the role of ideology, of stable generalization, in the political process. Only to a very limited extent has it been feasible to look in detail at the effect of ideological likenesses and differences on the course of reciprocal diplomatic, ideological, economic, and military influence. To have attempted an assessment of the impact of these ideological factors on the foreign policies of the two nation-states, or even on the flow of internal policy, would have gone beyond the circumscribed scope of the present undertaking. We cannot refrain, however, from formulating a few propositions that deserve sustained investigation in more intensive research on the political process.

First of all, it is worth noting the broader significance of the fact that in the daily flow of news and comment neither the elite of India nor the elite of the United States was greatly preoccupied with each other. *When the elites (and a fortiori the rank and file) of bodies politic are relatively inattentive to one another, their policy relations are left in the hands of elite elements who are recruited from two contrasting categories: (a) those who are chiefly concerned with broad national policy and (b) those who have distinctive and particular interests involving the nation-states in question.*

The leaders of newly-independent India were concerned with the United States principally as a source of economic support; the top leadership of the United States, on the other hand, examined India in terms of her significance for American security and the program for "containing communism" (or, more accurately, of containing the power of the principal polar opposite in the world arena). The effective foreign policy makers in both countries were able to initiate and execute common policies without succumbing to the day-to-day pressures generated by interest groups strategically located throughout their constituencies, or groups able to influence decision by the simple act of appealing to a highly emotionalized set of key symbols understood to carry explicit operational connotations. Contrast, in this regard, the limited freedom of action of official or unofficial elites of India or the United States in dealing with Great Britain. So far as Britain is an object of national policy, every sector of society is involved, and ideological considerations limit official options.

Our study of the role of articulate generalization in India and United States politics has gone far enough to suggest a basic model depicting the complex interplay among *specific policy demands, ideological systems, value ranking,* and *social change.* As a means of bringing these interconnections into the open, it is useful to point out that social change follows two paths: (a) *ecological* change, in which deliberate objectives and strategies play an insignificant part; (b) *executive* change, characterized by the focusing of collective attention and the mobilization of choice and decision. Many aggregate processes are ecological, such as population increase or decrease, or the dispersion of people in urban or rural centers or zones. The political process is the distinctive sector of premeditated manipulation, conflict, and conflict resolution.

More concretely, the most conspicuous feature of collective decision, particularly in a relatively democratic arena, is the promotion of specific policy demands. We have indicated how these specific demands—whether political party platforms, bureaucratic proposals, or whatever—are justified in terms of political myths (well established or counter-ideological). Typically the myth as a whole is not invoked in support of a given program; as a rule reliance is put on one or a few chosen doctrines, legal prescriptions, or popular images (miranda). *If demand A is successful, the overriding hypothesis is that subsequent demands (B,C) are likely to seek justification by invoking the ideology, or the ideological component, that coincides with the success of A.* This hypothetical formulation is compatible with the expansion of technical modernization and of planning in the early years of Indian independence, and of programs of economic aid by the United States.

The analysis has likewise drawn attention to a sequence in which *words* are widely disseminated in politics with few resulting changes in *deed*. Often the deed comes first; the use of self-justification occurs when criticism must be met. "Socialism," for example, has become a positively toned symbol of Indian politics without mobilizing effective support for radical change in the balance between governmental and private channels of production. In the vocabulary of United States politics "anticommunism" has been a slogan in the name of which a wide range of seemingly incompatible measures have been put into effect.

A conspicuous feature of India's growth is the conflict betwen traditional and modernizing tendencies. An unsettled question of enormous importance for the future is whether, regardless of ideology, specific modernizing demands will continue to obtain support. From the standpoint of a scientific observer there need be no difficulty *in principle* in redefining the general (hence ambiguous) postulates of a traditional system to include support for innovation. In particular countries, however, many political factors may block or slow down the acceptance of modernizing policies. Those elite elements who are accustomed to a particular set of decisions, justified in the name of basic doctrines, may fear loss of power if they redefine the traditional doctrine to include techno-scientific innovation.

We have alluded to the significant role in social change of modifications in the rank order of values, and it may be pertinent to spell this out to some extent in the context of our research. As scientific observers we find it convenient to classify specific policy demands according to the value-institution categories of our analysis of social process. We have seen that this is relatively simple if only the manifest content of policy proposals is taken into account. (A "tax," for instance, explicitly refers to wealth; a "hospital" statute deals with "well-being," and so on.) It is also feasible to classify the justifications in these categories. This operation, too, is uncomplicated. (A "tax," for example, may be justified in economic terms; a "hospital" in the vocabulary of well-being; or several values may be invoked in support of each measure.) It is practicable to describe *trends* in the *relative attention* given to each value, as we have done in part, thus disclosing changes that may occur in the ranking of these values.[2]

At present we cannot summarize pre- and post-independence trends with complete assurance. It is, nonetheless, highly probable that the elites of pre-independence India put tremendous emphasis on power, rectitude, respect, and affection, while post-independence India, pre-occupied with nation building, has laid more stress than before on wealth, skill, enlightenment, and well-being. The sequence probably moves from *deference* values to *welfare* values.[3]

It is common knowledge that with the spread of modern science-based technology profound transformations have harassed traditional institutions in every sector of an established society. Invariably associated with these transformations is the awakening of individuality, the strengthening of the ego core of the self-system, and the spread of freedom-generated anxieties, uncertainties, and achievements. In these colossal waves of change a revised scale of value ordering occurs at different rates for different individuals, pluralistic and territorial participants in social process. These transformations of fundamental predisposition mean that further changes are selectively encouraged in the priority sectors. Thus ideologies and operational techniques are appraised according to a modified scale of value realization.

[2] See Harold D. Lasswell, "The Uses of Content Analysis Data in Studying Social Change," *Social Sciences Information* 7 (1968), 57–70. (Paper originally presented at the International Conference on Comparative Research on Social Change and Regional Disparity Within and Between Nations with Special Reference to Southern Asia, New Delhi, 1967. Conference jointly organized by the Indian Statistical Institute and the International Social Science Council).

[3] The distinction between *welfare* and *deference* values is drawn in H. D. Lasswell and A. Kaplan, *Power and Society; A Framework for Political Inquiry* (New Haven: Yale University Press, 1950, pp. 55–56). Welfare values are "those whose possession to a certain degree is a necessary condition for the maintenance of the physical activity of the person." Deference values are "those that consist in being taken into consideration (in the acts of others and of the self)."

So far as the future is concerned there is as yet no clear answer to the question whether the incorporation of modern science and technology will proceed along a decisively different path in India than it did, for example, in the United States. The failures of the moralizing theme in the international arena suggest that wealth and power will come to play the prominent part characteristic of industrial societies to date.[4]

We do not, however, dismiss a further possibility, despite the short-range evidence that points in a contrary direction. Gandhi can be interpreted as a religious and moral leader of unparalleled success in synchronizing ideology with the political opportunities of Indian society. It is, however, doubtful whether his delicate blend of seemingly incompatible elements can recover from the forces that have already eroded its effectiveness. The cleavage between the secularized ethics of socialism and the religio-magical traditions of Indian culture is deep, if not deepening. Evidently Gandhi's assault on the respect structure of Hindu society set in motion collective movements that cannot be nourished by the precedents of European socialism or liberalism.

It is permissible to speculate about one line of future development, a construct that at the moment cannot be assigned high probability of realization. Perhaps the religio-ethical components of Indian tradition can be revivified by recovering or discovering the challenge of realizing human dignity in the life of each individual, and eventually of every pluralistic and territorial group in society. European socialism, communism, or liberalism are now handicapped by their identification with strategies that either exalt government and suppress men, or de-emphasize government and inadvertently exalt private oligarchies. Indian programs of a traditional sort are permeated with faiths and rituals that cramp the potential flowering of human life and talent. Nonetheless the traditional mood and ideological orientation of Indian society give expres-

---

[4] In his forthcoming study of Puerto Rico, Henry Wells draws attention to the importance of deference values to the elite that fostered Puerto Rican claims against Spanish rule. A significant change took place in the independence movement of post-Spanish days when Munoz perceived the latent concern of the rank and file of Puerto Rican society with the improvement of their welfare, and provided leadership in modernizing the island. It is worth exploring the hypothesis that many if not all sequences of modernization eventually restore the primacy of deference values, redefined with perspectives and operations appropriate to the new state of affairs. In this connection see Ralph Braibanti (ed.), *Political and Administrative Development* (Durham, N.C.: Duke University Press, forthcoming). See especially H. D. Lasswell and A. R. Holmberg, "Toward a General Theory of Directed Value Accumulation and Institutional Development" (Chapter 8). Further, consult H. F. Dobyns, A. R. Holmberg, M. E. Opler, and L. Sharp, *Methods for Analyzing Social Change* (Department of Anthropology, Cornell University, Ithaca, New York, 1967).

sion to an all-pervading concern with the dignity of human life and experience. Hence the fundamental approach is contextual, therefore capable of orchestrating the channels of personal, pluralized, and territorial expression according to their optimal effectiveness in value shaping and sharing. The revolution of science, technology, and production can be accompanied by more sweeping revolutions of respect, rectitude, and love that correlate enlightenment and skills with security and abundance.

The future development of the United States is, in some features, less problematic than that of India. As we have had ample occasion to demonstrate, the power goals of the United States are perceived as instrumental rather than ultimate objectives of national policy. There is no evidence that world domination, for example, is part of the American dream or that violence is a welcome way of life either at home or abroad. Despite these perspectives there are no grounds for assuming that national policy will be less firm in the world arena than it has been in the recent past. The policy makers of the United States are committed—publicly and privately—to policies of world reconstruction designed to overcome present gaps in the system of public order, and to cut down the waste of resources used to nourish the institution of war. The problem, as usual, is how to bring about by strategies of persuasion a profoundly revolutionary change in the arena of world politics. Up to the present the tendencies toward militancy, or, more generally, toward a subtle transformation of American society into a garrison-police state, have been held in check. The pursuit of multiple values and the institutions of a relatively individualistic, pluralistic, and democratic body politic have been sufficiently strong to sustain "minor wars" and huge expenditures on "the absolute weapon." So far as political science can say at present, the future equilibrium patterns exhibited by these conflicting forces will depend as much on Moscow or Peking as on New York or New Delhi. In the light of available knowledge political scientists can do little more than express concern for the long-term erosion of civilian society and multi-valued goals usually associated with prolonged military crises.

Interestingly enough our data failed to reflect one of the major points made by analysts of highly industrialized societies. The allusion is to the alleged tendency of such societies to alienate large sectors of their population from a shared sense of power. Traditional Marxism emphasized the probable alienation of "toilers" and "workers." More recently social scientists have been addressing themselves to the failures of identity believed to characterize the young or the middle levels of executive or technical talent. These apprehensions were perceived by the American elite of the fifties, at least, as low priority problems. Even the relatively sudden and belated respect revolution of the Negro—accompanied by more intense demands to participate effectively in power and in all values—had low visibility. Perhaps the conspicuousness of ethnic tension resulted in deflecting the elite from noticing some of the non-ethnic deprivations and resentments germinating among the young or the technologically obsolescent.

We are impressed by the evidence that United States politics is increasingly affected by the data-gathering, data-analyzing approach that results from extending the scientific frame of reference to all events. We commented on the role of intellectuals; and we see evidence that qualified specialists are obtaining opportunities to perform the complex tasks of planning and appraisal required to improve the realism of the decision processes of government and the choosing processes of society. The implication for the future is that the potentialities of man for enlightenment will continue to play an enlarging role in American civilization.

If professional philosophers overrate the influence of abstractions on human conduct, students of politics often go to the opposite extreme. They tend to emphasize the fact that political history is full of contradictory and preposterous applications of basic assumptions. But political history also contains many instances of the long-range effect of abstract ideas, such as the demand for human dignity (as against indignity). Despite certain outrageous deviations from any tenable conception of human dignity in India or the United States, we cannot fail to be impressed by the perpetual challenge offered by such fundamental value criteria to the appraisal of political and social institutions. Nehru was fully justified in attaching enormous importance to his role of ideologist to independent India. Nor was a President such as Eisenhower or a candidate such as Stevenson wasting his time when he sought to express the significance of America's political heritage in the configuration of current issues. If men and nations cannot be entirely devoted to the perfecting of ideology, they cannot be wholly unaffected by ideological images and aspirations for man and society.

APPENDIXES

APPENDIX A

TABLE 1

SPOKESMEN ORIGINATING STATEMENTS IN THE UNITED STATES AND INDIA, 1950–1958[a]

(Number of different spokesmen in each year and percentage of all spokesmen making statements each year)

YEAR	United States		India	
	NUMBER	PERCENT	NUMBER	PERCENT
1950	27	18.9	12	14.3
1951	27	18.9	12	14.3
1952	33	23.1	14	16.7
1953	36	25.2	12	14.3
1954	29	20.3	7	8.3
1955	18	12.6	32	38.1
1956	24	16.8	15	17.9
1957	29	20.3	16	19.0
1958[a]	10	7.0	9	10.7
Total	(233)[b]		(129)[b]	

[a] 1958 is for first six months only in this and in all other tables.
[b] Counts separately same speaker in different calendar years.
NOTE: Percentages in this and other tables may not add up to one hundred because of rounding.

TABLE 2

SPOKESMEN AND STATEMENTS BY OCCUPATION IN THE UNITED STATES AND INDIA, 1950–1958

| | United States | | | | India | | | |
| | Speakers | | Statements | | Speakers | | Statements | |
OCCUPATIONS	NUMBER	PERCENT	NUMBER	PERCENT	NUMBER	PERCENT	NUMBER	PERCENT
1. Diplomatic	11	7.69	71	5.01	7	8.33	110	7.60
2. Military	12	8.39	74	5.22	1	1.19	10	0.69
3. Presidents and Prime Ministers[a]	3	2.09	451	31.82	2	2.38	912	63.07
4. Cabinet and high officials	27	18.88	257	18.13	8	9.52	79	5.46
5. Judiciary	4	2.79	12	0.84	1	1.19	2	0.13
6. Legislature[b]	50	34.96	218	15.38	20	23.80	51	3.52
7. State government	6	4.19	225	15.87[c]	15	17.85	124	8.57
8. Political parties	7	4.89	15	1.05	15	17.85	94	6.50
9. Labor	8	5.99	27	1.90	3	3.57	6	0.41
10. Business	4	2.79	13	0.91	2	2.38	10	0.69
11. Intellectuals	6	4.19	41	2.89	—	—	—	—
12. Associations	5	3.49	13	0.91	10	11.90	48	3.31
Total	143	100	1417	100	84	100	1446	100

[a] Includes the Presidents of the United States; Presidents and Prime Ministers of India.

[b] Congress for the United States; Parliament for India.

[c] The high American percentage is primarily to be accounted by the presence of Adlai Stevenson, then governor of Illinois and running as the Democratic party's candidate for the presidency.

TABLE 3

DEGREE OF PRESS CONCENTRATION ON ELITE SPOKESMEN:
CUMULATIVE NUMBER OF SPEAKERS ACCOUNTING FOR
CUMULATIVE NUMBER OF STATEMENTS IN INDIA, 1950–1958

Speakers			Statements		
Number of Speakers Who Made Given Number of Statements	Cumulative Number of Speakers		Number of Statements Made by Given Speakers	Cumulative Number of Statements	
	NUMBER	PERCENT		NUMBER	PERCENT
1	1	1.2	798[a]	798	55.2
1	2	2.4	114	912	63.1
1	3	3.5	86	998	69.0
1	4	4.8	44	1042	72.1
1	5	6.0	39	1081	74.8
3	8	9.5	66 (22 each)	1147	79.3
1	9	10.7	21	1168	80.8
1	10	11.9	18	1186	82.0
1	11	13.1	14	1200	83.0
1	12	14.3	12	1212	83.8
1	13	15.5	11	1223	84.6
1	14	16.7	10	1233	85.3
2	16	19.0	18 (9 each)	1251	86.5
3	19	22.6	24 (8 each)	1275	88.2
5	24	28.6	35 (7 each)	1310	90.6
2	26	31.0	12 (6 each)	1322	91.4
3	29	34.5	15 (5 each)	1337	92.5
5	34	40.5	20 (4 each)	1357	93.8
11	45	53.6	33 (3 each)	1390	96.1
17	62	73.8	34 (2 each)	1424	98.5
22	84	99.9[b]	22 (1 each)	1446	99.9[b]

[a] Prime Minister Nehru.
[b] Does not add to 100 percent because of rounding.

TABLE 4

DEGREE OF PRESS CONCENTRATION ON ELITE SPOKESMEN:
CUMULATIVE NUMBER OF SPEAKERS ACCOUNTING FOR
CUMULATIVE NUMBER OF STATEMENTS IN
UNITED STATES, 1950–1958

Speakers			Statements		
Number of Speakers Who Made Given Number of Statements	Cumulative Number of Speakers		Number of Statements Made by Given Speakers	Cumulative Number of Statements	
	NUMBER	PERCENT		NUMBER	PERCENT
1	1	.7	324	324	22.9
1	2	1.4	158	482	34.0
1	3	2.1	125	607	42.8
1	4	2.8	73	680	48.0
1	5	3.5	46	726	51.2
1	6	4.2	45	771	54.4
2	8	5.6	68 (34 each)	839	59.2
2	10	7.0	46 (23 each)	885	62.5
3	13	9.1	51 (17 each)	936	66.1
1	14	9.8	16	952	67.2
1	15	10.5	15	967	68.2
3	18	12.6	39 (13 each)	1006	71.0
1	19	13.3	12	1018	71.8
2	21	14.7	22 (11 each)	1040	73.4
4	25	17.5	40 (10 each)	1080	76.2
2	27	18.9	18 (9 each)	1098	77.5
3	30	21.0	24 (8 each)	1122	79.2
4	34	23.8	28 (7 each)	1150	81.2
6	40	28.0	36 (6 each)	1186	83.7
11	51	35.7	55 (5 each)	1241	87.6
8	59	41.3	32 (4 each)	1273	89.8
19	78	54.5	57 (3 each)	1330	93.9
22	100	69.9	44 (2 each)	1374	97.0
43	143	99.9[a]	43 (1 each)	1417	99.9[a]

[a] Does not add to 100 percent because of rounding.

TABLE 5

FOCUS OF ATTENTION: AMERICAN AND INDIAN SPOKESMEN, 1950–1958

ITEM	United States		India	
	NUMBER	PERCENT	NUMBER	PERCENT
Inner arena	1207	50.3	1502	58.4
Economic	106	4.4	227	8.8
Political				
orientations	370	15.4	644	25.1
Operations	343	14.3	358	13.9
Other[a]	388	16.2	273	10.6
Outer arena	1192	49.7	1066	41.5
Nonregional	694	28.9	451	17.6
Regional	498	20.8	615	23.9
India–United States[b]	5	0.2	27	1.1
General regional	75	3.1	45	1.8
Asian (except India)	176	7.3	438	16.9
Middle East	40	1.7	4	0.2
Africa	4	0.2	21	0.8
Europe	198	8.3	80	3.1
South America	0	0	0	0
Total[c]	2399	100.0	2568	99.9

[a] Primarily statements pertaining to personalities.

[b] For the United States this item includes *only* references to India, for India, *only* references to the United States.

[c] These totals differ from the totals in Tables 3 and 4. The discrepancy is accounted for by the fact that some statements were tabulated under more than one topic (that is, a statement might refer to both politics and economics, or to both India and Pakistan).

TABLE 6A

FOCUS OF ATTENTION: INNER ARENA ITEMS ONLY, UNITED STATES AND INDIA, 1950–1958

SUBJECT OF STATEMENT	United States		India	
	NUMBER	PERCENT	NUMBER	PERCENT
All Inner Arena	1207	100.00	1502	100.00
Economic:				
General	12	.99	44	2.93
Business	14	1.16	29	1.93
Government	8	.66	25	1.66
Planning	0	.00	42	2.80
Labor	36	2.98	36	2.40
Agriculture	9	.75	48	3.20
Landownership	0	.00	3	.20
Natural resources	12	.99	0	.00
Business cycles	8	.66	0	.00
Prices, inflation	7	.58	0	.00
Political:				
Orientations				
Self-Image	175	14.50	297	19.77
National symbols	25	2.07	6	.40
History	1	.08	55	3.67
National goals and values	40	3.31	71	4.73
Unity	58	4.81	153	10.19
Doctrines	71	5.88	62	4.13
Operations				
Law and order	16	1.33	51	3.40
Political institutions	148	12.26	88	5.86
Political parties	144	11.93	203	13.52
Political process	26	2.15	16	1.07
Center-state relations	9	.75	0	.00
Other:				
Religion-morality	26	2.15	28	1.86
Social problems	34	2.82	121	8.06
Civil rights	38	3.15	0	.00
Enlightenment	46	3.81	44	2.93
Communications	8	0.66	0	.00
Personalities	236	19.55	80	5.33

FOCUS OF ATTENTION: OUTER ARENA ITEMS ONLY
DEALING WITH SPECIFIC REGIONS
UNITED STATES AND INDIA, 1950–1958

RAPHIC .RENCE	United States		India	
	NUMBER	PERCENT	NUMBER	PERCENT
Regional Items	498	100.00	615	100.00
ia	5	1.0		
ted States			27	4.4
neral References	(75)	(15.0)	(45)	(7.3)
Great powers	0	.0	6	1.0
Free world	49	9.8	0	.0
The West	12	2.4	13	2.1
Neutrals	4	.8	7	1.1
Underdeveloped countries	10	2.0	1	.2
Bandung Conf.	0	.0	18	2.9
ian Nations (excluding India)	(176)	(35.3)	(438)	(71.2)
Asians	14	2.8	9	1.5
Southeast Asia	0	.0	10	1.6
Indo-China	6	1.2	0	.0
South Asia (general)	0	.0	4	.6
Pakistan	0	.0	116	18.9
Kashmir	0	.0	132	21.5
Tibet	0	.0	7	1.1
Portuguese colonies	0	.0	72	11.7
Far East	1	.2	0	.0
China	38	7.6	80	13.0
Formosa	18	3.6	7	1.1
Korea	91	18.3	1	.2
Japan	8	1.6	0	.0
Middle East	(40) 40	8.0	(4) 4	.7
Africa (South of the Sahara)	(4) 4	.8	(21) 21	3.4
Europe	(198)	(39.8)	(80)	(13.0)
General References	29	5.8	0	.0
Britain and commonwealth	17	3.4	27	4.4
Cyprus	0	.0	2	.3
France	7	1.4	0	.0
Austria	2	.4	0	.0
Greece	3	.6	0	.0
Germany	10	2.0	4	.7
Yugoslavia	2	.4	0	.0
Poland	3	.6	0	.0
Hungary	8	1.6	0	.0
USSR	117	23.5	47	7.6

Appendix A

TABLE 6B

FOCUS OF ATTENTION: INNER ARENA IT[
UNITED STATES AND INDIA, 1950–1

SUBJECT OF STATEMENT	United States		NUM
	NUMBER	PERCENT	
All Inner Arena	1207		15(
Economic:	106	100.00	22
General	12	11.32	4.
Business	14	13.20	2ς
Government	8	7.54	25
Planning	0	.00	42
Labor	36	33.96	36
Agriculture	9	8.49	48
Landownership	0	.00	3
Natural resources	12	11.32	0
Business cycles	8	7.54	0
Prices, inflation	7	6.60	0
Political:	713	100.00	1002
Orientations	(370)		(644)
Self-Image	175	24.53	297
National symbols	25	3.50	6
Past History	1	.14	55
National goals and values	40	5.61	71
Unity	58	8.13	153
Doctrines	71	9.95	62
Operations	(343)		(358)
Law and order	16	2.24	51
Political institutions	148	20.75	88
Political parties	144	20.19	203
Political process	26	3.64	16
Center-state relations	9	1.26	0
Other:	388	100.00	273
Religious-morality	26	6.70	28
Social problems	34	8.76	121
Civil rights	38	9.79	0
Enlightenment	46	11.83	44
Communications	8	2.06	0
Personalities	236	60.82	80

TABLE 7B

FOCUS OF ATTENTION: OUTER ARENA ITEMS ONLY, UNITED STATES AND INDIA, 1950–1958

SUBJECT OF STATEMENT	United States		India	
	NUMBER	PERCENT	NUMBER	PERCENT
All outer arena	1192	100.0	1066	100.0
Nonregional	694	(58.2)	451	(42.4)
General	(409)	(34.3)	(298)	(28.0)
World problems	40	3.4	153	14.3
Doctrines	91	7.6	21	2.0
Personalities	26	2.2	22	2.1
War and peace	215	18.0	71	6.7
United Nations	37	3.1	31	2.9
Foreign policy	(159)	(13.3)	(147)	(13.8)
Military policy	(126)	(10.6)	(6)	(.6)
Defense	105	8.8	0	.0
NATO	18	1.5	6	.6
EDC	1	.1	0	.0
Baghdad Pact	1	.1	0	.0
SEATO	1	.1	0	.0
Regional	(498)	(41.8)	(615)	(57.7)
India	5	.4	0	.0
United States	0	.0	27	2.5
General regional references	(75)	(6.3)	(45)	(4.2)
Great Powers	0	.0	6	.6
Free World	49	4.1	0	.0
The West	12	1.0	13	1.2
Neutrals	4	.3	7	.7
Underdeveloped countries	10	.8	1	.1
Bandung Conference	0	.0	18	1.6
Asia	(176)	(14.8)	(438)	(41.0)
General	14	1.2	9	.8
Southeast Asia	0	.0	10	.9
Indo-China	6	.5	0	.0
South Asia	0	.0	4	.4
Pakistan	0	.0	116	10.8
Kashmir	0	.0	132	12.4
Tibet	0	.0	7	.7
Portuguese colonies	0	.0	72	6.8
Far East (general)	1	.1	0	.0

TABLE 7B (Cont.)

SUBJECT OF STATEMENT	United States		India	
	NUMBER	PERCENT	NUMBER	PERCENT
China	38	3.2	80	7.5
Formosa	18	1.5	7	.7
Korea	91	7.6	1	.1
Japan	8	.7	0	.0
Middle East	(40) 40	3.4	(4) 4	.4
Africa (south of the Sahara)	(4) 4	.3	(21) 21	2.0
Europe	(198)	(16.6)	(80)	(7.5)
General References	29	2.4	0	.0
Britain and commonwealth	17	1.4	27	2.5
Cyprus	0	.0	2	.2
France	7	.6	0	.0
Austria	2	.2	0	.0
Greece	3	.3	0	.0
Germany	10	.8	4	.4
Yugoslavia	2	.2	0	.0
Poland	3	.3	0	.0
Hungary	8	.7	0	.0
USSR	117	9.8	47	4.4
South America	(0)	0.0	(0)	0.0

TABLE 8

SELF-IMAGES: INDIA AND THE UNITED STATES

VALUE	United States		India	
	NUMBER	PERCENT	NUMBER	PERCENT
Power	31	28	46	21
Enlightenment	15	15	27	13
Wealth	2	2	17	8
Well-being	6	6	31	14
Skill	13	13	15	7
Affection	4	4	20	9
Respect	17	16	18	8
Rectitude	17	16	49	20
Total	105	100	223	100

APPENDIX B

A Dean Wilbur Schramm published a study of the World's Press in 1959 from which the data immediately following are taken. Wilbur Schramm, *One Day in the World's Press: Fourteen Great Newspapers on a Day of Crisis, November 2, 1956.* Stanford, Stanford University Press, 1959. His list of prestige papers was:

1.	Moscow	*Pravda*
2.	Paris	*Le Monde*
3.	Warsaw	*Trybuna Ludu*
4.	Frankfurt	*Frankfürter Allgemeine Zeitung*
5.	Prague	*Rude Pravo*
6.	Stockholm	*Dagens Nyheter*
7.	Belgrade	*Borba*
8.	Cairo	*Al Ahram*
9.	Peking	*Jen-Min Jin-Pao*
10.	Tokyo	*Asahi*
11.	Buenos Aires	*La Prense*
12.	Bombay and Delhi	*Times of India*
13.	London	The *Times*
14.	New York	The New York *Times*

Concerning the two papers used in the present study:

The New York *Times* (New York)

    Morning, daily and Sunday. Circulation: 570,000 weekdays; 1,168,000 Sundays. Published by The New York Times Company.

The *Times of India* (Bombay and Delhi)

    Morning, seven days a week. Circulation: about 100,000. Published by Bennett Coleman & Co., Ltd.

B Comparative information on the use of general media of communication in 1956 is from *World Communications: Press, Film, Television*, UNESCO, 3rd Edition, 1956.

PRESS

	Daily Newspapers	Total Daily Circulation
India	330	2,500,000
United States	1,786	55,000,000

RADIO

	Transmitters	Receivers
India	48	695,000
United States	2,569 AM (Stations)	127,000,000
	653 FM (Stations)	

FILM

	Cinemas	Feature Films Produced
India	2,933	259 (in one year)
United States	19,000	354 (in one year)

NEWSPRINT

	Production	Consumption
India	—	68,000 (metric tons per year)
United States	970,000	5,470,000 (metric tons per year)

TELEVISION

	Transmitters	Receivers
India	—	—
United States	413 (stations)	35,000,000

POPULATION

	Total
India	372,000,000
United States	159,629,000

ILLITERACY

India	80 to 85 percent
United States	2 to 3 percent

C   Further details on The *Times of India* are from G. B. Gates-Reed, ed., *The Indian Press Year Book*, 1956, London & Madras, The Indian Press Publications, 1956. Published daily simultaneously from Bombay and Delhi. "Policy—Independent Liberal, supporter of Democratic Government." Circulation ABC (January to June 1955) combined Delhi and Bombay editions: 97,290.

Circulation breakdown by states:
1. Greater Bombay: 40,137
2. Bombay State: 25,721
3. Madras: 1313
4. Andhra: 406
5. West Bengal: 648

6. Uttar Pradesh: 3131
7. Madhya Pradesh: 2921
8. East Punjab: 1610
9. Bihar: 378
10. Assam: 41
11. Orissa: 36
12. Himachal Pradesh: 9
13. Hyderabad: 2451
14. Madhya Bharat: 1907
15. Mysore: 833
16. PEPSU: 140
17. Rajasthan: 1804
18. Saurashtra: 2450
19. Travancore-Cochin: 163
20. Vindhya Pradesh: 101
21. Delhi: 5738
22. Jammu and Kashmir: 548

Outside India: Pakistan: 1784; Ceylon: 71; other countries: 261.

In advertisements the *Times of India* describes itself as "India's leading daily, with the largest circulation of any newspaper in the East." If the East includes Japan, this certainly is not the case. If "East" includes East India, it is not the case, either. Most likely the statement was accurate decades ago.

D The period covered in the present analysis is January 1950, to June 1958. The issues of the first and fifteenth of the month were used. (When the *Times of India* was not published on these dates, the issue of the following day was substituted.) The "front page" means the stories that appeared on page 1 *plus* the continuation of the stories inside the issue. The procedure was to note all national speakers (Indians in India, Americans in the United States) and to use quoted statements (or paraphrases).

The *Times of India* and the New York *Times* print on pages of approximately the same size (20 inches long in both cases; width 15½ inches in the *Times of India*, 14 inches in the New York *Times*). Both pages employ eight columns. The New York *Times* continues its stories at much greater length than the *Times of India*, and prints more news than the latter. The amount of elite comment, however, is approximately the same.

Each sentence quoted (or paraphrased) is classified according to "who" said it and "what" was said. The communicators are recorded according to role (official, private, and so forth). The content of the communications is classified according to self and other image, and arena of reference (external, internal); and the value involved (power enlightenment, and so on). The categories were subdivided in great detail.

The categories were applied by one of us, subject to occasional checking by the other to see that the basic definitions were applied in the same way. Studies of content analysis have shown that each coder tends to stabilize his interpretation of a given set of categories and remain self-consistent within it. In the present investigation the procedure of content analysis was being used as a deliberate act of self-discipline to provide a check on tendencies to characterize the trend of political communication in impressionistic fashion. Thus the purpose has not been to contribute to the technique of content analysis, but rather to employ simple methods to discover whether future research can fruitfully be addressed to certain problems of political generalization in the language of politics. For the frame of reference used here see Harold D. Lasswell, Nathan Leites and Associates, *The Language of Politics: Studies in Quantitative Semantics* (New York, George W. Stewart, 1949, republished 1966 by the M.I.T. Press, 1966); Robert Rubenstein and Harold D. Lasswell, *The Sharing of Power in a Psychiatric Hospital* (New Haven, Yale University Press, 1966), chapter 7. For more sophisticated techniques see the forthcoming analysis of *American Party Platforms* by Zvi Namenwirth and Harold D. Lasswell which employs the "Lasswell Value Dictionary" within the framework of the procedures described by Philip J. Stone and associates, *The General Enquirer Method* (Cambridge, Mass. M.I.T. Press, 1966).

E The speakers are listed according to the position they held at the time they were quoted. There were 143 Americans.

Diplomatic Service/Delegates to International Organizations
   1. Lewis Douglas
   2. Benjamin Cohen
   3. W. Aldrich
   4. Eleanor Roosevelt
   5. E. Gross
   6. Ralph Bunche
   7. Warren Austin
   8. Henry Cabot Lodge
   9. John Peurifoy
  10. James Conant
  11. James Wadsworth

Armed Forces
   1. Forrest Sherman
   2. Lucius Clay
   3. George Marshall
   4. Douglas MacArthur
   5. Omar Bradley
   6. Alfred Gruenther
   7. William Leahy
   8. Henry Crommelin
   9. Matthew Ridgway
  10. Curtis Lemay
  11. Arthur Radford
  12. Nathan Twining

Presidents
   1. Dwight Eisenhower
   2. Harry Truman
   3. Herbert Hoover

Vice Presidents
1. A. W. Barkley
2. Richard Nixon

Cabinet and High Federal Officials
1. William Foster
2. Oscar Ewing
3. Charles Wilson
4. Louis Johnson
5. A. Harriman
6. John Foster Dulles
7. Roy V. Peel
8. David Lilienthal
9. Paul Hoffman
10. Dean Acheson
11. Frank Pace, Jr.
12. Henry Fowler
13. Robert Anderson
14. John Hannah
15. Ezra Taft Benson
16. Charles Thomas
17. Lewis Strauss
18. Oveta Culp Hobby
19. Harold Stassen
20. Lincoln White
21. Gabriel Hauge
22. Robert Hill
23. Lloyd Wright
24. Wilber Brucker
25. Neil McElroy

Judiciary
1. Myles Lane
2. William O. Douglas
3. Herbert Brownell
4. Jacob Javits

House of Representatives
1. Joseph Martin (R–Mass.)
2. John Lyle, Jr. (D–Texas)
3. Pat Sutton (D–Tenn.)
4. Sam Rayburn (D–Texas.)
5. Charles Eaton (R–N.J.)
6. John Dingell (D–Mich.)
7. Robert Crosser (D–Ohio)
8. Frank Clef (D–Kentucky)
9. Patrick Hillings (R–Cal.)
10. Kenneth Keating (R–N.Y.)
11. Thomas Dodd (D–Conn.)

12. John McCormack (D–Mass.)
13. John Rooney (D–N.Y.)

Senate

1. E. W. McFarland (D–Ariz.)
2. Hubert Humphrey (D–Minn.)
3. Paul Douglas (D–Ill.)
4. E. Dirksen (R–Ill.)
5. Francis Case (R–S.D.)
6. John Bricker (R–Ohio)
7. Kenneth Wherry (R–Neb.)
8. Robert Taft (R–Ohio)
9. Joseph McCarthy (R–Wis.)
10. William Knowland (R–Cal.)
11. Estes Kefauver (D–Tenn.)
12. Lyndon Johnson (D–Texas)
13. Tom Connally (D–Texas)
14. Harry Byrd (D–Virginia)
15. Styles Bridges (R–N.H.)
16. Brian McMahon (D–Conn.)
17. H. R. O'Connor (D–Maryland)
18. Alexander Wiley (R–Wis.)
19. Homer Ferguson (R–Wis.)
20. William Fulbright (D–Ark.)
21. Albert Gore (D–Tenn.)
22. Herbert Lehman (D–N.Y.)
23. Wayne Morse (D–Oregon)
24. H. Alexander Smith (R–N.H.)
25. Charles Tobey (R–N.H.)
26. Ralph Flanders (R–Vt.)
27. Walter George (D–Ga.)
28. Irving Ives (R–N.Y.)
29. William Jenner (R–Ind.)
30. Theodore Green (D–R.I.)
31. Mike Mansfield (D–Mont.)
32. John McClellan (D–Ark.)
33. Richard Russell (D–Ga.)
34. John Sparkman (D–Ala.)
35. Stuart Symington (D–Mo.)
36. Herbert Walters (D–Mo.)
37. Bourke Hickenlooper (R–Iowa)

State Governors

1. James Byrnes (S.C.)
2. Earl Warren (Cal.)
3. Thomas Dewey (N.Y.)
4. Adlai Stevenson (Ill.)
5. Orval Faubas (Ark.)
6. Luis Munoz Marin (Puerto Rico)

Labor
1. George Meany
2. Walter Reuther
3. Joseph Ryan
4. Louis Hollander
5. W. P. Randolph
6. John F. English
7. James Hoffa
8. Philip Murray

Business
1. Bernard Baruch
2. John D. Biggers
3. G. G. Gurley
4. John A. Stephens

Political Parties
1. John Hamilton—Eastern campaign manager for Senator Taft
2. Katherine Brown—Republican national committeewoman (Ohio)
3. Jonathan Daniels—Democratic National Committeeman (N.C.)
4. Gael Sullivan—Campaign manager for Senator Kefauver
5. Arthur Summerfield—Republican national committeeman (Mich.)
6. Leonard Hall—Chairman Republican National Committee
7. Carmine DeSapio—Democrat (N.Y.)

Professors and Authors
1. Lyman Bryson
2. Corliss Lamont
3. Grayson Kirk
4. William Jansen—superintendent of schools, N.Y.
5. Isidor Rabi
6. Howard Fast

Private Groups
1. Lewis Gough—American Legion
2. Donald Wilson—American Legion
3. Thurgood Marshall—NAACP
4. Bryant Bowles—National Association for Advancement of White People
5. Louis Orr—President, National Conference of Presidents and Other Officers of State Medical Associations

F There were 84 Indians:
Diplomatic Service/Delegates to International Organizations
1. S. Radharkrishman
2. Setalvad
3. Mrs. V. L. Pandit
4. Dr. Sita Ram
5. B. N. Rau
6. V. K. Krishna Menon
7. R. Jaipal

Army
    1. General Cariappa
President of India
    1. Rajendra Prasad
Central Cabinet
    1. Sardar Patel
    2. Jawaharlal Nehru
    3. Sri Prakasa
    4. John Matthai
    5. Jagjivan Ram
    6. G. L. Nanda
    7. T. T. Krishnamachari
    8. C. D. Deshmukh
    9. K. N. Katju
Judiciary
    1. Sir Arthur Trevor Harries
Parliament
    1. N. R. M. Swamy (Commonwealth party)
    2. P. Tandon (Congress)
    3. B. R. Ambedkar
    4. G. Mavlankar (Congress—speaker of the Lok Sabha)
    5. Misra (Congress)
    6. N. C. Chatterjee (Hindu Mahasabha)
    7. N. V. Gadgil (Congress)
    8. Y. B. Gandhi (Congress)
    9. G. H. Deshpande
   10. Hiren Mukherjee (Communist)
   11. Raghuramiah (Congress)
   12. Jaipal Singh (Independent)
   13. Lanka Sundaram (Independent)
   14. A. M. Thomas
   15. Firoz Gandhi (Congress)
   16. Pandit Bhargava
   17. Mrs. Chakravarty
   18. Mahendra Pratap
   19. Anup Singh
   20. Supakar
State Governors
    1. Bajpai (Bombay)
    2. Diwakar (Bihar)
    3. Mahtab (Bombay)
State Cabinets
    1. G. B. Pant (Uttar Pradesh)
    2. Sheikh Abdullah (Kashmir)
    3. Morarji Desai (Bombay)
    4. Hanumantaiya (Mysore)
    5. T. R. Narvane (Bombay)

    6. P. T. Pillai (Travancore–Cochin)
    7. Y. Chavan (Bombay)
State Legislatures
    1. Peter Alvares (Bombay)
    2. G. M. Sadiq (Kashmir)
    3. K. N. Sehgal (Punjab)
    4. Govinda Menon (Travancore–Cochin)
    5. T. V. Thomas (Travancore–Cochin)
Political Parties: Congress Party
    1. Mohammed Taher
    2. Seth Govind Das
    3. S. K. Patil
    4. V. Shah
    5. U. N. Dhebar
Praja Socialist Party
    1. Asoka Mehta
    2. J. P. Narayan
    3. Acharya Kripalani
    4. P. Tricumdas
    5. I. Desai
Communist Party
    1. A. K. Gopalan
    2. Ajoy Ghosh
Hindu Mahasabha
    1. N. B. Khare
Jan Sangh
    1. P. Misra
Miscellaneous
    1. C. R. Rajagopalachari
Labor
    1. G. D. Ambedkar (Rashtriya Mill Mazdor Sangh)
    2. Tripathi (Indian National Trade Union Congress)
    3. B. N. Ghosh (National Federation of Post and Telegraph Employees)
Industrialists
    1. Seth Ramakrishna Dalmia
    2. A. D. Shroff
Associations
    1. Kumarappa (President, All-India Village Industries Association)
    2. G. Ramachandran (Talimi Sangh)
    3. Vinoba Bhave (Bhoodan movement initiator)
    4. Chinai (Swadeshi League)
    5. T. B. Chunha (Goa Liberation Movement)
    6. P. Gaitonde (Goa Liberation Movement)
    7. S. M. Joshi (Goa Liberation Movement)
    8. Nath Pai (Goa Liberation Movement)
    9. I. Yagnik (Mahagujerat Janata Parishad)
    10. Salebhoy Abdul Kadar (India-China Friendship Committee)

SELECTED
BIBLIOGRAPHY
ON INDIAN GOVERNMENT
AND SOCIETY

HISTORY: POLITICAL AND CULTURAL

Prepared by the Bharatiya Vidya Bhavan under the editorship of R. C. Majumdar. *The History and Culture of the Indian People* (Bombay), 10 vols. One of the best general histories of India.

Bhasham, A. L., *The Wonder That Was India* (New York, 1954). Excellent for the ancient period.

Nehru, Jawaharlal, *The Discovery of India* (London, 1956). Good not only for the overview of Indian history which it presents, but because it gives an insight into the specific manner in which an Indian intellectual viewed his own history.

INDIAN POLITICAL PHILOSOPHY:
ANCIENT AND MEDIEVAL

The following are representative of the classical works in this subject:

Kangle, R. P. (ed.), *The Kautilya Arthasastra,* 3 vols. (Poona, 1965). Original text, translation, notes, and commentaries.

Muller, Franz (tr.), *The Laws of Manu,* Vol. 25 of the Sacred Books of the East (Oxford, 1886).

Roy, Pratap Chandra (tr.), "Santiparvan," *Mahabharata,* Vol. 7. (Calcutta).

Sarkar, B. K. (tr.), *Sukraniti* (Allahabad, 1914). An excellent example of a medieval compendium of political thought.

RECENT INDIAN HISTORY AND THE
FREEDOM MOVEMENT

Azad, Abul Kalam, *India Wins Freedom* (Bombay, 1959). Excellent for some unusual insights into the period preceding independence, by one of the outstanding participants in the freedom movement.

Desai, A. R., *The Social Background of Indian Nationalism* (Bombay, 1959). Provides the socioeconomic context within which the freedom movement arose.

Philips, C. H., *The Evolution of India and Pakistan, 1858–1947* (London, 1962). Contains a selection of abbreviated documents for this period.

Sitaramayya, B. Pattabhi, *History of the Indian National Congress*, 2 vols. (Bombay, 1946). The official history of the Congress, with insights and documents pertaining to the history of the movement as well as to the general period of the freedom struggle.

POLITICAL INSTITUTIONS AND BEHAVIOR

Harrison, Selig, *India: The Most Dangerous Decades* (Princeton, 1960). A provocative discussion especially pertaining to the influence of the language issue upon Indian political behavior, with prognoses for the future.

Morris-Jones, W. H., *Parliament in India* (London, 1957). A thoroughly documented, detailed description of the functioning of this institution during the first decade of independent India.

Park, Richard L., and Irene Tinker (eds.), *Leadership and Political Institutions in India* (Princeton, 1959). Contains papers presented in a symposium on these topics, which are still useful for commentary on politics and elites during the 1950s.

Philips, C. H., *Politics and Society in India* (London, 1963). Contains essays by anthropologists, historians as well as political scientists, including an especially fine discussion of Indian political styles by W. H. Morris-Jones, "India's Political Idioms," pp. 133–154.

Rudolph, Lloyd I., and Susanne H. Rudolph, *The Modernity of Tradition: Political Development in India* (Chicago, 1967). Essays on Indian political behavior in a social and cultural context.

Sirsikar, V. M., "A Study of Political Workers in Poona," *Journal of the University of Poona*, Vol. 13 (1967), pp. 77–158. A detailed survey of the background and attitudes of middle-rank political cadres of various parties in an important Indian city.

Somjee, A. H., *Voting Behaviour in an Indian Village* (Baroda, 1959). A rather good attempt to present the dimensions of electoral behavior in an Indian village.

ADMINISTRATIVE BEHAVIOR

Bendix, Reinhard, "Public Authority in a Developing Political Community: The Case of India," *Archives Européennes de Sociologie*, 4 (1963), pp. 39–85.

An insightful discussion of administration and local politics in rural India.

Eldersveld, Samuel J. *et al., The Citizen and the Administrator in a Developing Democracy* (New Delhi, 1968). Presents highly informative and provocative results of a detailed survey of both administrators, and rural and urban citizens of Delhi state.

Panjabi, Kewal L. (ed.), *The Civil Servants in India* (Bombay, 1965). Contains revealing, short autobiographical sketches by members of the Indian Civil Service who have manned the highest administrative posts during the British period as well as after Independence.

URBAN INDIA

Misra, B. B., *The Indian Middle Classes* (Oxford, 1961). A carefully documented historical study of the rise of the middle classes in India.

Popegamage, A., and P. V. Veeraraghavan, *Status Images in Changing India* (Bombay, 1967). Presents the results of an excellent UNESCO-sponsored survey, conducted in two different regions of India, comparing the backgrounds and attitudes of both rural and urban samples within each region.

Turner, Roy (ed.), *India's Urban Future* (Berkeley, 1962). A collection of papers on political, social and economic problems pertaining to India's urban areas.

ANTHROPOLOGICAL STUDIES

Carstairs, G. Morris, *The Twice-Born* (London, 1961). An attempt to apply a psychoanalytic framework to the analysis of high-caste Hindu rural society.

Wiser, William and Charlotte, *The Hindu-Jajmani System* (Lucknow, 1958). A classical study on a fundamental form of economic relationship in rural India.

The following are examples of anthropological village studies of a general nature:

Baden-Powell, B. H., *The Indian Village Community* (New Haven, 1957). This study was first published in 1896.

Dube, S. C., *Indian Village* (Ithaca, 1955).

Marriott, McKim (ed.), *Village India* (Chicago, 1955).

Srinivas, M. N., *Religion and Society among the Coorgs of South India* (London, 1952).

———— (ed.), *India's Villages* (Calcutta, 1955).

The following place heavy emphasis upon concomitants of changing configurations of power in village India:

Bailey, F. G., *Caste and the Economic Frontier* (Manchester, 1957).

————, *Tribe, Caste and Nation* (Manchester, 1960).

————, *Politics and Social Change* (Bombay, 1963). A study conducted in Orissa which attempts to view the electoral process at the village level and as it extends upward to the district level.

Be´eille, André, *Caste, Class and Power* (Bombay, 1966).
Orᵢnstein, Henry, *Gaon: Conflict and Cohesion in an Indian Village* (Princeton, 1965).
Sivertsen, Dagfinn, *When Caste Barriers Fall* (Aarhus, Denmark, 1963).
Srinivas, M. N., *Social Change in Modern India* (Bombay, 1966). Essays.

ECONOMIC PROBLEMS

Bettleheim, Charles, *L'Inde Indépendente* (Paris, 1962). A general analysis of Indian problems, with major stress upon economic factors.
Dutt, Romesh, *The Economic History of India,* 2 vols. (Delhi, 1960). Originally published in 1903, these volumes cover the period from 1757 to 1900.
Habib, Irfan, *The Agrarian System of Mughal India* (Bombay, 1963).
Vivesvaraya, M., *Planned Economy for India* (Bangalore, 1934). One of the first attempts to conceptualize planning for India, now considered a classic.

The following are concerned with rural economic problems:

Epstein, T. Scarlett, *Economic Development and Social Change in South India* (Manchester, 1962). An excellent comparative analysis of two Mysore villages, in which the author—an anthro-economist—demonstrates how differing economic structures affect the type and extent of socioeconomic change.
Fukutake, Tadashi *et al., The Socio-Economic Structure of the Indian Village* (Tokyo, 1964). Detailed results of two surveys conducted in villages in Gujerat and West Bengal.
Kumar, Dharma, *Land and Caste in South India* (Cambridge, 1965). An historical study of nineteenth-century agricultural labor in Madras.
Neale, Walter C., *Economic Change in Rural India* (New Haven, 1962). A well-documented study of land tenure legislation and practice in Uttar Pradesh between 1800 and 1955.
Reserve Bank of India, *Rural Credit Follow-Up Survey, 1958–1959.* (Bombay, 1961). A statistical analysis and review of socioeconomic problems besetting the rural Indian.
Singh, Baljit, *Next Step in Village India* (Bombay, 1961). Provides insight into the relationship between local political behavior and economic relationships.
Thorner, Daniel, and Alice Thorner, *Land and Labour in India* (London, 1962). Provocative essays, based on the authors' field work, drawing attention to important economic problems.

CULTURE AND SOCIETY

Kapp, William, *Hindu Culture, Economic Development and Economic Planning in India* (Bombay, 1963).
Mukerji, D. P., *Diversities* (New Delhi, 1958). The last published collection of essays—on economics, sociology and culture—by an outstanding Indian sociologist.

Singer, Milton (ed.), *Traditional India: Structure and Change* (Philadelphia, 1959). An unusually refreshing collection of essays by scholars in the arts, history as well as the social sciences.

COMMUNICATIONS

Internal Communications Processes:

Damle, Y. B., *Communication of Modern Ideas and Knowledge in Indian Villages* (Cambridge, 1955). A field study relating access to communication, and level of knowledge in villages varying in distance from the city of Poona.

Majundar, D. N., *Caste and Communication in an Indian Village* (Bombay, 1958).

Mathur, J. C., and Paul Neurath, *An Indian Experiment in Farm Radio Forums* (Paris, 1959). A detailed account of various programs presented, and the reactions of listeners to them.

National Institute of Community Development, *Perception of the National Emergency in Village India* (Mussoorie, 1963). A statistical analysis of interviews with over three thousand villagers throughout India regarding their reactions to and sources of information about the Chinese aggression.

Opler, Morris E., and Rudra Dutt Singh, "The Extensions of an Indian Village," *Journal of Asian Studies*, 16 (1956), pp. 5–10. An excellent account of the various links which a village has with the outside world.

Rao, Y. V. Lakshmana, *Communication and Development* (Minneapolis, 1966). A field study of two Andhra villages.

Thakur, B. S. *et al.*, *Villagers and the News* (Hyderabad, 1963). Based on an empirical survey.

Internal Communications and Images of America in India:

Coelho, George, *Changing Images of America: A Study of Indian Students' Perceptions* (Glencoe, 1958).

Davis, Frederick T., *America in the Indian Press: A Study of News Flow and Usage* (Cambridge, 1957).

International Press Institute, *The Flow of News* (Zurich, 1953).

———, *As Others See Us: U.S.A., Britain, Germany, France, Italy, India* (Zurich, 1954).

Shridharani, Krishnalal, *The Journalist in India: A Study of the Press Corps* (Cambridge, 1956).

Useem, John and Ruth, *The Western Educated Man in India* (New York, 1955).

Images of India in America:

Arora, Satish K., "The Process of Foreign Policy Formulation: A Study of Communications, Images and Attitudes" (Ph.D. Dissertation, Cornell University, 1959).

Isaacs, Harold, *Scratches on Our Minds* (New York, 1958).

Jones, Dorothy B., *The Portrayal of China and India on the American Screen* (Cambridge, 1955).

INDIAN FOREIGN POLICY: INTERNATIONAL RELATIONS

Indian Council of World Affairs, *Defense and Security in the Indian Ocean* (New Delhi, 1958).

Kundra, J. C., *Indian Foreign Policy, 1947–1954* (Groningen, 1955). Good for background on the subject.

Mende, Tibor, *Nehru: Conversations on India and World Affairs* (New York, 1956). Provides insight into the Prime Minister's thinking on foreign policy, as well as India's domestic problems.

Panikkar, K. M., *Asia and Western Dominance* (London, 1953). An important survey of Asian history from 1498–1945, with a stress on international relations.

———, *Problems of Indian Defence* (Bombay, 1960).

Rajkumar, N. V., *The Background of India's Foreign Policy* (Delhi, 1952), a Congress Party publication.

INDO-AMERICAN RELATIONS

Arora, Satish K., *American Foreign Policy Towards India* (New Delhi, 1954).

Indian Council of World Affairs, *Indian-American Relations* (New Delhi, 1950).

Talbot, P., and S. L. Poplai, *India and America* (New York, 1958).

INDEXES

INDEX OF NAMES

INDEX OF SUBJECTS